THE TRIVIAL SUBLIME

The Trivial Sublime

Theology and American Poetics

Linda Munk
Assistant Professor of English
University of Toronto

St. Martin's Press

© Linda Munk 1992

All rights reserved. No reproduction, copy or transmission of
this publication may be made without written permission.

No paragraph of this publication may be reproduced, copied or
transmitted save with written permission or in accordance with
the provisions of the Copyright, Designs and Patents Act 1988,
or under the terms of any licence permitting limited copying
issued by the Copyright Licensing Agency, 90 Tottenham Court
Road, London W1P 9HE.

Any person who does any unauthorised act in relation to this
publication may be liable to criminal prosecution and civil
claims for damages.

First published in Great Britain 1992 by
THE MACMILLAN PRESS LTD
Houndmills, Basingstoke, Hampshire RG21 2XS
and London
Companies and representatives
throughout the world

This book is published in Macmillan's *Studies in Literature and Religion* series.
General Editor: David Jasper

A catalogue record for this book is available from the British Library.

ISBN 0–333–53987–7

Printed in Great Britain by
Antony Rowe Ltd, Chippenham, Wiltshire

First published in the United States of America 1992 by
Scholarly and Reference Division,
ST. MARTIN'S PRESS, INC.,
175 Fifth Avenue,
New York, N.Y. 10010

ISBN 0–312–08561–3

Library of Congress Cataloging-in-Publication Data
Munk, Linda.
 The trivial sublime: theology and American poetics / Linda Munk.
  p.   cm.
 Includes index.
 ISBN 0–312–08561–3
 1. Religious poetry, American—History and criticism. 2. Sublime,
The, in literature. 3. Theology in literature. 4. God in
literature. 5. Poetics. I. Title.
PS310.R4M86
811.009'382—dc20   92-19511
                                                                    CIP

Contents

Acknowledgments		vi
General Editor's Preface by David Jasper		vii
The Trivial Sublime / Ex-tracts		1
1	Emerson: This Almost Insignificant Signifier	22
2	*In Nomine Diaboli*: An Extreme Interpretation of *Billy Budd*	40
3	Giving Umbrage: The Song of Songs which is Whitman's	60
4	Recycling Language: Emily Dickinson's Religious Wordplay	83
5	Robert Frost: The Design of Violence	107
6	Understanding Understatement: Biblical Typology and "The Displaced Person"	119
7	His Dazzling Absence: The Shekinah in Jonathan Edwards	136
Notes		163
Index		192

Acknowledgments

I am indebted to the Social Sciences and Humanities Research Council of Canada for generous funding; to St. Chad's College, University of Durham, for electing me to the Macmillan Fellowship in 1989–90; and to David Jasper, the director of the Centre for the Study of Literature and Theology at the University of Glasgow. Two scholars have been unsparing with their learning: Eleanor Cook and Robert Hayward. Charles Lock has not only shared his unbounded scholarship, but has been the most scrupulous of readers.

Chapters of this work incorporate or adapt material from essays that have previously been published: "Recycling Language: Emily Dickinson's Religious Wordplay," in *Emerson Society Quarterly: A Journal of the American Renaissance*; "Understanding Understatement: Biblical Typology and 'The Displaced Person,'" in *Literature and Theology*; "The Design of Violence," in *Literature and Theology*; "His Dazzling Absence: Jonathan Edwards and the Shekinah," in *Early American Literature*.

General Editor's Preface

To be fascinated by theology is to be fascinated by words. The theologian works through and beyond language. The same is true of the poet, and both poet and theologian must track words patiently and exactly in both meaning and mystery.

For Ralph Waldo Emerson, as Linda Munk comments, the words of God are never fixed or even consistent, yet these fugitives are infinitely precious and endlessly demanding. In these chapters on American literature, Munk relentlessly pursues the language of religion from its biblical roots in the Judaeo-Christian tradition and through the poetics of modern literature. The result is a remarkable and demanding book, its themes spreading into numerous areas of the relationship between literature and theology, into our postmodern world, and across a spectrum of theological issues.

The study of detail can become a journey into the trivial, yet apparent trivia may also open windows upon matters of crucial, even sublime importance. It is easy for language, and particularly religious language, to become embedded in the norms of customary use, until, "words are revived by a new relation between words". Poets, like Emily Dickinson or Robert Frost, release worlds which were in danger of becoming sterile and return them to the complex, often violent, beautiful realms of what Emerson calls the "common every day". Theology and its forms must then accept new responsibilities and become subject to the demands of a new "literalism" within the workings of poetry.

Whitman returns us to the body; Frost reminds us of the design of violence. The pun, irony, plurisignificance – the infinite complexity of language and the business of the poet takes us back to the heart of theology and its ancient symbols. Mystery, not meaning: a dazzling absence, not unwholesome presence – these are Linda Munk's preoccupations in this remarkable, learned and unsettling book.

David Jasper
GENERAL EDITOR

And in this he shewyd me a lytille thynge, the quantyte of a haselle nutte, lyggande in the palme of my hande, and to my vndyrstandynge that, it was as rownde as any balle. I lokede ther opon and thought: Whate maye this be? And I was annswerde generaly thus: It is alle that ys made. I merveylede howe that it myght laste, for me thought it myght falle sodaynly to nought for litille.

Julian of Norwich

The Trivial Sublime / Ex-tracts

"Thomas of Celano tells us that the saint picked up every piece of parchment which he found on the ground, even if it were from a pagan book. Asked by a disciple why he did so, Francis answered: 'Fili mi, litterae sunt ex quibus componitur gloriossimum Dei nomen.'"

Ernst Robert Curtius

* * *

"How were they to understand a writer whose greatest pride it was that 'the writing consists largely of quotations – the craziest mosaic technique imaginable' – and who placed the greatest emphasis on the six mottoes that preceded the study . . . ?"

Hannah Arendt, citing Walter Benjamin

* * *

"Can we rescue a word and discover a universe? Can we study a language, and awake to the Truth? Can we bury ourselves in a lexicon, and arise in the presence of God?"

Edwyn Clement Hoskyns

* * *

"Look at theological dictionary. 1855. Walt Whitman."

Walt Whitman

* * *

"My personal way has been from the observed detail to ever broadening units which rest, to an increasing degree, on speculation. It is, I think, the philological, the inductive way, which seeks to show significance in the apparently futile, in contrast to the deductive procedure which begins with units assumed as given . . . ."

Leo Spitzer

* * *

"I fear chiefly lest my expression may not be *extra-vagant* enough, may not wander far enough beyond the narrow limits of my daily experience, so as to be adequate to the truth of which I have been convinced."

Henry David Thoreau

* * *

"In the Talmud it is always of great importance to specify, for each saying, who said it. A true teaching is one in which the universal nature of the truth it announces does not obliterate the name or the identity of the person who said it. The Talmudic scholars even believe that the Messiah will come at the moment when everyone quotes what they have learned, in the name of the person they learned it from."

Emmanuel Levinas

* * *

"One must be able to make use of the trivial for the expression of the sublime."

Thomas Hardy, citing Havelock Ellis,
citing Jean François Millet

* * *

"Yet in his [Whitman's] later years particularly, he did think of his work in relation to painting. He said that 'the Leaves are really only Millet in another form.'"

F. O. Matthiessen

* * *

"To me the converging objects of the universe perpetually flow
All are written to me, and I must get what the writing means."

Walt Whitman

* * *

"The first step is the awareness of having been struck by a detail, followed by a conviction that this detail is connected basically with the work of art . . . . To begin by omitting this first step must doom any attempt at interpretation . . . ."
Leo Spitzer

* * *

"Singular & particular Detail is the Foundation of the Sublime."
William Blake

* * *

"Benjamin had a passion for small and even minute things; Scholem tells about his ambition to get one hundred lines onto the ordinary page of a notebook and about his admiration for two grains of wheat in the Jewish section of the Musée Cluny 'on which a kindred soul had inscribed the complete *Shema Israel*.' For him the size of an object was in an inverse ratio to its significance."
Hannah Arendt

* * *

"Now stamp the Lord's Prayer on a grain of rice . . . ."
Dylan Thomas

* * *

"The whole code of her [nature's] laws may be written on the thumbnail, or the signet of a ring."
Ralph Waldo Emerson

* * *

"Nichts is mir zu klein und ich liebe es trotzdem
und mal es auf Goldgrund und gross,
und halt es hoch, und ich weiss nicht wem
löst es die Seele los . . . ."
Rainer Maria Rilke

* * *

"The greatest poet hardly knows pettiness or triviality. If he breathes into anything that was before thought small it dilates with the grandeur and life of the universe."

Walt Whitman

* * *

"It is time to consider how Domenico Scarlatti condensed
so much music into so few bars
with never a crabbed turn or a congested cadence,
never a boast or a see-here . . . ."

Basil Bunting

* * *

"Miniature is one of the refuges of greatness."

Gaston Bachelard

* * *

"If 'compression is the first grace of style',
you have it. Contractibility is a virtue
as modesty is a virtue."

Marianne Moore

* * *

" . . . strength is compactness, not extent nor bulk."

William Blake

* * *

"The noble soul often illustrates itself in what the world rates as trivial: the grandeur and beauty of the spirit making the commonest action more luminous than the sun."

Walt Whitman

* * *

The Trivial Sublime / Ex-tracts

"We come here to a central paradox among the various ones that lurk in the oracular passages of Wordsworth's major period: the oxymoron of the humble-grand, the lofty-mean, the trivial-sublime . . . ."

M. H. Abrams

* * *

"'The smallest production of nature has the circle of its completeness within itself & I have only need of eyes to see with, in order to discover the relative proportions. I am perfectly sure that within this circle, however narrow, an entirely genuine existence is enclosed . . . . the works of nature are ever *a freshly uttered word of God.*' Goethe."

Ralph Waldo Emerson, citing Goethe

* * *

"The philologian will then continue the pursuit of the microscopic because he sees therein the microcosmic . . . ."

Leo Spitzer

* * *

"The microscope cannot find the animalcule, which is less perfect for being little. Eyes, ears, taste, smell, motion, resistance, appetite, and organs of reproduction that take hold on eternity – all find room to exist in the small creature."

Ralph Waldo Emerson

* * *

"Goethe said, quite as if he were talking about Stevens: 'It makes a great difference whether the poet seeks the particular in relation to the universal or contemplates the universal in the particular . . . . [In the first case] the particular functions as an example, as an instance of the universal; but the second indeed represents the very nature of poetry. He who grasps this particular as living essence also encompasses the universal.'"

Randall Jarrell

* * *

"From the essay on Goethe on, quotations are at the center of every work of Benjamin's. This very fact distinguishes his writings from scholarly works of all kinds in which it is the function of quotations to verify and document opinions, wherefore they can be safely relegated to the Notes. This is out of the question in Benjamin."

Hannah Arendt

* * *

"For Goethe, the guarantee of Spinoza, that the more we know individual things the more we know God, was a password to the most intimate apprehensions of the warm contours of physical existence . . . ."

Thomas McFarland

* * *

"Der Augenblick ist Ewigkeit."

Goethe

* * *

"In eternity there is indeed something true and sublime. But all these times and occasions are now and here. God himself culminates in the present moment, and will never be more divine in the lapse of all the ages. And we are enabled to apprehend at all what is sublime and noble only by the perpetual instilling and drenching of the reality which surrounds us."

Henry David Thoreau

* * *

"Longfellow:

In the elder days of art,
Builders wrought with greatest care
Each minute and unseen part,
For the gods are everywhere.

(Könnte mir als Motto dienen.)"

Ludwig Wittgenstein

* * *

"Philosophers before Wittgenstein had found that our lives are distorted or waylaid by illusion. But what other philosopher has found the antidote to illusion in the particular and repeated humility of remembering and tracking the use of humble words, looking philosophically as it were beneath our feet rather than over our heads?

Inquiring that way . . . I am in fact armed with names, before all with those of Emerson and Thoreau, whose emphasis on what they call the common, the everyday, the near, the low, I have in recent years repeatedly claimed as underwriting the ordinariness sought in the ordinary language methods of Wittgenstein and of Austin."

Stanley Cavell

* * *

"Ah! that I could reach with my words the force of that rhetoric of things in which the Divine Mind is conveyed to me day by day in what I call my life. A loaf of bread, an errand to the town, a temperate man, an intemperate man."

Ralph Waldo Emerson

* * *

"I think that the trivialness of life is, and personally to each one, ought to be seen to be, done away with by the Incarnation – or, I shd. say the difficulty wh. the trivialness of life presents ought to be. It is one adorable point of the incredible condescension of the Incarnation (the greatness of which no saint can have ever hoped to realize) that our Lord submitted not only to the pains of life . . . but also to the mean and trivial accidents of humanity."

Gerard Manley Hopkins

* * *

"The humility of the Incarnation derives its full force from the contrast with Christ's divine nature: man and God, lowly and sublime, *humilis et sublimis*; both the height and the depth are immeasurable and inconceivable: *peraltissima humilitas*."

Erich Auerbach

*   *   *

"Only rarely, however, did she [Emily Dickinson] bring a poem to a successful conclusion . . . . too often the poem expires in a teased-out and breathless obscurity. Often the imagery is both trivial and immense: is this an invitation to a walk or a consummation with the Godhead?"

Philip Larkin

*   *   *

"I remember once asking a seer to ask one among the gods who, as she believed, were standing about her in their symbolic bodies, what would become of a charming but seemingly trivial labour of a friend, and the form answering, 'the devastation of peoples and the overwhelming of cities.'"

William Butler Yeats

*   *   *

"Do you see that man who has just skipped out of the way of the tram? Consider, if he had been run over, how significant every act of his would at once become. I don't mean for the police inspector. I mean for anybody who knew him . . . . It is my idea of the significance of trivial things that I want to give the two or three unfortunate wretches who eventually read me."

James Joyce

*   *   *

"[Wordsworth] has endeavoured (not in vain) to aggrandize the trivial . . . . No one has shown the same imagination in raising trifles into importances."

William Hazlitt

*   *   *

"The unbelief of the age is attested by the loud condemnation of trifles."

Ralph Waldo Emerson

*   *   *

"The commerce between Man and his Maker cannot be carried on but by a process where much is represented in little, and the Infinite Being accommodates himself to finite capacity. In all this may be perceived the affinity between religion and poetry . . . ."

William Wordsworth

*   *   *

"One of the motives of American poetry since Emerson has been to remove the privilege of history; to refute the European afflatus with its claim upon privileged acts and monuments. It is American rhetorical practice to treat every detail as if it were equal to everything else . . . . "

Denis Donoghue

*   *   *

"But as Aby Warburg used to say to his students, 'God is in detail.'"

Ernst Robert Curtius

*   *   *

"Der liebe Gott steckt im Detail."

Aby Warburg, cited by E. H. Gombrich

*   *   *

"It is not . . . detail sought for its own sake . . . but . . . detail referred to a great end, – sought for the sake of the inestimable beauty which exists in the slightest and least of God's works . . . . There may be as much greatness of mind, as much nobility of manner in a master's treatment of the smallest features, as in his management of the most vast . . . ."

John Ruskin

* * *

"Yet readers will know that they are reading a poem informed by love because of the intensity of attention paid to this or that detail of the universe."

Joseph Brodsky

* * *

"There is everything in common between the relentless detail in which the boredom and pointlessness of Emma Bovary's life was built up, and the minutely articulated jumble of reflections behind the blank-faced *nana* in Manet's *Bar at the Folies-Bergère*; and both, in a sense, point forward to the 'objective,' molecular constellations of dabbed light from which Seurat assembled his figures on the speckled lawn of the Grande Jatte."

Robert Hughes

* * *

"But, of course, the attempt to discover significance in the detail, the habit of taking a detail of language as seriously as the meaning of a work of art . . . this is an outgrowth of the preestablished firm conviction, the 'axiom' of the philologian, that details are not an inchoate chance aggregation of dispersed material through which no light shines. The philologian must believe in the existence of some light from on high."

Leo Spitzer

* * *

> "he who wishes to see a Vision; a perfect Whole
> Must see it in its Minute Particulars"

William Blake

* * *

"A poet who can see the world in a grain of sand or a host of angels in the rising sun does not require the conventional props of sublime poetry. He can discover grandeur in or through the most ordinary aspects of human experience. This method, to anticipate, was Wordsworth's great contribution to the poetry of the religious sublime, although Blake too certainly at times cherishes in his poetry the small, the helpless, and the seemingly insignificant."

David B. Morris

*   *   *

"Instead of the sublime and beautiful; the near, the low, the common, was explored and poeticized . . . . I embrace the common, I explore and sit at the feet of the familiar, the low."

Ralph Waldo Emerson

*   *   *

"But God hath chosen the foolish things of the world to confound the wise; and God hath chosen the weak things of the world to confound the things which are mighty; And base things of the world, and things which are despised, hath God chosen, yea, and things which are not, to bring to nought things that are . . . ."

St. Paul

*   *   *

"This becomes in Browning a Pascalian or Blakean notion of the special closeness to God of the miniscule. We shall reach God best . . . by descending toward even more minute particulars until below the smallest of the small, rather than beyond the largest of the large, we reach the splendor of God."

J. Hillis Miller

*   *   *

"The Name comes close behind a stomach-cyst,
The simplest of creations, just a sac
That's mouth, heart, legs and belly at once, yet lives
And feels, and could do neither, we conclude,
If simplified still further one degree:
The small becomes the dreadful and immense!"

Robert Browning

* * *

"In his *Lectures on the Sacred Poetry of the Hebrews*, published in 1753, Robert Lowth identified as the paradoxical quality 'almost peculiar to the sacred poets' of the Old Testament a use of imagery which invests 'the most common and familiar with the greatest dignity.' The effect is that of a *humilitas-sublimitas;* or as Lowth puts it, 'the meanness of the image' and 'the plainness and inelegance of the expression' are used with such 'consistency' and 'propriety' that 'I do not scruple to pronounce it sublime.'"

M. H. Abrams

* * *

"In antique theory the sublime and elevated style was called *sermo gravis* or *sublimis;* the low style was *sermo remissus* or *humilis;* the two had to be kept strictly separated. In the world of Christianity, on the other hand, the two are merged, especially in Christ's Incarnation and Passion, which realize and combine *sublimitas* and *humilitas* in overwhelming measure."

Erich Auerbach

* * *

" . . . even beauty in the eighteenth century grew more and more sublime as it grew from the classical terms of *happy* to late-century *sad*, from *new* to *wild* . . . even from *mighty* to *little*, as the sublimity of passion came down to smallest essences, and the whole realm became one with the pathetic. This was the road that sublimity travelled . . . ."

Josephine Miles

* * *

"However, it may not be amiss to add . . . that, as the great extreme of dimension is sublime, so the last extreme of littleness is in some measure sublime likewise . . . ."

Edmund Burke

* * *

"We may venture to speak of atoms and monads in a relative sense; and it is certain that the smallest world is the most durable."

Friedrich Nietzsche

* * *

"Forms without matter are not visible to the eye, but they are known by the eye of the heart."

Maimonides

* * *

"In the thrust of a trembling glance my mind arrived at That Which Is. Then indeed I saw clearly *Your invisible things which are understood by the things that are made*; but I lacked the strength to hold my gaze fixed . . . ."

St. Augustine

* * *

"For the invisible things of him from the creation of the world are clearly seen, being understood by the things that are made, even his eternal power and Godhead . . . ."

St. Paul

* * *

"Those strange and mysticall transmigrations that I have observed in Silkwormes, turn'd my Philosophy into Divinity. There is in these workes of nature, which seeme to puzle reason, something Divine . . . ."

Sir Thomas Browne

* * *

"O to be a dragon,
a symbol of the power of Heaven – of silkworm
size or immense; at times invisible.
Felicitous phenomenon."

Marianne Moore

* * *

"If the only route to the intellect lies through the senses, belief in a supernatural Being finds itself insecure. God had to be saved, even if He had to marry the world of appearances. And so, in the natural sublime, He did."

Thomas Weiskel

* * *

"Through Whitman, Emily Dickinson, Marianne Moore and others, America has fostered the sense of size not only in greatness, but in smallness also, in the most minute and loving detail."

Josephine Miles

* * *

"The details of a thing can be the sign of a new world which, like all worlds, contains the attributes of greatness."

Gaston Bachelard

* * *

"The smaller the object, the more likely it seemed that it could contain in its concentrated form everything else; hence his [Benjamin's] delight that two grains of wheat should contain the entire *Shema Israel*, the very essence of Judaism, tiniest essence appearing on tiniest entity . . . ."

Hannah Arendt

* * *

"He that despiseth small things will perish by little and little."

Ralph Waldo Emerson

* * *

"Puritans had enough confidence in God's design to believe that no facts were too small or insignificant to be included in that design; everything could emblemize something."

Francis Murphy

The Trivial Sublime / Ex-tracts

* * *

"Wherefore, if God so clothe the grass of the field, which today is, and tomorrow is cast in the oven, shall he not much more clothe you, O ye of little faith?"

Jesus, according to St. Matthew

* * *

" . . . through every grass-blade . . . the glory of a present God still beams."

Thomas Carlyle

* * *

"Not a line is drawn without intention & that most discriminate & particular as Poetry admits not a Letter that is insignificant so Painting admits not a Grain of Sand or a Blade of Grass Insignificant."

William Blake

* * *

"A mote of sand, you know, a blade of grass –
What was so despicable as mere grass,
Except perhaps the life o' the worm or fly
Which fed there? These were small and men were great.
Well, sir, the old way's altered somewhat since,
And the world wears another aspect now:
Somebody turns our spyglass round, or else
Puts a new lens in it: grass, worm, fly grow big:
We find great things are made of little things,
And little things go lessening till at last
Comes God behind them. Talk of mountains now?
We talk of mould that heaps the mountains, mites
That throng the mould, and God that makes the mites."

Robert Browning

* * *

" . . . there is no fact in nature which does not carry the whole sense of nature; and the distinctions which we make in events, and in affairs, of low and high, honest and base, disappear when nature is used as a symbol."

Ralph Waldo Emerson

*   *   *

"The dissociation or dualism at the core of the eighteenth-century sublime had profoundly ideological implications, and the various forms of alienation reinforced by the sublime – between the familiar and the novel, the human and the natural, the low and the high – could not be shaken until these ideological correlatives were questioned in the ferment of social revolution. Yet the sublime moment brought the high and the low into dangerous proximity . . . ."

Thomas Weiskel

*   *   *

"At the beginning of the thirteenth century there appears in Italy a man who embodies, in exemplary fashion, the mixture we are discussing of *sublimitas* and *humilitas*, of ecstatically sublime immersion in God and humbly concrete everydayness – with a resulting irresolvable fusion of action and expression, of content and form. He is Saint Francis of Assisi."

Erich Auerbach

*   *   *

"And by an ultimate subversion, Wordsworth did not merely level the Neoclassic order, but turned it upside down, by preferring in his subjects the last over the first and by transforming the humble and the passive into the heroic, the low into the sublime, and the petty into the numinous."

M. H. Abrams

*   *   *

"The sublime enters into every thing even into a baker's score or a school boy's multiplication table as the light beams into privies and garrets."

Ralph Waldo Emerson

* * *

"[Ben 'Azzai] used to say, Despise not any man, and carp not at any thing; for thou wilt find that there is not any man that has not his hour, and not a thing that has not its place."

Pirque Aboth

* * *

"What stuns us into a realisation of our supersensible destiny is not, as Kant imagined, the formlessness of nature, but rather its unutterable particularity; and most particular and individual of all natural things is the mind of man."

Iris Murdoch

* * *

"Those masterful images because complete
Grew in pure mind but out of what began?
A mound of refuse or the sweepings of a street,
Old kettles, old bottles, and a broken can,
Old iron, old bones, old rags, that raving slut
Who keeps the till."

William Butler Yeats

* * *

"Is not the beauty that piques us in every object, in a straw, an old nail, a cobblestone in the road, the announcement that always our road lies *out* into nature, and not inward to the wearisome, odious anatomy of ourselves . . . ."

Ralph Waldo Emerson

* * *

" . . . and God is seen God
In the star, in the stone, in the flesh, in the soul and the clod."

Robert Browning

* * *

"Lowth, naturally, was more critically aware of the presence of 'low' terms in the Bible . . . . Viewed properly, he argued, some of the 'low' objects are not really low or mean at all. With some justification in historical fact . . . he pictured Hebrew society as 'simple and uniform in the greatest degree' . . . . Since in this classless society no employments were accounted mean, no objects were regarded as mean or degraded; therefore complete freedom is assumed in the poetic use of bottles, dishes, knives, potter's wheels, barns, wine vats, and other objects connected with the pursuits in which the Hebrew poets were 'educated from their earliest years.'"

Vincent Freimarck

* * *

"At all events, that Shakspeare stooped to accommodate himself to the People, is sufficiently apparent; and one of the most striking proofs of his almost omnipotent genius, is, that he could turn to such glorious purpose those materials which the pre-possessions of the age compelled him to make use of."

William Wordsworth

* * *

"For the ocean, nothing
is beneath consideration.
   The houses
of so many mussels and periwinkles
have been abandoned here, it's hopeless
to know what to salvage. Instead
I keep a lookout for beach glass –
amber of Budweiser, chrysoprase
of Almadén and Gallo . . . ."

Amy Clampitt

* * *

"There is nothing small or mean to the soul. It derives as great a joy from symbolizing the Godhead or his Universe under the form of a moth, or a gnat, as of a Lord of Hosts."

Ralph Waldo Emerson

The Trivial Sublime / Ex-tracts

*　　*　　*

"We have frequently said that small and trivial things are figures and foreshadowings of great things; thus, this day of ours, which is bounded by sunrise and sunset, bears the likeness of that great day which is circumscribed by the passing of a thousand years."

Lactantius, cited by Erich Auerbach

*　　*　　*

"If you would understand me go to the heights or water-shore
The nearest gnat is an explanation . . . ."

Walt Whitman

*　　*　　*

"I find you, Lord, in all Things and in all
my fellow creatures, pulsing with your life;
as a tiny seed you sleep in what is small
and in the vast you vastly yield yourself."

Rainer Maria Rilke, trans. Stephen Mitchell

*　　*　　*

"Lord clear my misted sight that I
May hence view thy Divinity;
Some sparks whereof thou up dost hasp
Within this little downy wasp,
In whose small corporation we
A school and a schoolmaster see . . . ."

Edward Taylor

*　　*　　*

" . . . what reason may not goe to Schoole to the wisdome of Bees, Aunts, and Spiders? what wise hand teacheth them to doe what reason cannot teach us? ruder heads stand amazed at those prodigious pieces of nature, Whales, Elephants, Dromidaries, and Camels; these I confesse, are the Colossus and Majestick pieces of her hand; but in these narrow Engines there is more curious Mathematicks, and the civilitie of these little Citizens, more neatly set forth the wisdom of their Maker . . . ."

Sir Thomas Browne

*   *   *

"Beasts, we have said partake of Understanding. If any man deny this, there is a ready way of settling the question. Let him give a careful perusal to . . . Kirby and Spence's Introduction to Entomology."

Samuel Taylor Coleridge

*   *   *

"Kirby and Spence tell us that the battles of ants have long been celebrated and the dates of them recorded . . . ."

Henry David Thoreau

*   *   *

"The instincts of the ant are very unimportant considered as the ant's; but the moment a ray of relation is seen to extend from it to man, and the little drudge is seen to be a monitor, a little body with a mighty heart, then all its habits . . . become sublime."

Ralph Waldo Emerson

*   *   *

> "The ant's a centaur in his dragon world.
> Pull down thy vanity, it is not man
> Made courage, or made order, or made grace,
>   Pull down thy vanity, I say pull down.
> Learn of the green world what can be thy place
> In scaled invention or true artistry,
> Pull down thy vanity . . . ."

Ezra Pound

*   *   *

"And, behold, the Lord passed by, and a great and strong wind rent the mountains, and brake in pieces the rocks before the Lord; but

the Lord was not in the wind; and after the wind an earthquake; but the Lord was not in the earthquake: And after the earthquake a fire; but the Lord was not in the fire: and after the fire a still small voice."
(1 Kings 19:11–12)

*   *   *

"Is not the sublime felt in an analysis as well as in a creation?"
Ralph Waldo Emerson

*   *   *

"Then sighing . . . we return to the sound of our own tongue . . . ."
St. Augustine

1
Emerson: This Almost Insignificant Signifier

> This signifier of little, this discourse that doesn't amount to much, is like all ghosts: errant. It rolls (*kulindeitai*) this way and that like someone who has lost his way, who doesn't know where he is going, having strayed from the right path, the right direction, the right of rectitude, the norm; but also like someone who has lost his rights, an outlaw, a pervert, a ruffian, a vagrant, a bum. Wandering in the streets, he doesn't even know who he is . . . . uprooted, anonymous, unattached to any house or country, this almost insignificant signifier is at everyone's disposal . . . .
>
> Jacques Derrida[1]

Thus licensed, one searches through Emerson's *Journals and Miscellaneous Notebooks* for this errant and almost insignificant signifier, *ce signifiant presque insignifiant* ("it is not insignificant; it simply signifies little, and always the same thing"). Three entries, all written on December 28, 1834:

> I honor him who made himself of no reputation.

> "He made himself of no reputation." The words have a divine sound.

> Excite the soul, & the weather & the town & your condition in the world all disappear, the world itself loses its solidity, nothing remains but the soul & the Divine Presence in which it lives.
>
> (*JMN* IV: 380, 382, 383)[2]

Three months later, in March 1835, Emerson writes that one "had better live in the country, & see little society, & make himself of no reputation" (*JMN* V: 24). Years later (June, 1852), mocking the local

"Medium," Miss Bridge, and her "knuckle dispensation," he calls it "the Rat-revelation, the Gospel that comes by taps in the wall, & thumps in the table-drawer. The spirits make themselves of no reputation. They are rats and mice of Society" (*JMN* XIII: 62).

With the phrase "He made himself of no reputation," Emerson is citing Paul's letter to the Philippians, in particular, these verses on the Incarnation:

> Let this mind be in you, which was also in Christ Jesus: Who, being in the form of God, thought it not robbery to be equal with God: But made himself of no reputation [*heauton ekenosen*] and took upon him the form of a servant, and was made in the likeness of men: And being found in fashion as a man, he humbled himself [*etapeinosen*], and became obedient unto death, even the death of the cross. (Phil. 2:5ff; AV)

The Authorized Version renders the Greek *ekenosen* as "made himself of no reputation," a phrase that manages to gloss the original without actually translating it. The verb *ekenosen* (*kenoun*) means "to empty oneself." The Vulgate stays close to the Greek: "Sed semet ipsum exinanivit formam servi accipiens." Likewise the Revised Standard Version: "but emptied himself, taking the form of a servant." As background and as context for the present study of Emerson, both English translations of *ekenosen* or *kenosis* should be held in mind: (1) the self-emptying or "self-exinanition" of Christ; (2) Christ's humbling himself (*tapeinosis*), abasing himself, making himself of no particular honour or distinction, of no reputation, of almost no significance.

What Paul intended to convey by the phrase *heauton ekenosen* is endlessly disputed by theologians. According to an entry in the *Theological Dictionary of the New Testament*, what is meant by the kenotic passage from Philippians

> is that the heavenly Christ did not selfishly exploit His divine form and mode of being, but by His own decision emptied himself of it or laid it by, taking the form of a servant by becoming man . . . . The best commentary is to be found in 2 Cor 8:9 "he became a beggar even though (of himself and up to this point) he was rich."[3]

Several commentators invoke (the problematic) 2 Corinthians 8:9 as a gloss on Paul's idiosyncratic use of *kenosis*: "though he was rich, yet for your sakes he became poor, that ye through his poverty might be rich." The biblical chiasmus is a model of reciprocity (he was rich and became poor; you were poor and became rich): several of the early Fathers, meditating on the kenotic model, imagined that by the self-emptying of the divine *logos*, we were able fill ourselves with divinity. St. Bernard, for example, as paraphrased by Jaroslav Pelikan, believed:

> What made [Salvation] possible was "the self-emptying of God"; what made it possible was "the opportunity to fill ourselves with him." To be filled with God through redemption was "to be deified."[4]

The most valuable and comprehensive study of Philippians 2, verses 5–11, is R. P. Martin's *Carmen Christi* (1967). If we insist upon the literal meaning of *kenosis*, Martin tells us, then we must "begin with the question, Of what did Christ empty himself in His resolve not to cling to, or clutch at, divine equality, but to take the form of a servant?" It seems there have been, generally speaking, three answers to this question. (1) Some theologians contend that at the Incarnation, Christ emptied himself of the divine or pre-existent nature. (2) Others contend that Christ emptied or divested himself, not of his divine nature, but "of the glories, the prerogatives, of Deity." (3) Still others assert that Christ emptied himself of "the conditions of glory and majesty." One theologian, writing in 1911, takes the verb *ekenosen* "in a general way as 'He poured out Himself', teaching that He did not 'consider the equality with God as an opportunity of self-aggrandizement', but effaced Himself and all thought of self and poured out his fulness to enrich others."[5] Walter Lock argues for an antithetical definition: *kenosis*, he writes, "means little more than that He accepted the limitations implied in incarnation . . . and was probably suggested to St Paul as the antithesis to the conception of the fulness (*pleroma*) of God which dwelt essentially in his Son."[6]

*   *   *

This wandering and inconclusive reading of Emerson will first explore one sense of *kenosis*: the out-pouring or self-emptying of the divine fulness or pleroma. Appropriating St. John's *logos* doctrine of the Word made flesh, Emerson implies that *kenosis* and the Word made flesh occur continually, in the most humble circumstances:

"Each of us is a part of eternity and immensity, a god walking in flesh, and the wildest fable that was ever invented, is less strange than this reality."[7] Compare this entry from the Journals: "God manifest in the flesh of every man is a perfect rule of social life. Justify yourself to an infinite Being in the ostler, and dandy, and stranger, and you shall never repent" (*JMN* V: 126). Throughout Emerson's writings, one comes upon passages like these that suggest the divinity of each person, and of every object or natural "fact":

> Of the universal mind each individual mind is *one more incarnation*. All its properties consist in him. (237; italics added)

> The world proceeds from the same spirit as the body of man. It is *a remoter and inferior incarnation of God* . . . . It is therefore to us the present expositor of the divine mind. (42; italics added)

> One mode of the divine teaching is *the incarnation of the spirit in a form*, – in forms, like my own." (390; italics added) [Cf. Paul's kenotic passage: "and took upon him the form of a servant."]

> I affirmed that we were Spirits now incarnated & should always be Spirits incarnated. Our thought is the income of God. (*JMN* V: 499)

> The divine circulations never rest or linger. Nature is the *incarnation of a thought*, and turns to thought again, as ice becomes water and gas. *The world is mind precipitated*; and the volatile essence is forever escaping again into the state of free thought. (555; italics added)

In Emerson's kenotic model, all things in and of the world (nature, the human body, forms visible and invisible) "preëxist in necessary Ideas in the mind of God . . . . A Fact is the end or last issue of spirit" (25). Put otherwise, for Emerson, *the earth and the fulness thereof is divine thought incarnate*. From an idea or thought in the divine mind the world issues or emanates or "proceeds," first as a substance named variously "volatile essence," or "currents," or "divine circulations"; and then as "Fact": "I proceed from God now & ever shall so proceed" (*JMN* V: 499). Thus the pre-existent (or pre-incarnate) "Ideas" of God, in translation, are continually embodied, for God expresses Himself literally, literally expressing Himself in the forms of persons and things of the world: "There seems to be a necessity in spirit to manifest itself in material forms," we read in the early *Nature* (25). For Emerson, "the definition of *spiritual* should be, *that which is its own evidence*" (475). Nature, then, is divine evidentness (sign, token, trace, mark, proof), composed of an infinite number of divine or spiritual Facts. "God himself does not speak prose, but communicates with us by hints, omens, inference, and dark resemblances in objects lying all around us."[8]

But no matter how the Divine evidences itself, it is always in transition, pausing only temporarily in each form or fact, taking on fleeting and fugitive otherness as it passes. (Asked in 1851 if he believed in God, Emerson answered, "when I speak of God, I prefer to say: It – It.")[9] For Emerson, the words of God are never fixed, never settled or consistent:

> These manifold tenacious qualities, this chemistry and vegetation, these metals and animals, which seem to stand there for their own sake, are means and methods only, – *are words of God, and as fugitive as other words*. (410; italics added)

> For all symbols are fluxional; all language is vehicular and transitive, and is good, as ferries and horses are, for conveyance, not as farms and houses are, for homestead. (463)

> First innuendos, then broad hints, then smart taps are given, suggesting that nothing stands still in nature but death; that the creation is on wheels, in transit, always passing into something else, streaming into something higher; that matter is not what it appears; – that chemistry can blow it all into gas.[10]

Thus the world as text, divine discourse, is fragmentary and discontinuous. Words of God, objects lying around, are "fugitive" – fleeting, vagrant, errant, shifting, vagabond, unsettled. "There are no fixtures in nature," Emerson contends. "The universe is fluid and volatile" (403). "Thin or solid, everything is in flight."[11] "The whole world is the flux of matter over the wires of thought to the pole or points where it would build" (965). "Who looks upon a river in a meditative hour, and is not reminded of the flux of all things? Throw a stone into the stream, and the circles that propagate themselves are the beautiful type of all influence" (21).

I shall focus narrowly on an "incarnational" passage cited above: "The divine circulations never rest or linger. Nature is the incarnation of a thought, and turns to thought again, as ice becomes water and gas. The world is mind precipitated; and the volatile essence is forever escaping again into the state of free thought" (555). Issuing forth, emanating, proceeding from a divine "thought" (cf. *logos* / word), what Emerson calls "the volatile essence" incarnates itself as one of the facts or signs in nature, which then "turns to thought again, as ice becomes water and gas." The same model of transformation and conversion appears in a Journal entry for 1845 and then passes into the late essay "Poetry and Imagination": "All forms are fluent and as the bird alights on the bough & pauses for rest, then plunges into the air again on its way, so the thoughts of God pause but for a moment in any form, but pass into a new form, as if by touching the earth again in burial, to acquire new energy" (*JMN* IX: 301). "Nothing is so fleeting as form; yet never does it quite deny itself" (242). The thoughts of God ("the stream of power and wisdom which animates all whom it floats" [309]), are continually issued, incarnated, buried, and re-incarnated.

Attempting to grasp Emerson's elusive model of thought, I return to his statement, "The world is mind precipitated." In an early lecture, "The Method of Nature," we learn that nature "is the memory of the mind. That which once existed as pure law has now taken body [cf. "incarnate"] as Nature. It existed already in the mind *in solution; now it has been precipitated, and the bright sediment is the world.*" Three paragraphs later, in a passage that recalls Jonathan Edwards, Emerson writes: "The wholeness we admire in the order of the world is the result of *infinite distribution . . . . Every natural fact is an emanation,* and that from which it emanates is an emanation also, and from every emanation is a new emanation" (118–19; italics added). Further on he asks the following:

> Are there not moments in the history of heaven when the human race was not counted by individuals, but was only *the Influenced,* was *God in distribution,* God rushing into multiform benefit? (125; italics added)

Another metaphor of divine in-fluence appears in the so-called "Divinity School Address": "In how many churches, by how many prophets, tell me, is man made sensible that he is an infinite Soul; that the earth and heavens are passing into his mind; that he is drinking forever the soul of God?" (84). Compare the essay "Circles": "I accuse myself of sloth and unprofitableness day by day; but when these waves of God flow into me, I no longer reckon lost time" (411). At the end of *Nature*, Emerson's "Orphic poet" teaches that

> Nature is not fixed but fluid. Spirit alters, moulds, makes it. The immobility or bruteness of nature, is the absence of spirit; to pure spirit, it is fluid, it is volatile, it is obedient. (48)

What is meant by a key phrase of Emerson's cited above, "God in distribution"? The word *distribution* can mean spreading abroad (as of seeds or words), dispersing, division into parts, bestowing in portions. What are these parts, portions, bits and pieces, made of? One clue may be Emerson's statement: *The world is mind precipitated*. In its chemical sense, *to precipitate* means "to deposit in a solid form from solution in a liquid"; "to deposit from suspension or admixture in a liquid as sediment" (*OED*). (Cf: "the bright sediment is the world.") The roots of the verb *to precipitate* are the Latin *prae*, before, and *caput*, head. As soon as anything is precipitated it may rush headlong ("God rushing into multiform benefits"), or it may plunge into some condition. Which is apparently Emerson's model: "As the bird alights on the bough, then plunges into the air again, so the thoughts of God pause but for a moment in any form. All thinking is analogizing, and 'tis the use of life to learn metonymy."[12] Compare this central passage from "Experience":

> Like a bird which alights nowhere, but hops perpetually from bough to bough, is the Power which abides in no man and in no woman, but for a moment speaks from this one, and for another moment from that one. (477)

(The Spirit bloweth . . . .) Formulated otherwise, "all nature is the rapid efflux of goodness executing and organizing itself" (407).

To recapitulate: according to Emerson, all forms pre-exist as Ideas "in solution" in the mind of God. These divine Ideas are "precipitated" as something called "God in distribution" or God in "infinite distribution." At some point in this process, the divine essence rushes into, influences (flows into) and deposits itself as "the bright sediment [which] is the world." Buried fleetingly in one form or "fact" or sign or token or trace – embodied, incarnated – the divine currents or divine discourse re-turn, like so many poetic tropes, to the mind of God. ("God himself does not speak prose, but communicates with us by hints, omens, inference, and dark resemblances in objects lying all around us.") Whereupon divine Ideas promptly throw themselves, pour themselves, plunge headlong, recirculate, into another, metonymic, "natural fact." "The true doctrine of omnipresence is, that God reappears with all his parts in every moss and cobweb. The value of the universe contrives to throw itself [cf. *precipitate*] into every point" (289). At each point (at each stage of the discourse) the value of the universe epitomizes itself, condenses itself, re-presents itself. At no point is it utterly insignificant.

*   *   *

One of Emerson's Journal entries for December 10, 1830, reads: "God is the substratum of all souls. Is not that the solution of the riddle of sympathy?" (*JMN* III: 213). How in Emerson's wandering discourse does one kind of "solution" (i.e. the answer to a problem) accord with Ideas that are "in solution" (in a state of flux, unsettled) in the mind of God?

> That which once existed as pure law, has now taken body as Nature. It existed already in the mind in solution; now it has been precipitated, and the bright sediment is the world. (118)

Whatever existed, or pre-existed, in God's mind in "solution" (from the Latin *solvere*, to loosen) has been precipitated. In *Nature* (1836), we are told that whenever "a spiritual life has been imparted to nature," then "the solid seeming block of matter has been pervaded and dissolved by a thought" (36). We are also told: "Man is the dwarf of himself. Once he was permeated and dissolved by spirit. He filled nature with his overflowing currents" (46). Loosening themselves, rushing in solution into otherness, the out-pourings of God permeate and dissolve the solidity of the matter of fact and the solidity of the self ("how transparent all things are & show God through every part & angle" [*JMN* V: 176]). Thus the crucial and epiphanic "transparent eyeball" passage from *Nature*, where Emerson, dissolved by the "currents of the Universal Being," becomes "part or particle of God" (or of God in distribution):

> In the woods, we return to reason and faith . . . . Standing on the bare ground, – my head bathed by the blithe air, and uplifted into infinite space, – all mean egotism vanishes. I become a

transparent eyeball; I am nothing; I see all; the currents of the Universal Being circulate through me; I am part or particle of God. (10)

At that moment Emerson is anonymous, uprooted, unattached to any house or country: "The name of the nearest friend sounds then foreign and accidental," almost immaterial. Compare an excerpt from the Journals, cited at the outset of the present study: "Excite the soul, & the weather & the town & your condition in the world all disappear, the world itself loses its solidity, nothing remains but the soul & the Divine Presence in which it lives" (*JMN* IV: 383).

> All things are *dissolved to their centre* by their cause, and, in the universal miracle, petty and particular miracles disappear. (270; italics added)
>
> The universe is fluid and volatile . . . . Our globe seen by God is a transparent law, not a mass of facts. *The law dissolves the fact* and holds it fluid. (403; italics added)
>
> Thought *dissolves the material universe* by carrying the mind up into a sphere where all is plastic. (956; italics added)
>
> We sidle towards the problem. If we cld. speak *the direct, solving word*, it wld. solve us too; we should die, or be liberated as the gas in the great gas of the atmosphere. (*JMN* IX: 259–60; italics added)
>
> Every solid in the universe is ready to become fluid on the approach of the mind, and *the power to flux it* is the measure of the mind. If the wall remain adamant, it accuses the want of thought. To a subtler force, it will stream into new forms . . . . (964)

*   *   *

God is the "substratum of all souls"; thus God is the essence or sub-stance that underlies and dissolves reality. ("All the forms are fugitive / But the substances survive.")[13] "Every correspondence we observe in mind and matter suggests a substance older and deeper than either of these nobilities."[14] Throughout Emerson's writings, one finds that the divine solvent or substance is metonymy for what he elsewhere names "stuff" or "one hidden stuff":

the universe is represented in every one of its particles....
Everything is made of one hidden stuff.... The true doctrine of
omnipresence is, that God reappears with all his parts in every
moss and cobweb. (289; italics added)

I do not know if all matter will be found to be made of one
element, as oxygen or hydrogen, at last, but the world of manners
and actions is *wrought of one stuff,* and, begin where we will,
we are pretty sure in a short space to be mumbling our ten
commandments. (367; italics added)

... so poor is nature with all her craft, that, from the beginning
to the end of the universe, *she has but one stuff,* – but one stuff with
its two ends, to serve up all her dream-like variety. Compound it
how she will, star, sand, fire, water, tree, man, *it is still one stuff,*
and betrays the same properties. (547; italics added)

The Same, the Same: *friend and foe are of one stuff;* the ploughman,
the plough, and the furrow, are of one stuff; and *the stuff is such,
and so much, that the variations of form are unimportant.* (638; italics
added)

The diamond and the lampblack it seems are the *same substance*
differently arranged. (*JMN* V: 233)

The divine stuff or "substance" is unnameable, we are told, for
to name is to limit the unboundable: "Fortune, Minerva, Muse,
Holy Ghost, – these are quaint names, too narrow to cover this
unbounded substance. The baffled intellect must still kneel before
this cause which refuses to be named, – ineffable cause ... " (485).
A name is a definition, a particularity, a limit; for Emerson there
is only analogy, and the only trope is metonymy: "All thinking is
analogizing, and 'tis the use of life to learn metonymy." Names for
the divine and ineffable stuff are therefore interchangeable: "For
all things proceed out of this same spirit, which is differently
named love, justice, temperance, in its different applications, just
as the ocean receives different names on the several shores which
it washes" (77).

*   *   *

Near the end of Emerson's *Nature* (1836), natural facts or material
forms are referred to as "*scoriae*":

> There seems to be a necessity in spirit to manifest itself in material forms.... A Fact is the end or last issue of spirit. The visible creation is the terminus or circumference of the invisible world. "Material objects," said a French philosopher, "are necessarily kinds of *scoriae* of the substantial thoughts of the Creator, which must always preserve an exact relation to their first origin; in other words, visible nature must have a spiritual and moral side." (25)

This unnamed "French philosopher" is the Catholic priest Guillaume Oegger, whose *Le vrai Messie; ou l'Ancien et le Nouveau Testaments, examinés d'après les Principes de la Nature* (Paris, 1829), in Elizabeth Peabody's manuscript translation, reached Emerson in the summer of 1835.[15]

Focusing on Emerson's use of *scoriae* in the passage from *Nature* above, Kenneth Burke overhears what he perceives as "strong hints of a fecal motive": "I have found," Burke informs us, "that readers seldom look up the word *scoriae*. It comes from the same root as 'scatological.' Here it conceives the realm of matter as nothing other than God's offal."[16] While it is true that the Latin *scoriae* stems from the Greek word for dung, the Latin word *scoria* (pl. *scoriae*) means dross, the slag that remains after the smelting out of a metal from its ore. *Scoriae* may be rejected by refiners; it may also be ejected by volcanoes. In the latter context, the phrase "bright sediment" evokes the shining scoriform crust that appears wherever lava settles down.

In Emerson's Journal for November 10, 1836, two months after *Nature* was published, there is the following use of *scoriae*:

> Language clothes nature as the air clothes the earth, taking the exact form & pressure of every object. Only words that are new fit exactly the thing, those that are old *like old scoriae that have been long exposed to the air & sunshine*, have lost the sharpness of their mould & fit loosely. (*JMN* V: 246; italics added)

It is not dung that *scoriae* evokes in this Journal entry, but an old, loose, scoriform crust that no longer fits or clings. If the earth was once thought to be the sediment of the Flood, Emerson imagines an unending, eruptive outpouring of a sort of divine lava (from *lavare*, to wash), emanating (from *manare*, to flow), rolling in a great rush from the loosened thoughts of God, and depositing its *scoriae* or sediment as "natural facts." "A Fact is the end or last issue of spirit" (25). More to the point, Emerson's Journal entry resonates with and can be glossed by Oegger's striking comments on divine language:

> The truths of salvation [Oegger writes] were unavoidably enveloped in a human language by Him who came from eternal splendors to visit our obscure retreat; and to have the pure gold and silver of doctrine and truth, we must know how to separate his language from the dross and the scoriae.[17]

In other words, the "fecal motive" overheard by Burke is fecal in the sense of its etymon, *faex*, which refers to dregs – the dregs or sediment left in a wine glass, for example, or the "bright sediment" which is the world. Or to cite the one thing that Emerson recalled from a conversation with Amos Bronson Alcott: "The grass, the earth seemed to him [Alcott] 'the refuse of the spirit'" (*JMN* V: 178).[18]

*　　*　　*

The present discussion of *kenosis* in terms of the divine self-emptying or out-pouring took its point of departure from Emerson's Journal entries of December 28, 1834:

> I honor him who made himself of no reputation.
>
> "He made himself of no reputation." The words have a divine sound. (*JMN* IV: 380, 382)

I intend now to examine Emerson's writings for a further sense of *kenosis* (he emptied himself) and of *tapeinosis* (he humbled himself): for persons and things of no esteem, no reputation, of almost no significance – persons who, like the suffering servant in Isaiah 53 (the biblical type of the "servant" of Philippians 2), may be despised and rejected. Here is a Journal entry for 1838:

> Day creeps after day, each full of facts – dull, strange, despised things that we cannot enough despise . . . . And presently the aroused intellect finds gold & gems in one of these scorned facts, then finds . . . that *a fact is an Epiphany of God* . . . . And because nothing chances . . . in these *motes & dust* he can read *the writing of the True Life* & of *a startling sublimity*." (*JMN* VII: 29; italics added)

Divine discourse, then, may inscribe itself in motes and dust – signifiers that are almost insignificant, practically immaterial ("every thing in nature, even motes and feathers, go [sic] by law" [364]). The "aroused intellect" can dissolve these trivial facts, thereby deciphering "the writing of the True Life." Compare a Journal entry for April 1836: "I at least fully believe that God is in every place, & that, if the mind is excited, it may see him, & in him an infinite wisdom in every object that passes before us" (*JMN* V: 150). Compare too a passage cited earlier in the present study: "Excite the soul, & the weather & the town & your condition in the world all disappear, the world itself loses its solidity, nothing remains but the soul & the Divine Presence in which it lives" (*JMN* IV: 383). The fragment above with its startlingly sublime motes and dust, ciphers of God, accords remarkably with a passage from the late essay, "Beauty" (1860):

> The feat of the imagination is in showing the convertibility of everything into every other thing. Facts which had never before left their stark common sense suddenly figure as Eleusian mysteries.... *All the facts in Nature are nouns of the intellect, and make the grammar of the eternal language*.... *Chaff and dust begin to sparkle, and are clothed about with immortality.* (1111; italics added)

Chaff and dust (refuse of the spirit) are normally accounted trivial; deciphered or undeciphered, however, such facts "make the grammar of the eternal language." All natural objects, Emerson claims, are "like words of a sentence; and if their true order is found, the poet can read their divine significance orderly as in a Bible."[19] Things at everyone's disposal comprise Emerson's "rhetoric of things": "Ah! that I could reach with my words the force of that rhetoric of things in which the Divine Mind is conveyed to me day by day in what I call my life. A loaf of bread, an errand to the town, a temperate man, an industrious man" (*JMN* VII: 488). From Emerson's Journals, here are further examples of almost but not quite insignificant signifiers:

> [January 3, 1834] To Goethe there was no trifle. Glauber picked up what every body else threw away. Cuvier made much of humblest facts. (*JMN* IV: 255; cf. *JMN* V: 134)

[July 18, 1834] What is there of the divine in a load of bricks? What is there of the divine in a barber's shop or a privy? Much. All. (*JMN* IV: 307)

[December 21, 1834] Wherever is life, wherever is God, there the Universe evolves itself as from a centre to its boundless irradiation. Whosoever therefore apprehends the infinite, and every man can, brings all worth & significance into that spot of space where he stands though it be a ditch, a potato-field, a work bench . . . . (*JMN* IV: 367)

[May 15, 1835] Trifles move us more than laws. (*JMN* V: 42)

[November 3, 1836] The sublime enters into every thing even into a baker's score or a school boy's multiplication table, as the Light beams into privies & garrets. (*JMN* V: 240)

[July 17, 1837] Cowley & Donne are philosophers. To their insight there is no trifle. (*JMN* V: 348)

[August 4, 1837] I embrace the common; I explore and sit at the feet of the familiar, the low . . . ." (*JMN* V: 352)

The last of these remarkable excerpts is woven into "The American Scholar" (1837).

> . . . I embrace the common, I explore and sit at the feet of the familiar, the low . . . . What would we really know the meaning of? The meal in the firkin; the milk in the pan; the ballad in the street; the news of the boat; the glance of the eye; the form and gait of the body; – show me the ultimate reason of these matters; *show me the sublime presence of the highest spiritual cause lurking, as always it does lurk, in these suburbs and extremities of nature;* let me see every trifle bristling with the polarity that ranges it instantly on an eternal law; and the shop, the plough, and the ledger, referred to the like cause by which light undulates and poets sing; – and the world lies no longer a dull miscellany and lumber-room, but has form and order; there is no trifle; there is no puzzle [for Emerson there is always a solution]; but one design unites and animates the farthest pinnacle and the lowest trench. (68–69; italics added)

Wherever and whenever the "sublime presence of the highest spiritual cause [is] lurking" – and for Emerson the sublime presence lurks in every form – "there is no trifle." "The deepest pleasure comes I think from the occult belief that *an unknown meaning & consequence lurk in the common every day fact* . . . " (*JMN* V: 212–13; italics added).

* * *

In the late essay "Poetry and Imagination" we come upon the phrase, "the lurking method."[20] And indeed, from time to time, one discovers in Emerson's writings a "lurking" divinity, a fugitive, a vagabond, an anonymous and uprooted signifier, hiding out in "these suburbs and extremities of nature." The biblical type of the lurking divinity is Isaiah 45:15: "Verily thou art a God that hidest thyself, O God of Israel, the Saviour." Compare Emerson's Journals: "From month to month, from year to year I come never nearer to definite speaking of him. He hideth himself. I cannot speak of him without faltering. I unsay as fast as I say my words" (*JMN* V: 76–77).[21] Perhaps the most evocative and compelling of Emerson's "lurking" texts is this Journal entry for April 1867:

> He or That which in despair of naming aright, some have called the *Newness*, – as the Hebrews did not like to pronounce the word, – *he lurks, he hides*, he who is success, reality, joy, power – that which constitutes Heaven, which reconciles impossibilities . . . .
>
> 'Tis all alike, – astronomy, metaphysics, sword, spade, pencil, or instruments and arts yet to be invented, – this is the inventor, the worth-giver, the worth. This is He that shall come; or if he come not, nothing comes: *He that disappears in the moment when we go to celebrate Him.* If we go to burn those that blame our celebration, He appears in them. The Divine Newness. Hoe and spade, sword and pen, cities, pictures, gardens, laws, bibles, are prized only because they were means He sometimes used. So with astronomy, music, arithmetic, castes, feudalism, – we kiss with devotion these hems of his garment, – we mistake them for Him; they crumble to ashes on our lips.[22]

The phrase "He that disappears in the moment when we go to celebrate him") recalls Jesus at Emmaus: "And it came to pass, as he sat at meat with them, he took bread, and blessed it, and brake, and gave it to them. And their eyes were opened, and they knew him; and he vanished out of their sight" (Luke 24:29–30). Thus the moment of transparency, wherein the Emersonian "axis of vision" coincides with the axis of things.

A section of Emerson's Journal entry above recalls a central passage from his late essay, "Works and Days" (1856):

> He lurks, *he* hides, – *he* who is success, reality, joy and power.... 'Tis the old secret of the gods that they come in low disguises. 'Tis the vulgar great who come dizened with gold and jewels. Real kings hide away their crowns in their wardrobes, and affect a plain and poor exterior. In the Norse legend of our ancestors, Odin dwells in a fisher's hut and patches a boat.... So in our history, Jesus is born in a barn and his twelve peers are fishermen.... We owe to genius always the same debt, of lifting the curtain from the common, and showing us that divinities are sitting disguised in the seeming gang of gypsies and pedlars.[23]

The moment the curtain is lifted, the divinity hiding among outlaws and vagrants disappears. No sooner is the disguise revealed than it is at once concealed. The passage directly above suggests a context for this from Emerson's "Experience" (1844):

> I carry the keys of my castle in my hand, ready to throw them at the feet of my lord, whenever and in what disguise soever he shall appear. I know he is in the neighborhood hidden among vagabonds. (475)

"When the gods come among men," Emerson writes, "they are not known. Jesus was not; Socrates and Shakespeare were not" (251).

> The persons who constitute the natural aristocracy, are not found in the actual aristocracy, *or only on its edge*; as the chemical energy of the spectrum is found to be greatest just outside of the spectrum. Yet that is the infirmity of the seneschals, who do not know their sovereign, when he appears. (527; italics added)[24]

Uprooted, disguised among those of no reputation – vagabonds, gypsies, pedlars – hidden on society's edges and margins and outskirts, on the "exterior circumference" of the spectrum, the Newness lurks. Whereupon, at the moment of recognition (the moment of transparency) he or she or it vanishes to assume yet another guise. Emerson's essay "Spiritual Laws" ends with the lurking Newness disguised in the form of a female servant. ("It is a sublime illustration of the Christian doctrine of Humility, – the fact that God is the Servant of the universe" [*JMN* V: 165].)

> Let a man believe in God, and not in names and places and persons. Let the great soul incarnated in some woman's form, poor and sad and single, in some Dolly or Joan, go out to service, and sweep chambers and scour floors, and its effulgent daybeams cannot be muffled or hid, but to sweep and scour will instantly appear supreme and beautiful actions, the top and radiance of human life, and all people will get mops and brooms; until, lo! suddenly the great soul has enshrined itself in some other form . . . .
>
> We know the authentic effects of the true fire through every one of its million disguises. (323)

*   *   *

"A man is a method," Emerson declares (311). There is a tenuous connection to be drawn between persons and things of no reputation (the discourse that doesn't amount to much) and Emerson's errant style of argumentation, which "rolls this way and that like someone who has lost his way, who doesn't know where he is going," like someone who never gets to the point.[25] The substance of Emerson's method may lurk in Sermon LXXVI, delivered eight times between May 1830 and August 1836, just two weeks before *Nature* was published. "Jesus taught as one having authority," Emerson says, citing Matthew 7:29. "How was he able to give this dignity to his instructions?"

> He was not a subtile reasoner. It is the fame of a few men that they have analyzed every action and every thought of man into its first elements; that they have received nothing until it was proved, and have shaken the evidence of the best authenticated facts . . . . Others there are who have applied the same ingenuity to better purpose . . . to fortify with impregnable reason every useful custom, every important truth. Neither of these sorts of skill was the merit of Jesus of whose instructions it is one of the most remarkable features, that *he does not reason at all. He proves nothing by argument.* He simply asserts, and appeals

to his divine commission. Christianity could not be defended if it looked to its author for a systematic account of its pretensions arranged by the rules of logic.[26] (italics added)

About those who had failed to understand Emerson's "Divinity School Address" of 1838, Henry James observed: "They were so provincial . . . they were shocked at his ceasing to care for the prayer and the sermon. They might have perceived that he *was* the prayer and the sermon: not in the least a secularizer, but in his own subtle insinuating way a sanctifier." Emerson, according to James, "is a striking exception to the general rule that writings live in the last resort by their form . . . ." And he added: "we have the impression that the search for a fashion and a manner on which he was always engaged never really came to a conclusion; it draws itself out through his later writings – it drew itself out through his later lectures, like a sort of renunciation of success."[27]

2

In Nomine Diaboli: An Extreme Interpretation of *Billy Budd*

> We must speak by the card, or equivocation will undo us.
>
> *Hamlet* V.i.129

> And though all evils may be assuaged; all evils can not be done away with. For evil is the chronic malady of the universe; and checked in one place, breaks forth in another.
>
> Herman Melville, *Mardi*

"Melville is Shakespearean in the energies of his prose," notes Geoffrey Hartman in *The Fate of Reading*, "and in him too there is a strange fire in the form of pun and wordplay. But what if an entire story, and one as moving as *Billy Budd*, were basically derived from a pun or quibble? Would our astonishment survive our distaste?" And Hartman continues by uncovering a radical link between trivial wordplay and the trivial sublime:

> *Billy Budd* is, probably, so entrenched as a modern classic that the extreme interpretation can only honor it. Vilest things become themselves in it. Yet so much remains unresolved, or hinges on what seems like an accident, that the whole thing quizzes us in an uncomfortable way. Thomas Rymer averred that too much depended on Othello's loss of a handkerchief; and too much, it can be argued, turns on Billy's tendency to stutter.
>
> But the relation of trivial to important is always problematized in fiction. The Biblical drama revolves around "An Apple," as Milton's Satan disdainfully points out. The Rape of Troy seems very different from the Rape of a Lock; but did not both "mighty

contests," as Pope suggests, spring from "trivial things," that is, "amorous causes"? And what is smaller yet more charged than verbal signs, so that, as the Talmud says, "Life and Death are in the hands of the tongue"?

It may be strangely appropriate if *Billy Budd* were punbegotten. The fact that the hero stutters points to either a pathological or a sacred condition; and his name (quite apart from possible mythic allusions) seems to collapse on itself, as if alliteration and stuttering blended to suggest a sacred pathology. . . .

Like Melville himself as narrator, I feel myself delaying, hesitating to come to the point. In the beginning was the Word, and the Word was with God. But there is no such Word here. It is the absence of the word which dooms Billy Budd . . . . What is the condition of the word in Melville's tale?[1]

In response, Hartman alludes to Chapter 10 of *Billy Budd* wherein Claggart, "passing along the battery in a bay of which the mess was lodged," remarks to Billy: "Handsomely done, my lad! And handsome is as handsome did it, too!" (119).[2] No one, says Hartman, expects Claggart's statement to be "very meaningful in a personal or prophetic way. Yet when Billy strikes Claggart he fulfills, literally, that passing phrase. He is that Hand. In consequence he dies at the 'main-yard arm.'" At this point in his essay, Hartman elaborates on the sublimity of the lowly and common pun:

> Hidden wordplay is common enough in fiction and easily overvalued. It shows the condensing power or contaminating energy of the creative mind. Yet, however common, is it not also a fearful feature, a matter for woe and wonder? All at once, in *Billy Budd*, a casual phrase takes on prophetic status. A passing remark becomes part of a fatal series. A figure puts on literal truth and words are dangerous again.[3]

The unfallen Billy Budd may be doomed, not by the "absence of the word," but by the presence of an equivocal and fallen language that he cannot grasp. Like "young Adam before the Fall" (208), Billy is "one to whom not yet has been proffered the questionable apple of knowledge."

> . . . with little or no sharpness of faculty or any trace of the wisdom of the serpent, nor yet quite a dove, he possessed

> that kind and degree of intelligence going along with . . . one to whom not yet has been proffered the questionable apple of knowledge. He was illiterate; he could not read but he could sing, and like the illiterate nightingale was sometimes the composer of his own song. (42)
>
> By his original constitution aided by the cooperating influence of his lot, Billy in many respects was little more than a sort of upright barbarian, much such perhaps as Adam presumably might have been ere the urbane Serpent wriggled himself into his company. (44)

Thus Billy's "mentor," the Dansker, wonders "what might eventually befall a nature like that, dropped into a world not without some mantraps . . . and where such innocence as man is capable of does yet in a moral emergency not always sharpen the faculties or enlighten the will" (111).

Derek Attridge has argued that "the possibility of the pun is the mark of our fallen condition."[4] In *Billy Budd*, the mark of Billy's ignorant, unfallen condition is the impossibility of *recognizing* the pun. When near the end of Melville's narrative, Billy is shown "lying between the two guns, as nipped in the vice of fate" (304), the urbane reader infers that Billy is: (1) gripped in an two-jawed, winding instrument or mantrap; (2) pinched off, cut off, nipped in the bud; (3) wounded by the vice, depravity of Claggart. What the vice grasps is not itself, but a "novice" (116). ("Thus, like the formal Vice, Iniquity, / I moralize two meanings in one word [*Richard III*, III.i.82].) Arrested in "the pre-lapsarian state of language" (to use a phrase of Christopher Ricks's),[5] Billy has been "dropped" into a strange world of double-talk. As Melville explains, "Billy . . . was yet by no means of a satirical turn. The will to it and the sinister dexterity were alike wanting. To deal in double meanings and insinuations of any sort was quite foreign to his nature" (30). In the words of F. O. Matthiessen:

> his [Billy's] simplicity was completely baffled by anything equivocal; he had no knowledge of the bad, no understanding even of indirection. Honest and open hearted, he concluded everyone else to be likewise. In such an undeveloped nature the only overt flaw was a blemish in his physical perfection, a liability to a severe blockage in his speech under moments of emotional pressure. Melville deliberately recurred in this detail

In Nomine Diaboli: An Extreme Interpretation of Billy Budd

to his memory of "the beautiful woman in one of Hawthorne's minor tales," that is to say, to "The Birthmark".... [6]

Hawthorne's "The Birth-mark," with its double language and "deeply impressive moral," circles on Georgiana's "visible mark" (or "impress"), whose shape "bore not a little similarity to the human hand, though of the smallest pygmy size." The hand is stamped on Georgina's face. "It was [Hawthorne reports] the fatal flaw of humanity, which Nature, in one shape or another, stamps ineffaceably on all her productions...."[7] In marked contrast, the flaw of Billy Budd (who has been "impressed" into the H.M.S. *Bellipotent*, a man-of-war) is no "visible blemish... but an occasional liability to a vocal defect."

> Though in the hour of elemental uproar or peril he was everything that a sailor should be, yet under sudden provocation of strong heart-feeling his voice, otherwise singularly musical, as if expressive of the harmony within, was apt to develop an organic hesitancy, in fact more or less of a stutter or even worse. In this particular Billy was a striking instance that the arch interferer, the envious marplot of Eden, still has more or less to do with every human consignment to this planet of Earth. In every case, one way or another he is sure to slip in his little card, as much as to remind us – I too have a hand here. (48)

To explicate the name that is impressed, marked, inscribed, signed, on the calling card of "the arch interferer" is the pursuit of the present chapter.

*   *   *

"a literary sin"

Some divergences or bypaths, Melville remarks, "have an enticement not readily to be withstood." Erring into such a bypath, we "can promise ourselves that pleasure which is wickedly said to be in sinning, for a literary sin the divergence will be" (58). As Milton's Satan knew, one of the pleasures in sinning is the pleasure in sinuous and wriggling words. Thus we turn towards the *handsome/hand* pun in *Billy Budd*, of which Hartman has observed: "A passing remark becomes part of a fatal series. A figure puts on literal truth and words are dangerous again." His paradigm recalls Emerson's *Nature*: "Every word which is used to express a moral or intellectual fact, if traced to its root, is found to be borrowed from some material appearance" (20).[8] Compare a passage from Emerson's essay, "The Poet":

> For, though the origin of most of our words is forgotten, each word was at first a stroke of genius, and obtained currency, because for the moment it symbolized the world to the first speaker and to the hearer. The etymologist finds the deadest word to have been once a brilliant picture. (457)

For example, when the word *handsome* is returned to its "literal truth" (its original, concrete sense), it signifies "easy to handle or manipulate" (*OED* 1). Likewise the adjective *upright* ("Billy in many respects was little more than a sort of upright barbarian"), which may be used to express a moral fact ("strictly honourable"); traced to its root, *upright* means "erect," "vertical," a sense still current. Likewise, as a moral, even a sinful, fact, *insinuate* means "to ingratiate oneself," "to hint obliquely"; whereas in its radical sense, *insinuate* means "to wind, curve, bend oneself into," and "to enter through a narrow way."

When Melville uses the word *handsome* in a manner suggestive of its "literal truth" ("easy to handle"), *handsome* insists also on its prevailing and current sense: "having a fine form or figure" (*OED* 6). The dextrous play of difference between the etymon of *handsome* and its figural issue informs a not uncharacteristic passage from Emerson's "Experience":

> I take this evanescence and lubricity of all objects, which lets them slip through our fingers then when we clutch hardest, to be the most unhandsome part of our condition. (473)[9]

Here are two not unrelated lines from Emerson's "Prudence":

> Let him, if he have hands, handle. (360)

> The thought is not then taken hold of by the right handle. (366)

Marking dextrously the two lines above, one suddenly recalls an apparently innocent passage from Emerson's Journals:

We would speak the words of Jesus & use his name only, as if we would play the tunes of Handel only, or learn Handel's music, instead of becoming Handels ourselves.... (*JMN* V: 492–93)

*　　*　　*

getting a handle on Claggart

"Since punning is considered crass," Frederick Ahl observes, "the critic has no scholarly obligation to look for puns and full license to explain them away if efforts to avoid acknowledging their odious presence fail."[10] Take as a striking instance of bi-lingual wordplay the give-away name of the insinuating Claggart, clearly begotten of the German verb *klagen* (to complain, to lament), and explained away by critics, even though Melville tells us that "there lurked a bit of accent in [Claggart's] speech" (93).[11] *Der Kläger* is a plaintiff, complainant; *anklagen* means to accuse; *die Anklage* is a charge or accusation; *der Ankläger* is the accuser. In late High German (to follow Duden's *Herkunftswörterbuch*), *Kläger* was written *clagare*. John (Hans?) Claggart is the sinisterly dextrous master-at-arms, whose nature is to obstruct Billy and to accuse him falsely:

> If Claggart was a false witness – that closed the affair. And therefore, before trying the accusation, he [Captain Vere] would first practically test the accuser.... (215)

> Claggart deliberately advanced within a short range of Billy and ... briefly recapitulated the accusation. (221)

> Meanwhile, the accuser's eyes ... underwent a phenomenal change.... (222)

> "Speak, man!" said Captain Vere to the transfixed one, struck by his [Billy's] aspect even more than by Claggart's. "Speak! Defend yourself!" Which appeal caused but a strange dumb gesturing and gurgling in Billy; amazement at such an accusation so suddenly sprung on inexperienced nonage; this, and, it may be, horror of the accuser's eyes, serving to bring out his lurking defect.... (223)

Claggart's literary antecedents include Milton's Satan, "The tempter ere th' accuser of mankind" (*PL* IV, 10), and *his* model, the biblical accuser, Satan.

The name Satan is the Hebrew word *satan* transferred to English: according to Rabbi Klein's *Etymological Dictionary*, the Hebrew noun *satan* derives from a verb meaning "he acted as an adversary of, showed enmity to; he charged, accused."[12] In the Septuagint (LXX; the early Greek version of the Hebrew Bible) the Greek word *diabolos* was used to render the Hebrew *satan*: "And the Lord said unto Satan [*diabolo*], Whence comest thou?" (Job 1:7). In the New Testament, as in the Apocrypha, *satanas* and *diabolos* both appear: Paul tends to use the word *satanas* (*diabolos* is used in Ephesians): "Wherefore we would have come unto you, even I Paul . . . but Satan [*satanas*] hindered us" (1 Thess. 2:18). *Diabolos* appears in the Pastoral Epistles:

> For men shall be lovers of their own selves, covetous, boasters, proud, blasphemers, disobedient to parents, unthankful, unholy,
> Without natural affections, trucebreakers, false accusers [*diaboloi*], incontinent, fierce despisers of those that are good. (2 Timothy 3:2–3, AV)

Like a lion stalking its prey, the devil is the adversary of mankind: "Be sober, be vigilant; because your adversary [*antidikos*] the devil [*diabolos*], as a roaring lion, walketh about, seeking whom he may devour" (1 Peter 5:8). Satan's original sin is said to be envy: "through envy of the devil [*diaboloi*] came death into the world: and they that do hold of his side do find it" (Wisdom 2:24).

Denominating Claggart, Melville alludes to a certain lexicon "based on Holy Writ": "And indeed, if that lexicon which is based on Holy Writ were any longer popular, one might with less difficulty define and denominate certain phenomenal men" (130). That lexicon may be Kitto's *Cyclopaedia of Biblical Literature* (1845; 10th edition, New York, 1853), from which the following is excerpted:[13]

> Devil (*Diabolos*) is the more frequent term of designation given to Satan in the New Testament. Both Satan and devil are in several instances applied to the same being (Rev. xii.9). "That old serpent, the devil and Satan" . . . . Devil is the translation of *diabolos*, from the verb *diaballo*, "to thrust through," "to carry over," and, tropically, "to inform against," "to accuse." He is also called the accuser of the brethren (Rev. xii.10).

Literature, Hartman hypothesizes, writing on Derrida's *Glas*, "is the elaboration of a specular name";[14] or in Jonathan Culler's terms,

In Nomine Diaboli: *An Extreme Interpretation of* Billy Budd 47

it is "a punning exfoliation of the proper name."[15] In *Glas*, Derrida speaks of "the great stake [*enjeu*] of literary discourse":

> I do say discourse: patient, crafty [*rusée*], quasi animal or vegetable, untiring, monumental, derisory too, but on the whole holding itself up to derision, transformation of his proper name, *rebus*, into things, into the name of things.[16]

What if *Billy Budd* were derived, not finally from a pun or quibble on the word *handsome* (as Hartman has suggested), but from the proper name *Diabolos*, ingeniously and patiently and craftily transformed? In June 1851, during the final stages of work on *Moby-Dick*, Melville wrote to Hawthorne: "This is the book's motto (the secret one), *Ego non baptiso te in nomine* – but make out the rest yourself." In *Moby-Dick*, that motto has become Ahab's blasphemous incantation over his harpoon: "Ego non baptizo te in nomine patris, sed in nomine diaboli!"[17]

In the Septuagint and the New Testament, the Greek word *diabolos* is a term of designation given to Satan, the adversary and accuser. Traced to its etymon, *diabolos* is found to be borrowed from several material appearances. According to Liddell and Scott, *diaballo* signifies: (1) throw or carry over or across; (2) set at variance, set against, bring into discredit, to be filled with suspicion or resentment against another; (3) attack a man's character, calumniate, accuse, complain of, speak or state slanderously. Under the entry for *devil*, the *OED* gives: "in Jewish and Christian use 'the Devil, Satan', a specific application of *diabolos* 'accuser, calumniator, slanderer, traducer', f. *diaballein* to slander traduce, *lit.* to throw across, f. *dia* through, across + *ballein* to cast." If *Billy Budd* is "punbegotten," it is surely begotten from a artfully-extended pun on the etymological meanings of *diabolos*. To take over our previous citation from Emerson, the name *diabolos*, though its origin is forgotten, "was at first a stroke of genius and obtained currency."

In a crucial passage, we are told by Melville that Billy Budd has

> an occasional liability to a vocal defect . . . . under sudden provocation of strong heart-feeling his voice . . . was apt to develop an organic hesitancy, in fact more or less of a *stutter* or even worse. In this particular Billy was a *striking* instance that the arch *interferer*, the envious marplot of Eden, still has more or less to do with every human consignment to this planet of Earth. In every case,

one way or another he is sure to slip in his little card, as much as to remind us – I too have a hand here. (48; italics added)

Again, the Greek verb *diaballein*, traced to its root, signifies "to thrust, to strike through, to throw across," a vivid etymology that recalls "The Quarter-Deck" chapter in *Moby-Dick*:

If man will strike, strike through the mask! How can the prisoner reach outside except by thrusting through the wall? To me, the white whale is that wall, shoved near to me.[18]

Given what Hayford and Sealts in their edition of *Billy Budd* have called "Melville's meticulous regard not only for words themselves but for natural fact" (168n), it is not unremarkable that the verb *stutter* ("to speak with continued involuntary repetition of sound or syllables"; "to stammer") is cognate with the German *stossen*, "to push," "to thrust," "to strike." Furthermore, the English *interferer* ("the arch interferer, the envious marplot of Eden"), when traced to its root via the Old French *s'entreferir*, means "to strike each other." Billy, Melville explains, "was a striking instance that the arch interferer, the envious marplot of Eden still has more or less to do with every human consignment to this planet of earth"; "'But Billy came [Captain Graveling says]; and it was like a Catholic priest striking peace in an Irish shindy'" (20); "the Nore Mutiny was what a strike in the fire brigade would be to London threatened by general arson" (51); "Any tangible object associated with some striking incident of the service is converted into a monument" (345). In its final state, Leaf 137 reads, "[Claggart] let escape an ironic inkling . . . as to what it was that had first moved him against Billy, namely, his significant personal beauty"; in an earlier stage of composition, however, the closing words read: "his striking personal beauty." Vere announces to the martial court:

"Quite aside from any conceivable motive actuating the master-at-arms . . . a martial court must needs . . . confine its attention to the blow's consequence, which consequence is to be deemed not other wise than as the striker's deed." (256)

Other passages should be noted: "this struck [Vere] as a most immodest presumption" (201); "Claggart's envy struck deeper" (140); "Billy's aspect recalled to [Vere] that of a bright young schoolmate of his whom he had once seen struck by much the same startling impotence" (225); "'Struck dead by an angel of God'" (232); "As to the drumhead court, it struck the surgeon as impolitic, if nothing more" (235). Even, Billy had an "erring sense of uninstructed honor" (253). As for Billy's "beginnings," he was what Melville punningly calls "a presumable by-blow" (written "bye-blow" in the manuscript): "Yes, Billy Budd was a foundling, a presumable by-blow, and evidently, no ignoble one" (41). Billy is that blow's consequence.

* * *

"D-d-damme, I don't know what you are d-d-driving at, or what you mean . . . ." (Leaf 158)

"The pun . . . is not just an ambiguity that has crept into an utterance unawares, to embarrass or amuse before being dismissed; it is an ambiguity *unashamed of itself*, and this is what makes it a scandal and not just an inconvenience. In place of a context designed to suppress latent ambiguity, the pun is the product of a context deliberately constructed to enforce an ambiguity, to render impossible the choice between meanings, to leave the reader or hearer endlessly oscillating in semantic space."[19] Thus Derek Attridge, in words that suggest to me a link between Claggart, the unashamed scandal or *skandalon* of *Billy Budd*, and Melville's deliberately questionable language. Billy's "occasional liability," we are told, is his stuttering, stumbling, stammering. On occasion, Claggart, "the arch interferer," is Billy's liability, obstacle, impediment, hinderance, stumbling block. In Matthiessen's words, Billy's "only overt flaw was . . . a liability to a severe blockage in his speech under moments of emotional pressure."

Now in the Septuagint, the Greek word *skandalon* and its word group are used "for two sets of Hebrew terms with the different senses of striking or catching in a snare, and slipping or stumbling (with the transferred meaning 'occasion of sin')" (*Theological Dictionary of The New Testament*). Psalm 141: 4, for example, reads: "Keep me from the snares [*skandalon*] which they have laid for me." Compare Joshua 23:13: "but they shall be snares and traps [*skandala*] unto you, and scourges in your sides." Another meaning of *skandalon* (to follow Arndt and Gingrich's *Greek-English Lexicon of the New Testament*) is "temptation to sin, enticement to apostasy."

Thus in Wisdom 14:11, wooden idols are called "stumblingblocks [*skandala*] to the souls of men, and a snare to the feet of the unwise."

> Woe unto the world because of offenses [*skandalon*]! for it must needs be that offenses [*skandala*] come; but woe to that man by whom the offense [*skandalon*] cometh! Wherefore if thy hand or thy foot offend thee [*skandalizei*], cut them off . . . . (Matthew 18:7–8)

> But he [i.e., Jesus] turned, and said unto Peter, Get thee behind me, Satan [*satana*]: thou art an offense [*skandalon*] unto me. (Matthew 16:23)

Whereas in the Septuagint, *skandalon* can mean "both 'trap' and 'stumbling block' or 'cause of ruin,'" in other Greek literature, *skandalon* is used mostly in the figurative sense of a "snare for an enemy, cause of moral stumbling"; but it is "certainly an old word meaning 'trap'" (*OED*). The Dansker wonders "what might eventually befall a nature like that, dropped into a world not without some mantraps." And Squeak, one of Claggart's "more cunning corporals," goes about "laying little traps [cf. *skandala*] for the worriment of the foretopman" (147). One of the senses of the verb *scandalizo* is "to set traps." The "means" which Satan uses (we read in Kitto's *Cyclopaedia*) "are variously called wiles, darts, depths, snares, all deceivableness of unrighteousness."

Confronting Captain Vere in order to slander Billy Budd, Claggart insinuates that Billy is himself a trap: "You have but noted his fair cheek. A mantrap may be under the ruddy-tipped daisies" (207). Likewise, when Claggart repeats his accusation to Billy's face, Billy is "transfixed" (lit. pierced or thrust through) by Claggart's charge, "so suddenly sprung on inexperienced nonage." (The Greek word *skandalethron* means the "spring of a trap.") Given the dense and recoiling language of *Billy Budd*, it can be no accident that the English words *slander* and *scandal* spring from a common root, nor that the word *stammer* is cognate with *stumble*. (At one stage in the composition of Leaf 47, Melville replaced the word *stammer* with *stutter*.) "The fact that the hero stutters," says Hartman of *Billy Budd*, "points to either a pathological or a sacred condition." More directly, it may point to the pathological Claggart, the double tongued man-trap and *skandalon* of Melville's narrative, and Billy's equivocal "liability."

A further etymological point: in the *OED* the verb *to clog* (whose derivation is said to be "obscure," but which appears to be cognate with the Middle English *klogge*, "a log of wood") is defined as: "To load so as to entangle or impede the motion of." In its figurative sense, *clog* may mean: "To hinder, impede, obstruct (actions)"; "to choke up so as to hinder free passage, to obstruct." On Leaf 89 of the manuscript, Melville first wrote "Claggat," then altered it to read "Claggart." There is a pun on *Claggart / clog* in the scene of the "interview" between Claggart and Captain Vere: "as to Claggart ... his [Vere's] feelings partook ... of strong suspicion clogged by strange dubieties" (214). If the name *Claggart* has overtones of the biblical stumbling block or *scandalon*, it also evokes wooden planks, wooden blocks, and certainly the "jewel-block" in Melville's pun-ridden ballad, "Billy in the Darbies." Thus in Vere's cabin, when Billy's arm strikes the fatal blow, Claggart's body "fell over lengthwise like a heavy plank tilted from erectness" (226). Melville then remarks mordantly:

> To be prepared for burial, Claggart's body was delivered to certain officers of his mess. And here, not *to clog* the sequel with *lateral matters*, it may be added that at a suitable hour, the master-at-arms was committed to the sea. (295; italics added)

*   *   *

"secret currency"

In *The Language of Allegory*, Maureen Quilligan argues that the "plots of all allegorical narratives ... unfold as investigations into the literal truth inherent in individual words, considered in the context of their whole histories as words." The "plot" of the Book of Holiness, for example, "unfolds as Spenser's investigation into the meaning of one particular word: error. The etymology of the term, that in Latin means 'wandering,' names what the Redcrosse Knight and Una do throughout the greater part of the book."

> Spenser presents the wordplay obviously at first, then slowly builds the awareness of its structural significance. He repeats the word and its cognates often, keeping it before the reader. The process develops almost subliminally, for the reader is easily

distracted by events . . . . [20]

Appropriating Quilligan's phrasing, I venture that the leaves of *Billy Budd* unfold, exfoliate, as Melville's investigation into Claggart's "true antecedents" (95), or into the primary sense of one proper and improper name, Claggart/*Diabolos*/Satan, transformed "into things, into the name of things" (Derrida is cited). Again, according to Rabbi Klein, the Hebrew noun *satan* derives from a verb meaning "he acted as an adversary of, showed enmity to; *he charged*, accused" (italics added).

"And indeed," says Melville, "if that lexicon which is based on Holy Writ were any longer popular, one might with less difficulty define and denominate certain phenomenal men" (130). What does the loaded phrase "certain phenomenal men" refer to except to men who are characterized by a certain natural phenomenon? In Claggart's case, that phenomenon may be electrical. Claggart's nature, Melville tells us, is "surcharged with energy":

> With no power to annul the elemental evil in him, though readily enough he could hide it; apprehending the good, but powerless to be it; a nature like Claggart's, *surcharged with energy* as such natures almost invariably are, what recourse is left to it but to recoil upon itself and, like the scorpion for which the Creator alone is responsible, act out to the end the part allotted it. (142; italics added)

Having accumulated a surcharge or surplus or excess of energy, yet with "no power to annul the elemental evil in him," Claggart (like Milton's Satan, like an electric motor) has no recourse but to wind up recoiling upon himself. ("And like a devilish engine back recoils/Upon himself . . . " [*PL* IV, 17–18].) Electricity may be defined as an "abnormal condition of the atoms or molecules of a body usually due to an excess or deficiency of electrons" (*OED*). Positive electricity is a deficiency of electrons; negative electricity is an excess of electrons. This two-part model underlies polarity, compensation, magnetic attraction, and magnetic repulsion. Or as Emerson notes in "Compensation": "Polarity, or action and reaction, we meet in every part of nature . . . in electricity, galvanism, and chemical affinity."

> Superinduce magnetism at one end of a needle; the opposite magnetism takes place at the other end . . . . An inevitable

dualism bisects nature so that each thing is a half and suggests another to make it whole . . . . (286–87)

In *Billy Budd*, John Claggart, the accuser or *diabolos*, is portrayed as a driving (and driven) force, transmitting through an underground system of contacts and "compliant" connections what I take to be "the power of Satan" (Acts 26:18). In Melville's words, the master-at-arms was "a sort of chief of police *charged* among other matters with the duty of preserving order on the populous gun decks" (89; italics added). (Compare the puns on *charge* and on *discharge* made in *Paradise Lost* by Milton's Satan).[21] Melville's artfully-submerged pun in the phrase "among other matters" implies that, apart from Claggart, other forms of charged matter are on board – matters embodied in Claggart's so-called "corporals." If Claggart has an excess load of energy, these "corporals of the lower decks" (107), or "subordinates," placed under his "control," are "various converging wires of underground influence" (103). In electrical terms, they are conductors charged with transmitting and transforming Claggart's negative influence.

One night, a "mysterious emissary" of Claggart's, tempting Billy to some form of apostasy, makes what Melville terms an "overture": "'We are not the only impressed ones, Billy. There's a gang of us. – Couldn't you – help – at a pinch?'" (157) The suggestive word "pinch" with its erotic overtones resurfaces during Claggart's first "interview" with Vere: "'Not for nothing does he [Billy] insinuate himself into the good will of his shipmates, since at the least they will at a pinch say – all hands will – a good word for him, and at all hazards'" (207). All hands, including the emissary's hands, will at a pinch impress the Handsome Sailor. If Billy can't figure out what the emissary is "d-d-driving at" it is because the unfallen Billy is "illiterate" (he cannot read, and he iterates ill). Moreover he is utterly unequivocal, and Claggart's emissary is an "equivocal young person" (185). It was "the first time in his [Billy's] life that he had ever been personally approached in underhand intriguing fashion" (161):

The more he turned the matter over, the more he was nonplussed, and made uneasy and discomfited. In his disgustful recoil from an overture which, though he but ill comprehended, he instinctively knew must involve evil of some sort, Billy Budd was like a young horse fresh from the pasture suddenly inhaling a vile whiff from some chemical factory, and by repeated snortings trying to get it out of his nostrils and lungs. (162–63)

I shall focus on the the emissary's so-called "overture": (1) During the night, Billy is "stirred into semiconsciousness" by Claggart's "emissary," who whispers, "'Slip into the lee forechains, Billy; there is something in the wind'" (154). (2) Drowsy, but curious to know "what could be in the wind," Billy rises to meet the emissary, who holds up "two small objects faintly twinkling in the night-light" (157). (3) Emissaries (persons sent on a mission and charged with an odious or underhand object) may emit something subtle – light, sound, gases, odours, currency, and so on. (4) Claggart's emissary (Melville also calls him a "conspirator" [164]) makes some sort of "overture" to Billy; "inhaling" whatever was emitted, Billy associates it with a "vile" smell from a "chemical factory." (5) Put delicately, Claggart's emissary discharges something by means of an overture or aperture (scatological jokes about the devil are legion; and see the pun on "overture" made by Milton's Satan).[22] (6) Inhaling "a vile whiff" of whatever is in the wind (or con-*spiritus*), Billy "instinctively" knows it "must involve evil of some sort." The noxious, chemical overture from which Billy "recoil[s]" may represent an emission of energy that has influenced, flowed into, Billy. Compare Ahab's aside in *Moby-Dick*: "'Something shot from my dilated nostrils, he [Starbuck] has inhaled it in his lungs. Starbuck now is mine; cannot oppose me now, without rebellion.'" Whereupon Melville speaks of "the enchanted, tacit acquiescence of the mate . . . ."[23]

What may appear as a wilful reading of *Billy Budd* is supported in part by the scene of Billy's impressment by Lieutenant Ratcliffe, the boarding officer of the *Bellipotent*. At one time, Captain Graveling explains to Ratcliffe, "my forecastle was a rat-pit of quarrels."

> But Billy came; and it was like a Catholic priest striking peace in an Irish shindy. Not that he preached to them or said or did anything in particular; but *a virtue went out of him*, sugaring the sour ones. They took to him like hornets to treacle.[24] (20; italics added)

(In "Compensation" Emerson remarks reassuringly: "Every sweet has its sour; every evil its good" [287].) Billy's "virtue" is a sweet and active principle, that, in Graveling's words, "went out of him," influencing the rats on board as though Billy were Orpheus, charming wild animals and "striking peace" among the unruly crew of the Argonauts or as though he were Jesus, healing the multitude (see Luke 6:19). We recall that Billy "could not read but he could sing" (42); Claggart calls Billy "'the sweet and pleasant young fellow'" (123); and Melville alludes in passing to "the comely young David," (140) the sweet singer of the Bible. (Before he is hung, Billy's final words are "delivered in the clear melody of a singing bird on the point of launching from the twig" [318].) Billy's role as Orpheus, the fabulous enchanter, is reinforced by what I take to be a central remark of Vere's: "'With mankind . . . forms, measured forms, are everything; and that is the import couched in the story of Orpheus with his lyre spellbinding the wild denizens of the wood'" (333). Billy's power to enchant rats finds its parodic double in (the liar) Claggart's demonic power to galvanize and to control his corporals – the rat-like denizens of the *Bellipotent*.

Already we have met Claggart's "emissary" (or spy) who, when he is "espied" by Billy, is found to be: "Rather chubby too for a sailor . . . . In short the last man in the world, one would think, to be overburdened [cf. *surcharged*] with thoughts" (164). The word *chubby* recalls the word *plump* in the scene of Billy's impressment into the H.M.S. *Bellipotent* – a man-of-war "obliged to put to sea short of her proper complement of men."

> Plump upon Billy at first sight in the gangway the boarding officer, Lieutenant Ratcliffe pounced, even before the merchantman's crew was formally mustered on the quarter deck for his deliberate inspection. And him only he elected. For whether it was because the other men when ranged before him showed to ill advantage after Billy, or whether he had some scruples in view of the merchantman's being rather short-handed, however it might be, the officer contented himself with his first spontaneous choice. To the surprise of the ship's company, though much to the lieutenant's satisfaction, Billy made no demur. But indeed, any demur would have been as idle as the protests of a goldfinch popped into a cage. (12)

At one stage of Melville's composition, the final lines above read: "Billy made no demur to his capture. But indeed, any demur would have been as idle as a goldfinch popped into a wire cage." That at his impressment/capture Billy, the sweet singer, has been "popped into" a portable metal prison, may link him up to Claggart's "various converging wires of underground influence." In any case, it indicates that Billy, the song-bird, is caught in the snare of the *skandalon*. It also prepares us for the scene where Billy, "nipped in the vice of fate," is "lying prone in irons in one of the bays formed by the regular spacing of the guns comprising the batteries on either side" (300). Again, the word *battery* comes from the French *battre*, to strike, just as the verb *to pounce* is a variant of *to punch* – to strike a blow with the fist, or to pierce through.

Notice the number of animals on board Melville's ship: Billy as goldfinch and as the inauspicious nightingale; the rats lurking in the name of Lieutenant Ratcliffe, of Mrs. Radcliffe (125), *and* in the "official rattan" carried by Claggart (117). In addition we have the "urbane Serpent," the scorpion, the hornets, the dove, and the horse that inhales a "vile whiff" of evil. Captain Graveling of the *Rights-of-Man* is a "sea-dog"; and Billy, to whom Melville compares "a dog of St. Bernard's breed" (42), and a "dog of generous breed" (257), is "a cynosure" (the Greek word *kuwv* means dog) (1). We have manuscript evidence that Billy was envisioned as "animally heroic" (135c), a detail that may explain the reference to the "dog of St. Bernard's breed." In passing, Melville mentions "promiscuous lame ducks of morality" (96) and Guy Fawkes (pronounced "Fox" in America, and written "Fawks" in the manuscript [150]). The "ursine" Dansker with his "guarded cynicism" recognizes that Claggart's emissary is a "cat's paw"; moreover the Dansker has "small weasel eyes" (110), described also as "ferret eyes" (113). And then there is someone on board named Squeak,

> one of [Claggart's] more cunning corporals, a grizzled litle man, so nicknamed by the sailors on account of his squeaky voice and sharp visage ferreting about the dark corner of the lower decks after interlopers, satirically suggesting to them the idea of a rat in a cellar. (145)

Employed as Claggart's "implicit tool," Squeak (a "telltale") ingeniously transforms what he overhears, "perverting to his chief certain innocent frolics of the good-natured foretopman, besides inventing for his mouth sundry contumelious epithets he claimed to have overheard him let fall" (147). To what effect does Melville employ the word *ferreting* in his description of the rat-like Squeak if not (1) to echo the earlier description of Ratcliffe, pouncing on

Billy Budd; (2) to reinforce the description of Claggart's "peculiar ferreting genius" (102) and of the Dansker's "ferret eyes"; (3) to remind us that the ferret is a variety of the common polecat or *putorius foetidus*, whose Latin name signifies "a foul-smelling animal with a foul smell" (polecats, like skunks, are chemically repellent); (4) to recall the word *interferer* ("the arch interferer, the envious marplot of Eden"); (5) to hint at the ferrous content of some metals, and thus of the conductive or "compliant" nature of Claggart's various tools.

Let us connect the repellent nature of Claggart's emmisary and of his other ferreting corporals to the electrical and magnetic powers of some bodies to attract and to repel other bodies. Matthiessen speaks of "the ambiguous mixture of attraction and repulsion that governs Claggart's actions concerning Billy."[25] Describing "an antipathy spontaneous and profound" felt by Claggart for Billy, Melville employs the loaded phrase *"more or less of contact"* (126; italics added):

> Now there can exist no irritating juxtaposition of dissimilar personalities comparable to that which is possible aboard a great warship fully manned and at sea. There, every day among all ranks, almost every man comes into *more or less of contact* with every other man . . . . Imagine how all this might eventually operate on some peculiar human creature the direct reverse of a saint! (126; italics added)

An earlier draft of Leaf 126, cited directly above, included this:

> Imagine how . . . this abnormally recurring proximity or rubbing against his contrary might eventually operate on some peculiar human creature the direct reverse of a saint.

Alerted to the presence of electro-magnetic currents, direct and indirect, in *Billy Budd*, one overhears in Melville's seemingly innocent phrase "more or less" a signal of Claggart's interferring and charged hand: Billy "was apt to develop an organic hesitancy, in fact *more or less* of a stutter or even worse. In this particular Billy was a striking instance that the arch interferer . . . still has *more or less* to do with every human consignment to this planet of earth" (48; italics added). Claggart interprets "the affair of the spilled soup" as "the sly escape of a spontaneous feeling on Billy's part *more or less* answering to the antipathy on his own" (144; italics added). Claggart, "the arch interferer," has *"more or less* of contact" with Billy. Billy's so-called "occasional liability" may be occasioned by contact with his liability, Claggart, whose charge is carried by his "converging wires of underground influence."

Furthermore, the surcharged Claggart influences Captain Vere. In Chapter 18, intending to charge Billy with mutiny, Claggart requests an "interview" with Vere. Becoming "sensible of Claggart's presence," Vere feels "a vaguely repellent distaste":

> No sooner did the commander oberve who it was that now deferentially stood awaiting his notice when a peculiar expression came over him. It was not unlike that which uncontrollably will flit across the countenance of one at unawares encountering a person who, though known to him indeed, has hardly been long enough known for thorough knowledge, but something in whose aspect nevertheless now for the first provokes *a vaguely repellent distaste*. (195; italics added)

Describing this "interview" (with its eye-to-eye contact), Melville reiterates what he has said earlier: that Claggart is *"charged among other things* with police surveillance of the crew" (italics added). (Cf. "a sort of chief of police *charged* among other matters with the duty of preserving order on the populous gun decks" [89; italics added].) This is a signal that during the "interview" the highly "surcharged" Claggart may be subtly and electrically in-fluencing Vere, whose qualities are said to be "sterling" (80). Earlier, as Vere has one hand on the ship's "rigging," Melville notes "some minor matter *interrupting* the current of [Vere's] thoughts" (79; italics added). Alluding vaguely to a theory of contact electricity, Melville may imagine Claggart as interrupting, interferring with, tapping into, an electro-magnetic circuit. The word "current" is reiterated when Melville explains how the "appellation" Starry Vere "got currency." Concerning a rumour about Claggart's mysterious "former life," we are told: "The fact that nobody could substantiate this report was nothing against its secret currency" (94).

I also suspect that just as Milton's Satan disguises himself by entering the form of the serpent, so in *Billy Budd* Satan/*Diabolos* is incarnated temporarily in the "spare and tall" (90) form of John Claggart.[26] After the fatal blow, Vere and Billy attempt to raise the body of the master-at-arms: "The spare form flexibly acquiesced, but inertly. It was like handling a dead snake" (227). Melville's pun on *spare* may be a dead give-away: the adjective can mean lean or thin; as well, it can refer to something superfluous, something that can be spared, like a spare part in a devilish engine, or a spare and vacant room, or snakeskin. Vere and Billy lower the snake-like body; whereupon Vere's "aspect" changes noticeably. According to Melville, Vere has been "absorbed in taking in all the bearings of the event"; and given the charged nature of the scene and of magnetic bearings in general, what Vere has taken in is probably the phenomenal and elemental nature of Claggart/Satan. We recall that Claggart's body "fell over lengthwise like a heavy plank tilted from erectness" (226). Repeating the word "erectness," Melville writes:

> Regaining erectness Captain Vere with one hand covering his face stood to all appearances as impassive as the object at his feet. Was he *absorbed in taking in* all the bearings of the event . . . ? Slowly he uncovered his face; and the effect was as if the moon emerging from an eclipse should reappear with quite another aspect than that which had gone into hiding. (228; italics added)

Satan/Claggart, like the inconstant moon, has gone into hiding; a few moments later he reappears "with quite another aspect," which I take to be Vere's. Thus while the martial court is proceeding, and while the three hand-picked officers are being manipulated by Vere's rhetoric, Vere, "energize[d]" by something, paces the cabin to and fro like the biblical Satan (*diabolos*), who, when asked by God, "Whence comest thou?" answers: "From going to and fro in the earth, and from walking up and down in it" (Job 1:7).

> Turning, he [Vere] to-and-fro paced the cabin athwart; in the returning ascent to windward climbing the slant deck in the ship's lee roll . . . . (263)

*   *   *

"*the proximity of the malign*"

Too much, it can be argued wearily, is being made of Claggart's "surcharged" nature, of diabolic influence, and of electrical and magnetic undercurrents in *Billy Budd*.[27] Thus I present a Leaf of the manuscript, cancelled at some stage by Melville, where Billy's fatal blow is said to be "electrically energised." The passage as it appears in the genetic text, more or less:

> Yes, the young mute's blow, an athlete's, a blow electrically [>con energised x <x by] the inmost [<inmost] spasm of his heart, unintentionally had had upon its object the [p add all but] [>instantanious] operation of the divine judgement on Annannias. ([229a] 355)

Stated otherwise, the blow/"spasm of his heart" for which Billy is ultimately hung was "electrically energised," induced, by the proximity of the surcharged inductor, Claggart (cf. "under sudden provocation of strong heart-feeling his voice, otherwise singularly musical,..was apt to develop an organic hesitancy" [48]). Earlier, describing Billy's "ignorant innocence" of the presence of evil, Melville employs the telling phrase, "the proximity of the malign" (181).

At this critical juncture, and fascinated by the hidden nature of Claggart, we go back to Chapter 11, which opens: "What was the matter with the master-at-arms? And be the matter what it might, how could it have direct relation to Billy Budd, with whom prior to the affair of the spilled soup he had never come into any special contact official or otherwise?" (122). The word *contact* is a signal that we have wandered into the magnetic proximity of Claggart. The chapter ends with Melville's apology:

> *The point of the present story turning on the hidden nature* of the master-at-arms has necessitated this chapter. With an added hint or two in connection with the incident at the mess, the resumed narrative must be left to vindicate, as it may, its own credibility. (135; italics added)

Again Melville has set a verbal trap or *skandalon* for his readers. Normally a point does not turn on something. On the contrary: something turns on a point. "This is the point," we announce with conviction, "upon which the whole argument turns." Trying to unravel the set-down passage above, one finally asks whether the "hidden nature" of Claggart (on which the "point" of the story is said to turn) is not *itself* a point. Rephrased: is Claggart's phenomenal nature not the charged point on which Melville's

In Nomine Diaboli: *An Extreme Interpretation of* Billy Budd 61

narrative turns? Here I shall rehearse certain matters: (1) Those who know something about electricity speak of a metallic point at which electricity is charged or collected. (2) We have already met up with a kind of polecat, "ferreting about the dark corner of the lower decks," and Claggart is "a sort of chief of *pol*-ice *charged* among other matters with the duty of preserving order" (italics added). If Claggart indeed represents a contact point as I now suspect, it is a magnetic *pole*, defined thus: "Each of the two opposite points or regions on the surface of a magnet (when of elongated form, usually at its ends) at which the magnetic forces are manifested" (*OED* 5).[28]

Both Claggart and Billy are physically attractive. Yet the master-at-arms envies Billy's "good looks, cheery health, and frank enjoyment," Melville explains, "because these went along with a nature that, *as Claggart magnetically felt*, had in its simplicity never willed malice or experienced the reactionary bite of that serpent" (140; italics added). What are the connections between Claggart's electrical nature, his ability to in-fluence Vere, his power to galvanize the "compliant" and ferreting vermin of the *Bellipotent*, and his marked "animosity" (146) to Billy Budd? And what is the specific nature of the phenomenon that induces Billy to strike his diabolic accuser, Claggart? At this point, I turn to the subject of "animal magnetism," or mesmerism.

*   *   *

> "the diabolical incarnate and effective in some men"
>
> (Leaf 304)

Mesmerism, otherwise known as "animal magnetism," and popularized in the late eighteenth century by the Austrian physician, F. A. Mesmer (1733–1815), is a system or theory

> according to which a hypnotic state, usually accompanied by insensibility to pain and muscular rigidity, can be induced by an influence (at first known as "animal magnetism") exercised over the will and nervous system of the patient. (*OED*)

According to the *Encyclopedia Britannica* (13th edition), Dr. Mesmer in 1766 imagined that "stroking diseased bodies with magnets might effect a cure." A decade later, observing that a Swiss priest named Gassner "effected cures by manipulation alone," Mesmer imagined that an occult force "resided in himself by which he could influence others. He held that this force permeated the universe, and more especially affected the nervous system of men." What is unusual about Mesmer's system of hypnosis, it seems, is his postulate of "a special variety of magnetic fluid which he called *animal magnetism*." Witness Professor Westervelt, the "bearded enchanter" of Hawthorne's *The Blithedale Romance*, and "his universally pervasive fluid, as he affirmed it to be . . . . "[29]

Not only human subjects, but inanimate objects were thought to be mesmerisable. Trees, water, stones, and metals, for example, could be magnetized or mesmerized; thus an *OED* citation from 1840: "A thing not directly mesmerisable, but mesmerisable by contact with a directly mesmerisable metal." This citation makes me question the nature and purpose of those "glittering objects" ("two small objects faintly twinkling in the night-light"), held in front of Billy by Claggart's "emissary." "Where could the fellow get guineas? [Billy wonders] Why even spare buttons are not so plentiful at sea" (157; 162). The most common way of inducing a hypnotic state "consists in causing a person to look fixedly, for several minutes, with complete concentration, at a bright object placed above and in front of the eyes at so short a distance that the convergence of the optic axes can only be accomplished with effort" (*OED*, "hypnotism"). In the context of hypnosis or mesmerism or animal magnetism, Billy's phrase "spare buttons" recalls a chapter in *The Confidence-Man* called "Very Charming." There we meet Melville's insinuating "cosmopolitan," who speaks in a particular manner to the barber:

> Hard to say exactly what the manner was, any more than to hint it was sort of magical; in a benign way, not wholly unlike the manner, fabled or otherwise, of certain creatures in nature, which have the power of persuasive fascination – the power of holding another creature by the button of the eye, as it were, despite the serious disinclination, and, indeed, earnest protest of the victim.[30]

According to Smedley's *Occult Science* of 1855: "Magnetism by the eye is often more powerful than by the hands" (*OED*, "magnetism"). About Claggart's eye, Melville remarks: "It served Claggart in his office that his eye could cast a tutoring glance" (90). (The word *tutor* originally meant "to watch.") I am concerned with Claggart's office as mesmerist.

In Elizabeth S. Foster's invaluable Explanatory Notes to *The Confidence-Man*, Melville's interest in mesmerism is explicated:

> The wide interest in Mesmerism and animal magnetism in the mid-nineteenth century might be sufficient to account for Melville's inclusion of hypnotic spells in his stories were it not for the singular and consistent use that he makes of enchantments; with rare exceptions . . . they are the means of *the triumph of something malign*. The Magazines of the period were full of articles on Mesmerism and snake-charming . . . . (italics added)[31]

With the benefit of Foster's note, let us return to the scene in Captain Vere's cabin, where Claggart, having assumed the role of an "asylum physician," advances "within a short range of Billy" in order to hypnotize or to mesmerize him:

> With the measured step and calm collected air of an asylum physician approaching in the public hall some patient beginning to show indications of a coming paroxysm, Claggart deliberately advanced within a short range of Billy and, *mesmerically looking him in the eye*, briefly recapitulated the accusation.
> *Not at first did Billy take it in.* When he did, the rose-tan of his cheek looked *struck* as by white leprosy. He stood like one *impaled* and *gagged*. Meanwhile the accuser's eyes . . . underwent a *phenomenal* change . . . . The first *mesmeristic glance* was one of serpent fascination; the last was the paralyzing lurch of the torpedo fish.
> "Speak, man!" said Captain Vere to the transfixed one, *struck* by his aspect even more than by Claggart's. "Speak! Defend yourself!" Which appeal caused but a strange dumb gesturing and gurgling in Billy. (222–23; italics added)

Accused, charged falsely by the diabolical Claggart, Billy does not "at first . . . take it in." When he does "take it in," the pallid and shocked and spellbound Billy, "struck as by white leprosy," is "impaled" – struck through by Claggart's pointed accusation. (After the event, Melville speaks about "palliating circumstances" [267].)

The words *pole* and *pale*, as in wooden stakes, are doublets; whether we imagine magnetic poles or magnetized pales or magnetic needles or magnetic and pervasive fluid, Billy is in any case "transfixed" – pierced through, thrust through, struck through – by Claggart's "mesmeric glance." (Most of the etymological senses of the verb *diaballo* have converged in this crucial scene.) Then occurs the fatal blow/reaction, whereby the charge or current, accumulated in the insinuating coils of the accuser, and thrown/cast across to Billy, recoils on the mesmerist and enchanter, Claggart:

> The next instant, quick as the flame from a discharged cannon at night, his right arm shot out, and Claggart dropped to the deck. Whether intentionally or but owing to the young athlete's superior height, the blow had taken full effect upon the forehead . . . so that the body fell over lengthwise, like a heavy plank tilted from erectness. (226)

As Melville observes of a nature like Claggart's: "what recourse is left to it but to recoil upon itself and, like the scorpion for which the Creator alone is responsible, act out to the end the part allotted it" (142).

One further detail: during Billy's "execution by halter," his final words, "'God bless Captain Vere,'" have "a phenomenal effect" on the assembled crowd. The phenomenon is electrical:

> Without volition, as it were, as if indeed the ship's population were the vehicle of *some vocal current electric*, . . . came a resonant sympathetic echo: "God bless Captain Vere!" (318; italics added)

*   *   *

The pursuit of this chapter has been to decipher and then to exfoliate the name and signature impressed, marked, inscribed, engraved, on the calling card of "the arch interferer": "In every case, one way or another he is sure to slip in his little card, as much as to remind us – I too have a hand here" (48). Claggart's "hand was too small and shapely," we are told, "to have been accustomed to hard toil" (90). Throughout *Billy Budd*, Claggart's name is inscribed in a small and shapely hand, a running hand, a cursive and recursive hand. But even though Claggart shows his cards, Billy does not know what is on the cards, because he cannot decipher. It takes the wisdom of the serpent to recognize the insinuating presence of the *Diabolos*, and innocence is culpable; and according to Rabbi Klein, it is possible that the original meaning of the Latin *culpa* was "blow," in which case, he says, "it is probably cognate with the Greek *kolaphos*, "'a blow with the fist, a box on the ear.'"

3

Giving Umbrage: The Song of Songs which is Whitman's

> the body includes and is the meaning . . .
> Whitman, "Proto-Leaf" (1860)

I begin with a detail of Whitman's language: the phrase "under their umbrage," which appears in the 1855 preface to *Leaves of Grass*. "There will soon be no more priests," Whitman claims. "Their work is done. [. . . .] A new order shall arise and they shall be the priests of man, and every man shall be his own priest. The churches built *under their umbrage* shall be the churches of men and women"[1] (italics added).

Whitman's new order of priest may serve to redeem Emerson's emasculated and "merely spectral" preacher, the semblance and shadow of a man ridiculed in the Divinity School Address.[2] Against that spectre, Whitman's new order of priest embodies a figure or type or umbrage (a foreshadowing) of men and women to come. If the most common meaning of *umbrage* is shade or covering, the word may also carry the sense of displeasure (one may give umbrage, as Whitman knew); hence these intricate lines from Book IX of *Paradise Lost*:

> "O might I here [Adam says]
> In solitude live savage, in some glade
> Obscured, where highest woods impenetrable
> To star or sunlight, *spread their umbrage broad*,
> And brown as evening. Cover me ye pines,

Ye cedars, with innumerable boughs . . . . "

It is here that Adam and Eve

> "devise
> What best may for the present serve to hide
> The parts of each from other, that seem most
> To shame obnoxious, and unseemliest seen;
> Some tree whose broad smooth leaves together sewed,
> And girded on our loins, may cover round
> Those middle parts, that this newcomer, Shame,
> There sit not, and reproach us as unclean."
>
> (IX, 1084ff; italics added)

So Adam and Eve gather leaves from the banyan or fig tree, sewing them into what Milton calls "vain covering, if to hide / Their guilt and dreaded shame!"

Let us move from the shameful body-parts of our first parents to the body of the text, especially the shameful parts of the text, and its coverings. One approach of medieval hermeneutics assumed that truth or *veritas* was hidden *sub umbra et figura*, beneath shadow and figure.[3] In other words, to cite Brian Stock, "the text's meaning is disguised from the interpreter, who is animated by a skepticism, by a suspicion of the given, and by a desire to find the inner truth concealed beneath a dissimulating 'integument.'"[4] This integument I take to be the *literae cortex*, the shell or husk of literal meaning, presumed by exegetes to disguise and conceal the *nucleus spiritualis intelligentiae*, the "kernel of a Spiritual or Moral sense."[5] In the seventeenth century, John Bunyan considered the "Hard Texts" of the Bible "Nuts" to be cracked.[6]

The suspicious exegete, animated by a desire to find the inner truth hidden beneath the shell of literal meaning, may also be the embarrassed exegete, unwilling to admit the shameful meaning of the text. This leads to allegorizing, or to exegesis as allegory. In the context of suspicion, shadow, disguise, dissimulation, Puttenham's definition of allegory is apposite: "the figure of false semblant."[7] Following the author of Genesis, Milton has Adam and Eve disguise their shameful middle parts with leaves ("vain coverings"). Likewise biblical commentators have concealed the literal meaning of the Song of Songs, or Canticles, with spiritual and/or historical allegory, an approach that sometime in the first century assured the love songs a place in the biblical canon.[8] To cite E. Ann Matter's recent study of the Song, "very few Christian exegetes . . . before the modern age seemed to have questioned the premise of allegorical interpretation of the text . . . . There is no 'non-allegorical' Latin tradition of the Song of Songs commentary."[9]

It is not clear what Matter means by "the modern age." For in the eighteenth century, a few scholars, notably J. G. Herder and Thomas Percy, challenged allegorical readings of the Song.[10] Still, until the nineteenth century, when the "battle between the allegorists and literalists"[11] was waged openly, allegorical readings of the Song of Songs prevailed in the Church and in the Synagogue. In a much-cited passage, the tenth-century exegete, Rabbi Saadias ("Pseudo-Sa'adya"),[12] observing the "great diversity of opinions as regards the interpretation of this Song of Songs," says that the text "is like a lock, the key of which hath been lost."[13] Alluding directly to Saadias's metaphor of lock and key, Marvin H. Pope insists that:

> The quest for the supposedly lost key has been futile, for the door to the understanding of the Song was not locked, nor even shut, but has been wide open to any who dared to see and enter. The barrier has been a psychological aversion to the obvious, somewhat like the Emperor's New Clothes. The trouble has been that interpreters who dared acknowledge the plain sense of the Song were assailed as enemies of truth and decency. The allegorical charade thus persisted for centuries with only sporadic protests.[14]

One of these protests may have been Whitman's. The present study turns on my suspicion that some of the most sexually explicit passages of *Leaves of Grass* work specifically against the allegorical interpretation of the Song of Songs. We should now consider the context of that interpretation as it was received in the nineteenth century.

*   *   *

"In recent decades," Pope tells us, "there has been a general and growing tendency to reject allegory and freely admit the application of the Song to human physical love."[15] Thus in his recent study

Giving Umbrage: The Song of Songs which is Whitman's

of biblical poetry (1985), Robert Alter describes the Song of Songs as "the only surviving instance of purely secular love poetry from ancient Israel . . . . the continuous celebration of passion and its pleasure makes this the most consistently secular of all biblical texts . . . ."[16] Here Alter may depend on Rabbi Robert Gordis, who in 1954 wrote that while "fragments of secular poetry are imbedded in the Bible," the Song of Songs "is the only complete work which is entirely secular, indeed, sensuous, in character."[17]

> It is human love [Gordis writes], not that of a god, which is glorified in the Song, and that with a wealth of detail which rules out an allegorical interpretation. The entire book deals with concrete situations, whether of love's repining, or its satisfaction, of lovers' flirtations, estrangement and reunion.[18]

Both Alter and Gordis are anticipated by Bishop Thomas Percy (of the *Reliques*), who may be the first modern commentator to challenge directly allegorical readings of the Song. In his Preface to the Song of Solomon (1764), Percy censures those

> who have been so busily employed in opening and unfolding the allegorical meaning of this book as wholly to neglect that literal sense which ought to be the basis of their discoveries. If a sacred allegory may be defined a figurative discourse, which under a lower and more obvious meaning, delivers the most sublime and important truths; then it is the first duty of an expositor to ascertain the lower and more obvious meaning. For till this is done, it is impossible to discover what truths are couched under it.[19]

Percy's model of sublime and important truths "couched" under "a lower . . . meaning" of the Song suggests the "four-fold method" of interpretation and hierarchies of signification. Yet at the same time, he insists that commentators "ascertain" the low and literal sense of the text, a level that for centuries had been either ignored or denied outright. Confronted by the erotic imagery of the biblical text, exegetes had explained it away as the mystical love of Christ for his Spouse, or of Christ for the Church, or of God for Israel. Often, sacred allegory was superimposed like so many fig leaves to conceal entirely the low and plain sense of the Song.

There is a radical connection between allegorical exegesis and

Platonism, a model of thought whose unsuitability to the reading of Hebrew Scripture was clear to J. G. Herder. In *The Spirit of Hebrew Poetry* (1782; cited here in an 1833 American translation that Whitman may have known), Herder writes:

> The Platonism of love, as well as a monastic sanctity pertaining to the marriage relation, are foreign to the poetry of [the Jewish] people; but how delicate and refined sentiments, notwithstanding, pervade all the scenes in the garden of love in Solomon's songs.[20]

By ignoring this radical contrast between the "Platonism of love" and Hebrew thought, exegetes of the Song of Songs could contend that the fleshly kisses and embraces were designed to represent the inner and higher sense of the text. But if, as Herder says, there is not "the slightest intimation, or even the faintest trace"[21] of another sense concealed under the literal and obvious meaning of the Song, then allegorical readings are inappropriate. This was the opinion of George R. Noyes (1798–1868), Professor of Hebrew at Harvard, whose translations of and commentaries on biblical poetry were (according to Floyd Stovall) the "only significant American studies of the subject" available to Whitman.[22]

Noyes's commentary on the Canticles, or Song of Songs (1846), opens as follows: "As I do not regard the collection of songs, which goes under the name of the Song of Solomon, to have an express moral or religious design, perhaps it might have been expedient to pass it by in significant and prudent silence."[23] The word "moral" is a clue to Noyes's line of argument, for beneath his defense of the literal meaning of the Song, there is a moralizing and puritanizing agenda. To put that agenda briefly: if the Song of Songs is regarded as no more than "a specimen of the erotic poetry of the Hebrews," or "relics" of their "amatory poetry," then, like the songs of Anacreon or the idyls of Theocritus, "it will be treated with indifference by most readers, and consequently do them no harm. But if regarded as an inspired model and help for devotion, *its direct tendency is injurious to morals and religion*" (italics added).[24]

Attacking the "mystical" approach of allegorizers, Noyes contends that when the Song of Songs is "perverted and made to constitute an inspired model for the expression of feelings of devotion . . . . its direct effect must be to debase religion, and consequently *to promote immorality*" (italics added).[25] In part, Noyes is challenging the great biblical scholar, Moses Stuart (1780–1852), professor of sacred literature at Andover, whose Old Testament study of 1845 regards the Song "as expressing the warm and earnest desire of the soul after God, in language borrowed from that which characterises chaste affection between the Jews."[26] Against Stuart, Noyes argues that the erotic language of the Song has no precedent at all in Hebrew Scripture: it is "monstrous," he declares, to suppose that the love between "man and his Creator" should be set forth in the "amatory" language of human love. To this Noyes adds: "there is language in the Canticles which I could not apply to the Supreme Being in the manner required by the mystical [i.e., allegorical] theory, without feeling guilty of blasphemy."[27]

One further citation from an American divine: in his *A Brief Exposition of the Whole Book of Canticles, Or Song of Solomon* ("a work very usefull and seasonable to every Christian"), John Cotton defends "the amorousnesse of the dittie":

> the amorousnesse of the dittie will not stirre up wantonnesse in any age, if the words be well understood: but rather, by inflaming with heavenly love, will draw out, and burne up all earthly and carnall lust; and even as fire in the hand is drawne out by holding it to a stronger fire, or as the light and heat of the sun extinguisheth a kitchin fire; so doth heavenly love to Christ extinguish bare kitchin lusts.[28]

Before moving to Whitman, I want to turn briefly to Paul Ricoeur, who uses the terms "surface-structure" and "deep-structure" to speak about biblical texts.[29] His spatial, outer-inner metaphor suggests an intimate correspondence between the surface-structure of a text and the surface-structure of the body; or between the literal and "low" sense of a biblical text and the value of matter. (Indeed, for some medieval scholars, the word "*littera* is almost interchangeable with *corpus*.")[30] What I find most remarkable about the history of the Song of Songs is the fact that some Christian exegetes, among them Nicolas of Lyra (1270–1340), denied that the Song had *any* literal sense whatever.[31] For such a denial hints at ways of reading whereby the body is not a material, carnal body, but is only a semblance – the body allegorical. This we may call "docetic" hermeneutics (from the Greek *dokein*, to seem), an approach to the surface-structure or *littera* of the text that regards it, not as substance, but as mere shadow or umbrage. Unlike the bodies of Adam and Eve, docetic or phantom bodies have no middle parts; by analogy, then, docetic texts have no shameful parts. If commentaries on the Song of Songs indeed "tell a story of the triumph of the allegorical," as E. Ann Matter contends, they may also celebrate the triumph of Docetism.

To consider the correspondence between the surface-structure of the text and the surface-structure of the body, is to be reminded of Origen, whose third-century commentary on the Song of Songs includes this warning: "Everyone who is not yet rid of the vexations of flesh and blood and has not ceased to feel the passion of his bodily nature should refrain completely from reading this book." In the words of a modern scholar:

> When [Origen] was young he took too literally Jesus' hyperbole about cutting off bodily members that cause one to sin, and thus he castrated himself. Later in life he took too figuratively the Song of Songs and rejected its literal meaning. Eunuch Origen was sure that God never intended the book to be understood except as a purely spiritual drama of the inner life.[32]

This is not to say that Origen was single-minded: "*Allegoria*," as Angus Fletcher notes, "manifestly has two or more levels of meaning, and the apprehension of these must require at least two attitudes of mind."[33] Yet if Origen's approach to the Song of Songs appears to operate on two levels of signification (the bride of the word of God may be either the soul *or* the Church), neither level signifies the body, despite his use of "the word *eros* rather than *agape* . . . to describe the love of which the text speaks."[34] As Daniel Boyarin notes, Origen's allegorical method is founded "on a Platonic-Pauline theory of correspondence between the visible things of this world and the invisible things of God."[35]

One further issue, closely related to the Platonic-Pauline theory of correspondence, may be central to a reading of Whitman. The matter is best approached through Paul de Man, who remarks: "the allegorical sign refer[s] to another sign that precedes it. The meaning constituted by the allegorical sign can then consist only in the *repetition* . . . of a previous sign with which it can never coincide, since it is of the essence of this previous sign to be pure anteriority."[36] Phrased otherwise, in allegory there is an unbreachable, temporal gap between the literal or surface meaning of the text, and the prior or pre-text that it signifies. This temporal difference, and the deferment, must be sustained, for without it, the allegorical structure (and the ontological structure) collapses. Distinguishing allegory as writing from allegory as reading, one can posit a temporal gap in the allegorical method practiced by Origen and the School of Alexandria: a gap, that is, between the given or literal or surface meaning of the text, and the prior or hidden or spiritual truth that the literal meaning is presumed to signify.

Further, what de Man calls "pure anteriority" is radically involved with the idea of a disembodied truth. In other words, to consider the kernel of truth within the nut-shell as both valorized and prior to the low and literal cortex, is to stumble upon a Platonic model wherein the pre-existent soul is created before the body. This is crucial to the present discussion. In Platonism, as we know, the "most fundamental ontological distinction" is between the spiritual and the material.[37] The soul belongs to the divine spiritual realm; the body belongs to the lower material realm. The soul is trapped in the body just as the kernel of truth is trapped in a nutshell or husk of literal meaning. What this implies is that the allegorical approach to the Song of Songs somehow depends upon a Platonic mind-set. Or to cite Boyarin's concise formulation: "In order for the scripture to have an 'inner meaning', there must be an ontological structure that allows for inner meaning. Allegoresis is thus explicitly founded in a Platonic Universe."[38]

To the Greek idea of the pre-existent soul, we should compare the Hebrew model of creation out of nothing, *creatio ex nihilo*, whereby the world, including the human body and the human soul, was created by *fiat*, or by the expressed word of God. In sharp contrast to Platonism, the doctrine of creation *ex nihilo* insists that the soul is *not* anterior to the body, but that body and soul are created simultaneously. There is in Hebrew thought no "pure anteriority" that would privilege the human soul over the body. Adhering to de Man's model of allegory as temporality, one can venture that the spiritual sense of the Song of Songs is not prior to the literal or plain sense, but is in fact concurrent with it. To rephrase this: before exegetes like Origen and Philo and Augustine took over, the spiritual sense of the Song of Songs must have coincided with the literal sense. That coincidence or concurrence we may term (taking a hint from de Man)[39] correspondence: *not* the correspondence between low signs and their hidden, privileged, and prior meanings, but the atemporal correspondence between signs and other signs, without priority or privilege. To cite a first draft of

Whitman's *Leaves of Grass*: "As the shadow concurs with the body and comes not unless of the body, so the soul concurs with the body and comes not unless of the body, / As materials are so the soul."[40]

*   *   *

Earlier I suggested that some of the most sexually explicit passages of *Leaves of Grass* – particularly the 1855 text – may work against what Marvin Pope has called the "allegorical charade" of Song of Songs interpretation. Among Whitman's *Notes and Fragments* we find this cryptic note:

> What name? Religious Canticles. These perhaps ought to be the *brain* the *living spirit* (elusive, indescribable, indefinite) of all the "Leaves of Grass."
> Hymns of ecstasy and religious fervor.[41]

We are first alerted to the presence of what Whitman elsewhere calls "Hebrew canticles"[42] (the Song of Songs is called *Canticum Canticorum* in the Vulgate) by overhearing faint verbal coincidences between the Canticles (or Song of Solomon) and the poem Whitman would later call "Song of Myself."[43] Here is Whitman from line 6 of the poem that in 1855 began *Leaves of Grass*:[44]

> Houses and rooms are full of perfumes . . . . the shelves are crowded with perfumes,
> I breathe the fragrance myself, and know it and like it,
> The distillation would intoxicate me also, but I shall not let it.
>
> The atmosphere is not a perfume . . . . it has no taste of the distillation . . . . it is odorless,
> It is for my mouth forever . . . . I am in love with it,
> I will go to the bank by the wood and become undisguised and naked,
> I am mad for it to be in contact with me.
>
> The smoke of my own breath,
> Echoes, ripples and buzzed whispers . . . . loveroot, silk thread, crotch and vine [. . . .]
>
> [section 2]

In the third verse of the opening chapter of the Song of Songs we find perfumes also: "Because of the savour of thy good ointments thy name is as ointment poured forth" (1:3; AV). Whitman knew the Bible only in the King James version, but he may have known other translations of the Song of Songs. One of them, published in 1853 by the American scholar, George Burrowes, renders the same passage as:

> Thy perfumes are rich in fragrance;
> Thy name is perfume poured forth.[45]

And Professor Noyes of Harvard, in his 1846 translation of the Song, renders the identical passage:

> Because of the savour of thy precious perfumes
> (Thy name is like fragrant oil poured forth).[46]

Intrigued by the possible significance of this coincidence, one overhears other similarities between "Song of Myself" and the Song of Songs (the following are all cited from the AV). In the third chapter of the Song of Songs, for example, a question is asked, presumably by the maiden:

> Who is this that cometh out of the wilderness like pillars of smoke perfumed with myrrh and frankincense, with all the powders of the merchant? (3:6).

In muted counterpoint, Whitman rejects this perfumed smoke, praising instead: "The smoke of my own breath." If the perfumed lover of the Song of Songs comes out of the wilderness, Whitman retreats from the perfumed and confining rooms into the "odorless" wilderness, "to the bank by the wood," where he and his text will "become undisguised and naked." Once there, he evokes other, American fragrances:

> The sniff of green leaves and dry leaves, and of the shore and darkcolored sea-rocks, and of hay in the barn.

Later he will declare: "The scent of these arm-pits is aroma finer than prayer" (section 24).

76 The Trivial Sublime

Whitman celebrates his own undisguised and naked body. At the same time, he celebrates the correspondence or "tallying," to use his term, of body with soul, body with the natural world, body with *Leaves of Grass*. In an undated note, probably written in 1855–56, Whitman declares:

> My poems when complete should be *a unity*, in the same sense that the earth is, or that the human body, (senses, soul, trunk, feet, blood, viscera, man-root, eyes, hair) or that a perfect musical composition is.[47]

The 1855 preface instructs us to "read these leaves in the open air every season of every year of your life [. . .] and your very flesh shall be a great poem, and have the richest fluency, not only in its words but in the silent lines of its lips and face and between the lashes of your eyes and in every motion and joint of the body."[48] The topos is familiar: the lines of the face and the lines of the text coincide, as do perfumed rooms and the confining poetic *stanza* or chamber. (A first draft of *Leaves of Grass* reads: "I stifle in the confinement of rooms.")[49]

The correspondence between the written text and the body, between the text and its natural surrounding, between Whitman's expression and the literal ex-pressing of bodily fluids, creates the semantic tensions in *Leaves of Grass*. If there are indeed "silent lines" in his text, as Whitman says there are, we can read between them. Let us focus on two lines from section 2:

> A few light kisses . . . . a few embraces . . . . a reaching around of arms,
> The play of shine and shade on the tree as the supple boughs wag,

In the lines above, a temporal and spatial analogy is set up between the "supple boughs" of the tree and the supple arms of the lovers who embrace beneath the tree. Their "embraces," their "reaching around of arms" beneath the "shade," recall these lines from the Song of Songs:

> As the apple tree among the trees of the wood, so is my beloved among the sons. I sat down under his shadow [Vulgate: *sub umbra illius*] with great delight, and his fruit was sweet to my

Giving Umbrage: The Song of Songs which is Whitman's 77

taste.... His left hand is under my head, and his right hand doth embrace me. (2:3, 5)

(Cf. "His left hand should be under my head and his right hand should embrace me" [8:3].) In section 46 of "Song of Myself," the embrace of the Song of Songs is again overheard:

> My left hand hooks you round the waist,
> My right hand points to landscapes of continents, and a
>   plain public road.

Before moving to the sublime fifth section of "Song of Myself," with its sexual and textual marriage of body and soul, let us first consider these lines from section 3:

> Clear and sweet is my soul . . . . and clear and sweet is all
>   that is not my soul.
> Lack one lacks both . . . . and the unseen is proved by the
>   seen,
> Till that becomes unseen and receives proof in its turn.
> [. . . .]
> Welcome is every organ and attribute of me, and of any
>   man hearty and clean,
> Not an inch nor a particle of an inch is vile, and none
>   shall be less familiar than the rest.

Origen, we recall, castrated himself and the literal sense of the Song of Songs. Gregory the Great, in a moment of dualism, declared that "the more vile [*viliora*] the literal reference of scripture, the more useful its spiritual meaning."[50] With Whitman, however, we find ourselves in a text that insists upon restoring the physical and the literal sense of the Song of Songs. Not an inch of Whitman's text nor an inch of his body is "vile"; thus no level of meaning is either valorized or debased. In the following lines from section 5 of "Song of Myself," the embrace under the tree is expanded:

> I mind how we lay in June, such a transparent summer
>   morning;
> You settled your head athwart my hips and gently turned
>   over upon me,

> And parted the shirt from my bosom-bone, and plunged
>   your tongue to my barestript heart,
> And reached till you felt my beard, and reached till you
>   held my feet.
>
> Swiftly arose and spread around me the peace and joy and
>   knowledge that pass all the art and argument of the earth.

In the fourth line above, the word "reached" has been doubled (And reached till you felt my beard, and reached till you held my feet"), a detail that picks up and revises the embrace of section 2 with its phrase: "the reaching around of arms" (an etymological definition of "embrace"). More, I would point out the obvious: that Whitman's phrase "the peace . . . that pass all the art and argument of the earth" is an allusion to Paul's phrase, "the peace of God, which passeth all understanding" (Phil. 4:7). Earlier in the same epistle, Paul writes of "our vile body" (3:21; AV), a phrase that had surely provoked Whitman's sharp response: "Not an inch nor a particle of an inch is vile."

In section 6 of "Song of Myself," we hear the child asking, "What is the grass?"

> I guess it must be the flag of my disposition [Whitman answers],
>   out of hopeful green stuff woven.

That is one meaning. "Or I guess it is the handkerchief of the Lord"; "Or I guess the grass is itself a child"; "Or I guess it is a uniform hieroglyphic"; "And now it seems to me the beautiful uncut hair of graves." Whitman's images of woven textiles – the flag and the handkerchief – remind us that weavings and texts are related etymologically. To cite Brian Stock: the Latin verb *texo* "meant to weave, to plait, or to interlace, and hence, in a subsidiary sense, to compose." "From the eleventh century, *textus* began to refer more and more exclusively to the Bible . . . ." Yet at the same time, the word "never lost touch with its original, tangible associations. Cicero . . . speaks of 'tegumenta . . . corporum vel texta vel suta' ('the coverings of bodies or weavings or sowings') . . . ."[51]

It is the tallying of body with poem and with textile that gives us one context for Whitman's evocative phrase, "the flag of my disposition, out of hopeful green stuff woven." Further, it is not impossible that Whitman's flag has been brought in from the Song of Songs: "He brought me to the banqueting house, and his banner over me was love" (2:4). If in "Song of Myself" the grass is "the flag" of Whitman's sexual "disposition" (its leaves may be either "stiff or drooping in the fields" [section 5]), the grass also comprises the woven text of *Leaves of Grass*, whose first edition was carefully bound in "dark green cloth" with "rustic gold letters in the shape of leaves, tendrils and roots."[52] In case we overlook these stiff or drooping leaves, in the 1856 edition of *Leaves of Grass*, the flag of Whitman's disposition modulates into what he describes as, "This poem, drooping shy and unseen, that I always carry, and that all men carry."[53] We are moving close to those parts of the body censored by Origen and covered over with fig leaves by Adam. At the same time, we are confronting the low and literal sense of the Song of Songs.

Why does Whitman call a flag a flag, and not a banner? In the first instance his word choice is probably related to the potential doubleness of the word "flag," which signifies a banner *and* a kind of rush growing on moist ground. (In Job 8:11, Bildad asks in nice Hebrew parallelism: "Can the rush grow up without mire? can the flag grow without water?"; rushes or flags, of course, may be woven or plaited or interlaced.) In section 24 of "Song of Myself" the flag of Whitman's disposition becomes specifically the "washed sweet-flag" or calamus, which in turn will become the controlling metaphor of the 1860 *Calamus* poems. As Whitman later explained, calamus "is the very large & aromatic grass, or rush .... often called 'sweet flag.'" He speaks of its generous size ("the biggest & hardiest kind of spears of grass") and describes its scent ("fresh, aquatic, pungent bouquet").[54] What he does not say, however, is first, that the Latin word *calamus* means a writing instrument; and second, that the word appears in the King James version of the Song of Songs: "Spikenard and saffron; calamus and cinnamon, with all trees of frankincense; myrrh and aloes; with all the chief spices" (4:14).[55] The passage cited below, with its "washed sweet-flag," is the one Helen Vendler regards as "the most beautiful of all Whitman's renderings in the 1855 *Leaves*":[56]

> If I worship any particular thing it shall be some of
>   the spread of my body;
> Translucent mould of me it shall be you,
> Shaded ledges and rests, firm masculine coulter, it
>   shall be you,

> Whatever goes to the tilth of me it shall be you,
> You my rich blood, your milky stream pale strippings of my life;
> Breast that presses against other breasts it shall be you,
> My brain it shall be your occult convolutions,
> Root of washed sweet-flag, timorous pond-snipe, nest of guarded duplicate eggs, it shall be you,
> Mixed tussled hay of head and beard and brawn it shall be you,
> Trickling sap of maple, fibre of manly wheat, it shall be you.

The final line above evokes one of Whitman's first drafts: "Common things – the trickling sap that flows from the end of the manly maple."[57] What is most remarkable about this passage is its sustained series of metonymic shifts. Insisting upon the correspondence between the male body and the natural world, he insists also on analogies between the body and the text, including its exegesis. The phrase "some of the spread of my body" recalls section 5: "Swiftly arose and spread around me the peace and joy and knowledge that pass all the art and argument of the earth." To worship what Whitman describes as "some of the spread of my body" is to worship the spreading of seed or semen, the dissemination and expression and ejaculation of words, and the expanse or display of the body and of the open text. Seeds move sharply into focus with Whitman's image of the "coulter," the iron blade fixed in front of a plough that cuts vertically into the soil.

To imagine iron cutting into soil recalls Ernst Curtius's discussion of literary *topoi*, particularly of the iron stylus as a plough: an iron stylus was used by the Romans "for writing on wax tablets." "So early as Plato, we find the comparison between the dressing of a field and writing."[58] At some point in the evolution of the stylus/plough topos, the writing surface or parchment becomes metonymy for the field, and the ink becomes the seed. In Curtius's version of a scribal adage: "The white fields are the pages, the white plough the pen, the black ink the seeds."[59] But Curtius discreetly overlooks the obvious: the ink as semen, the writing implement (or *calamus*) as erect phallus. Thus in section 40 of "Song of Myself," Whitman can boast, "This day I am jetting the stuff of far more arrogant republics": the word "jetting" evokes the emission of semen (or in Whitman's phrase, "my own seminal wet" [section 7]) and the flow of jet-black ink. Curtius's unspoken topos of phallus as writing implement merges in Whitman's text with the well-known topos of sexual ploughing, where the soil and the lover's body, the phallus and the iron plough, correspond.[60] For example, in section 24 of "Song of Myself" we find "Broad muscular fields"; and in one of his fragments, which includes the words "Lovepivot" and "Lovejet," there is a "Tiller of Love."[61]

These and other correspondences between nature, the body, and Whitman's text may be clear enough; but there is something in "Song of Myself" that has been cunningly disguised. And that disguise takes us back to our theoretical concerns. The issue is best approached through Whitman's "timorous pond-snipe" in section 24:

> Root of washed sweet-flag, timorous pond-snipe, nest of
>   guarded duplicate eggs, it shall be you,
> Mixed tussled hay of head and beard and brawn it shall
>   be you.

First of all, and especially in this context, the word "timorous" comes straight to Whitman from Robert Burns's poem, "To a Mouse, On turning her up in her Nest, with the Plough, November, 1785." I should add that the word "coulter" (as in Whitman's phrase, "firm masculine coulter") appears in the fifth stanza of Burns's eight stanza poem. (Burns, according to Whitman, "was faithful to lowly things, customs, idioms, Scotland, the lasses, the peasants, and to his own robust nature.")[62] What Whitman has done, then, is to transform Burns's "wee" "tim'rous" mouse, turned up in 1785 in her nest "o' leaves an' stibble" with a coulter, into the "timorous pond-snipe" of 1855 with its "nest of guarded duplicate eggs." Snipes build their nests in marshy places where the sweet-flag or rush or calamus grows. Moreover, to follow Audubon, the snipe has a "very long bill." As for its breeding: "Four eggs in ground nest, in marsh or near it."[63] Another naturalist, John A. Livingston, informs us that the snipe, like its relative the woodcock, has "a truly enormous bill" with a "flexible tip." This bill is "essentially a probing instrument, for reaching deep into mud."[64]

Perhaps the pond-snipe's shyness is related to the truly enormous bill that it carries, and that all snipes carry. For Whitman's snipe is so timorous, that (to echo the title of Jean Starobinski's study of

Saussure's anagrams), it must hide and disguise a word beneath a word. In Saussure's language, the snipe is hiding an "hypogram," his term for the word hidden within the manifest word of an anagram. According to Saussure: "To write lines incorporating an anagram is necessarily to write lines based on that anagram and dominated by it."[65] Whether or not that is so in Whitman's text, the suspicious exegete anyway stumbles upon the unobvious: that the word hidden beneath *snipe* is *penis*. The letters have been "Mixed," to repeat Whitman's crossword clue of section 24. And if readers still miss the point about twoness, and about the contours of the male body, he adds the phrase, "guarded duplicate eggs," elsewhere described by Whitman as "man-nuts."[66]

To discover in Whitman's text a word hidden beneath or within a word suggests at first reading that we are back where we started: with allegorical charades, with the shameful, hidden parts of our first parents, and with the suspicious exegete, digging for sublime truths that she knows to be disguised *sub umbra* and beneath a dissimulating shell. But this would be to ignore the connection made by de Man between allegory and temporality. For de Man, as we have seen, the allegorical sign and the sign that precedes it "can never coincide": in allegory there is an unbreachable, temporal gap between the literal meaning of the text, and the prior text that it signifies and looks back to. Anagrams, however, are *not* allegorical, *nor* do they signify a prior text.[67] The two words in Whitman's anagram are in no way separated by space and time; on the contrary, each one corresponds or coincides or "tallies" with its anagrammatic other (or hidden self or hypogram). Because anagrams, unlike allegory, have no temporality, the word *snipe* cannot function as a sign of that which it so shyly conceals in the spread of its own body.

One last observation: just as the five letters of the word *snipe* can be transposed into that thing, stiff or drooping, that Whitman carries, and that all men carry, so can the same five letters that in *Paradise Lost* comprise those "pines" that "spread their umbrage broad" over Adam's unseemly middle parts ("Cover me ye pines,/Ye cedars, with innumerable boughs"). The pines give umbrage, and, anagrammatically, umbrage may be taken.

4
Recycling Language: Emily Dickinson's Religious Wordplay

Dickinson's copy of Emerson's *Essays, Second Series* is marked at the following passage from "The Poet":[1]

> Day and night, house and garden, a few books, a few actions, serve us as well as would all trades and all spectacles. We are far from having exhausted the significance of the few symbols we use. We can come to use them yet with a terrible simplicity. It does not need that a poem should be long. Every word was once a poem. Every relation is a new word. (457)[2]

When those "few symbols" are transformed, a "terrible simplicity" – the phrase can stand for all of Dickinson's poetry – is born. Words are revived by a new relation between words – metaphor, displacement, paradox, wordplay, juxtaposition. Richard Wilbur's observation that Dickinson "sent her whole Calvinist vocabulary into exile, telling it not to come back until it would subserve her own sense of things" is useful here.[3] Indeed, Dickinson turned her Calvinist vocabulary back on itself like a uroborus, the snake with its tail in its mouth. This study explores the nature of that transformation.[4]

I

The image of the uroborus is appropriate because it serves as an emblem for Emerson's cosmology, in particular, for his concept of language. Like all parts of Emerson's universe, words are in a constant state of transformation: "As the limestone of the continent consists of infinite masses of the shells of animalcules, so language is made up of images, or tropes, which now, in their secondary use, have long ceased to remind us of their poetic origins" (457). Emerson was especially concerned with the language of religion:

> The idioms of his [Christ's] language, and the figures of his rhetoric, have usurped the place of his truth; and churches are not built on his principles, but on his tropes.... He spoke of miracles; for he felt that man's life was a miracle, and all that man doth.... But the very word Miracle, as pronounced by Christian churches, gives a false impression; it is Monster. It is not one with the blowing clover and the falling rain. (80)

To believe that "Monster," the perverted and distorted word of Christ, can again be "Miracle" depends on the assumption that words can re-turn to their origins. It also depends on the conviction that "the corruption of man is followed by a corruption of language," and that both can be redeemed:

> When simplicity of character and the sovereignty of ideas is broken up by the prevalence of secondary desires, the desire of riches, the desire of pleasure, the desire of power, the desire of praise, – and duplicity and falsehood take place of simplicity and truth ... new imagery ceases to be created, and old words are perverted to stand for things which are not ....

The poet, however, can "pierce this rotten diction and fasten words again to visible things; so that picturesque language is at once a commanding certificate that he who employs it, is a man in alliance with truth and God" (23).

For Emerson, the "deadest word" was "once a brilliant picture" (457). When the etymologist traces to its root a word used to express an intellectual or moral fact, he will discover that it is "borrowed from some material appearance" – "*supercilious*," for example, means the "*raising of an eyebrow*"; "*transgression*" means the "*crossing of a line*" (20). Homer's images for "soul," "mind," "time," "courage," "emotion" are "intensely physical," Northrop Frye observes; they are "solidly anchored in physical images connected with bodily processes or with specific objects. The word *kairos*, which came to mean a crucial moment in time, originally meant the notch of an arrow."⁵ Emerson makes the same point in stating, "Words are signs of natural facts." To trace an intellectual fact back to its original material appearance is to revive the poetic value of a word or phrase, as Dickinson knew. I quote Margaret Schlauch:

> Poetic effect through etymology was achieved frequently by Emily Dickinson, whose influence can be felt pervasively in contemporary American poetry. She often vivified stale words by reaffirming the meaning of their parts, as when she makes *express* once again mean to "press out" in the physical sense, or *circuit* mean "going round about something."⁶

Religious language has its own Emersonian circularity. Because "Words are signs of natural facts," and "Nature is the symbol of spirit," all material forms "preëxist in necessary Ideas in the mind of God" (25). In simpler terms, the thoughts of God, in translation, are substantial. For Emerson, the creation and decreation of language proceeds from the Idea in God's mind, to a material form, to a word that signifies that form, to a corruption of that word or image. Thus "Miracle" degenerates to "Monster." The poet, however, can reverse this process by re-turning the distorted "Monster" to "Miracle" and once again translating it into the (substantial) blowing clover and falling rain. When the language of religion can be so recycled, new forms and rites are unnecessary:

> The evils of the church that now is, are manifest. The question returns, What shall we do? I confess, all attempts to project and establish a Cultus with new rites and forms, seem to me vain. Faith makes us, and not we it, and faith makes its own forms.... Rather let the breath of new life be breathed by you through the forms already existing. (91)

II

In *The Rhetoric of Religion*, Kenneth Burke reminds us that words have "wholly naturalistic, empirical reference. But they may be used analogically, to designate a further dimension, the 'supernatural.' Whether or not there is a realm of the 'supernatural,' there are *words* for it." The Calvinist vocabulary that Emerson and Dickinson inherited was made up of words that had originally been borrowed from the realm of everyday experience. But as Burke notes, "once a terminology has been developed for special theological purposes the order can become reversed. We can borrow back [compare "redeem"] the terms from the borrower, again secularizing to varying degrees the originally secular terms that had been given 'supernatural' connotations."[7] This two-part process of recycling – from secular to sacred and back to secular – effectively turns back religious language to its pre-Christian/classical meaning.

The Hebrew word for "holy" – *qodesh* – means literally the "separate" or, in Burke's terms, the "set apart," as does the Latin *sacer*. And language may be either natural or "set apart" depending on the realm to which it refers – this concept is central to the following discussion of Dickinson's religious language. In the cosmology of New England Puritanism, mankind exists in a natural system while God is outside the system, "set apart." In Emerson's cosmos, God is part of the world : "The true doctrine of omnipresence is, that God reappears with all his parts in every moss and cobweb" (289). And Emerson is part of God: "The currents of the Universal Being circulate through me; I am part or particle of God" (10).[8] When the traditional Puritan model is replaced by a model that includes God in every moss and cobweb, then the terminology of religion moves into every moss and cobweb as well; this is to say that religious language, like a social aristocracy, loses its separateness in a system where everything that exists is an analogue to all other existences.

Here I am taking over part of de Tocqueville's thought in "What Causes Democratic Nations to Incline towards Pantheism" and stretching it to include language:

> The idea of unity so possesses man . . . that if he thinks he has found it, he readily yields himself to repose in that belief. Not content with the discovery that there is nothing in the world but a creation and a Creator, he is still embarrassed by this primary division of things and seeks to expand and simplify his conception by including God and the universe in one great whole.[9]

Where God and the universe are "one great whole," it may be that language about God and language about the universe, become one great whole as well. Certainly for Carlyle the phrase "Natural

Supernaturalism" was no oxymoron, but rather his perception that everything we experience is a miracle of supernatural order: "Am I to view the Stupendous with stupid indifference, because I have seen it twice, or two-hundred, or two-million times?" For Carlyle, the cleverest trick of blind Custom, whose sphere we fight to transcend, is "her knack of persuading us that the Miraculous, by simple repetition, ceases to be Miraculous."[10] Emerson revises the idea: "The invariable mark of wisdom is to see the miraculous in the common" (47). And Dickinson, in an early letter to T. W. Higginson, writes,

> I was thinking, today – as I noticed, that the
> "Supernatural," was only the Natural, disclosed –
>
>> Not "Revelation" – 'tis – that waits,
>> But our unfurnished eyes –[11]

III

When Emerson wrote, "We can never see christianity from the catechism: – from the pastures, from a boat in the pond, from amidst the songs of wood-birds we possibly may" (409), he set up one method of recycling the language of religion. The Catechism is a book of instructions in the principles of the Christian religion. A catechism that is lower case and is not "set apart" can be any book of instructions – both texts take the form of a series of questions and answers. In order to "breathe new life" through the forms already existing, Emerson removes "catechism" from the church and places it in the pond, the pastures, and the woods, where all questions and answers can take place between man and nature directly: "The foregoing generations beheld God and nature face to face; we through their eyes. Why should not we also enjoy an original relation to the universe? . . . Why should not we have a . . . religion by revelation to us, and not a history of theirs?" (7).

In a similar fashion Emerson introduces "Pentecost" into an ordinary evening: "Conversation is a game of circles . . . . The parties are not to be judged by the spirit they partake and even express under this Pentecost . . . . Yet let us enjoy the cloven flame whilst it glows on our walls" (408). Here Emerson alludes to Acts 2 and the descent of the Holy Ghost on the followers of Christ:

And when the day of Pentecost was fully come, they were all with one accord in one place. And suddenly there came a sound from heaven as of a rushing mighty wind, and it filled all the house where they were sitting. And there appeared unto them cloven tongues like as of fire, and it sat upon each of them. (Acts 2:1–3; AV)

But Emerson specifies *this* Pentecost, and he misquotes and thus revises the term "cloven flame." In "Woodnotes II" he writes: "The least breath my boughs which tossed / Brings again the Pentecost."[12] Because nature is the symbol of spirit, revelation is direct and unmediated. Of course "Pentecost" had already been revised when Emerson took it up; originally it was the name for the Jewish harvest festival celebrated fifty days after the second day of the Passover. And "baptize" is handled in much the same way. Nature "does not leave another to baptize her but baptizes herself . . ." (457). Here Emerson means naming only, but certainly he alludes to the Christian sacrament and to the priest who ministers between God and man, as he did in the "Divinity School Address": "Let me admonish you . . . to go alone; to refuse the good models, even those most sacred in the imaginations of men, and dare to love God without mediator or veil" (88–89).

Thoreau, as described by R. W. B. Lewis, "had his own sacramental system, his own rite of baptism."[13] In *Walden* he writes: "I got up early and bathed in the pond; that was a religious exercise and one of the best things that I did."[14] Lewis rightly observes that one of the ways to discredit the inherited meaning of language is "to serve it up in an unfamiliar context";[15] certainly that is one method of reclaiming for secular purposes the rhetoric of religion. In the following passage, however, Thoreau performs two tricks. First of all he uses highly charged words – "sacrament," "inspired," "Heaven," "biblical," "grace," "revelation" – to describe a purification rite of "savage nations," the Mucclasse Indians and the Mexicans. Then he self-consciously defines "sacrament" in its most general sense to do what Emerson had done with "catechism," "baptize," and "Pentecost": to reclaim it from orthodoxy.

> I have scarcely heard of a truer sacrament, that is, as the dictionary defines it, "outward and visible sign of an inward and spiritual grace," than this, and I have no doubt that they were

originally inspired from Heaven to do thus, though they have no biblical record of the revelation.[16]

(Emerson's disciple Whitman goes so far with his demythologizing that in the 1855 text of "Song of Myself" he walks with a lowercase deity: "Walking the old hills of Judea with the beautiful gentle god by my side.")[17]

Such recycling does not negate the sense of the upper case. Words that had been appropriated and "set apart" to describe the supernatural can be borrowed back and reclaimed for secular use. James Joyce, for example, reclaims "epiphany," redefining it broadly as "a sudden spiritual manifestation, whether in the vulgarity of speech or of gesture or in a memorable phase of the mind itself."[18] But just as the Frog Prince can never be wholly rid of the frog gestalt, words such as "sacrament," "catechism," "baptize," "epiphany," after they are reclaimed from sacred use, still retain a trace of their former meaning: the idea of transformation includes at least one anterior form. A secularized "sacrament," then, is a word that alludes to its former theological meaning, always; thus a "sacrament" performed by "savage nations" is a "linking reference" (John Hollander's term)[19] that depends for its full poetic effect on the reader's knowing its orthodox or "set apart" meaning. The new image is presented as a revision of an earlier one, packing two meanings into one word: "sacrament," therefore, becomes a kind of pun, a "bisected Coach," to use Dickinson's phrase (Poem 1445), that holds Calvin on one side, and Emerson, Dickinson, and Thoreau on the other.

"These are the days when Birds come back" (Poem 130), one of Dickinson's great mutability poems, subtly transforms the language of orthodoxy, while Thoreau defiantly claims it as his own. Both poets, however, attempt to redeem the rhetoric of religion by associating it with early religious rites. I excerpt the final two stanzas of Dickinson's poem:

> Oh Sacrament of summer days,
> Oh Last Communion in the Haze –
> Permit a child to join.
>
> Thy sacred emblems to partake –
> Thy consecrated bread to take
> And thine immortal wine!

In the Indian Summer poems, as Martin Bickman observes, Dickinson "refashions" Christian symbols, and thus "manages to reinvest them with some of their most powerful archetypal meaning. She uncovers what Emerson would call the 'fossil poetry' of the Christian myth, giving us a personal and emotional etymology of it."[20] By taking over the imagery of the Lord's Supper to describe the dying year, Dickinson connects the death and resurrection of Christ with the pagan fertility gods who die in autumn, to return the following spring (Bickman links the poem to the mysteries of Eleusis). Her approach is ingenious, for as soon as "set apart" language is used to describe pre-Christian rituals, that language is effectively re-turned to its pre-Christian connotation. "Communion" and "Sacrament" are revised and thus recycled. And so are the "sacred emblems," which echo a passage from Emerson's *Nature*: "What is a farm but a mute gospel? The chaff and the wheat, weeds and plants, blight, rain, insects, sun, – it is a sacred emblem from the first furrow of spring to the last stack which the snow of winter overtakes in the fields" (29).

In another of Dickinson's elegiac lyrics, the song of crickets is a presentiment of death:

> Further in Summer than the Birds –
> Pathetic from the Grass
> A minor Nation celebrates
> It's unobtrusive Mass –
> No Ordinance be seen –
> So gradual the Grace
> A gentle Custom it becomes –
> Enlarging loneliness.
>
> Antiquest felt at Noon
> When August burning low
> Arise the Spectral Canticle
> Repose to typify –
> Remit as yet no Grace –
> No furrow on the Glow –
> But a Druidic Difference
> Enhances Nature now –

(Poem 1068)[21]

"Druidic," in the penultimate line, insists upon the pre-Christian setting of the poem, an exquisite, miniature Stonehenge hidden by tall grass. Dickinson establishes her paradigm of doubleness with a pun on "minor" in line 3, and also with a play on "Mass," which can stem from *missa* (the Lord's Supper; compare "Remit" l. 13), or *massa* ("the mass of people in a nation" – to quote from Dickinson's lexicon).[22] In either case the nation of crickets is celebrating a low mass. While the non-Christian meanings of "Ordinance" and "Grace" are obvious, the Christian meaning of "gradual" may not be: as a noun it can refer to "a grail; an ancient book of hymns and prayers."[23] A "Canticle" may simply be a song ; "Canticles" normally refers to the biblical Song of Songs. Dickinson uses upper case for "Mass," "Grace," "Canticle," and also for "Grass," Noon," and "Difference." Her capitalization is no indication of the relative sanctity of her poetic language; indeed, her indeterminable use of the upper case in this poem is itself a means of reclaiming the rhetoric of religion.

That Dickinson transforms the language of orthodoxy is clear. That she has done so without irony, however, is remarkable – her crickets in no way parody a requiem mass. (Besides, the elegiac and the ironic modes would tend in this context to displace one another.) In the animistic world of "Further in Summer," where insects are dignified with human feelings, Dickinson has returned "set apart" language to the "Antiquest" rituals of worship.

IV

Of the well known passages in Dickinson's letters to Higginson, one from letter 261 is perhaps the wittiest: "They are religious except me – and address an Eclipse, every morning – whom they call their 'Father.'" To "address an Eclipse" is to address an obscured heavenly body whose light has been intercepted – perhaps by the precepts of orthodoxy, perhaps by a thick cloud upon Mount Sinai. Moreover, Dickinson's lexicon defines "eclipse" as "literally a defect or failure." Her reference to astronomy recalls the whole pantheon of classical deities – Mars, Mercury, and so on – to turn the morning address into an absurd invocation. Emerson writes that "spirit is the Creator. Spirit has life in itself. And man in all ages and countries, embodies it in his language, as the FATHER" (21). Dickinson's "Eclipse," however, is a stone king of kings, and her attitude to him is unsettled, particularly in the early poems where she cannot resolve the tension between awe and irreverence. Richard Wilbur calls her "an unsteady congregation of one" (p. 127).

In Poem 61, Dickinson sets out to discredit the Eclipse by enclosing its so-called "Mansion" in quotation marks, a technique Northrop Frye would call "naive irony":[24]

> Papa above!
> Regard a Mouse
> O'erpowered by the Cat!
> Reserve within thy kingdom
> A "Mansion" for the Rat!
>
> Snug in seraphic Cupboards
> To nibble all the day,
> While unsuspecting Cycles
> Wheel solemnly away!

Lewis Carroll declares that there is "no surer way of making one's beliefs *unreal* than by learning to associate them with ludicrous ideas."[25] Dickinson plays with John 14: 2, "In my Father's House are many mansions," while she makes the Lord's Prayer sound absurd – Albert Gelpi calls the poem "a bad little girl's parody of the Lord's Prayer."[26] "Our Father" is reduced to "Papa," an unhallowed and domestic name if one is not speaking Italian. The Cat was led into temptation, and the Rat, when he enters the kingdom, will nibble his daily bread in a so-called "Mansion." The kingdom belongs to the Rat, the power to the Cat, the glory to the Cupboards. Dickinson had no sympathy for rats ("You remember my ideal cat has always a huge rat in its mouth, just going out of sight . . . "; letter 471), so that any "Mansion" reserved for one is equivocal, at best. And if this "Mansion" is ludicrous, what of the whole structure of belief that contains it?

Perhaps the most complex poem in which Dickinson employs naive irony is Poem 239. In three quatrains, she effectively revises *Paradise Lost*:

> "Heaven" – is what I cannot reach!
> The Apple on the Tree –
> Provided it do hopeless – hang –
> That – "Heaven" is – to Me!
>
> The Color, on the Cruising Cloud –

> The interdicted Land –
> Behind the Hill – the House behind –
> There – Paradise – is found!
>
> Her teazing Purples – Afternoons –
> The credulous – decoy –
> Enamored – of the Conjuror –
> That spurned us – Yesterday!

The Apple in stanza 1 is a synecdoche for both Heaven and Paradise – all are interdicted. Milton's tree itself is interdicted:

> In Paradise to Adam or his race
> Charged not to touch the interdicted tree.
> (*PL* VII, 45–46)

Dickinson's Apple that hangs "hopeless" (that she has no hope of reaching – her lexicon gives "to extend, to reach forward" as the primary sense of "hope") is a revision of Milton's pun on "fruitless," which plays on its literal and figurative meanings:

> Serpent, we might have spared our coming hither,
> Fruitless to me, though fruit be here to excess.
> (IX, 647–48)

Like Milton's serpent, Dickinson's Conjuror decoys the "credulous":

> So glistered the dire Snake, and into fraud
> Led Eve our credulous mother, to the tree
> Of prohibition, root of all our woe.
> (IX, 644–46)

And the Conjuror may decoy the reader as well, for Dickinson, like Milton, plays with roots. Her enigmatic closure – "the Conjuror –/That spurned us – Yesterday!" depends on her play with the etymon of "spurned," a "natural fact," to use Emerson's phrase, that means "to thrust back with the foot." Dickinson traces "spurned" to its original material appearance: when the Conjuror "spurned us" we fell. "It is very unhappy," Emerson says, "but too late to be helped, the discovery we have made that we exist. That discovery is called the Fall of Man" (487).[27]

The Miltonic Heaven is not Dickinson's. Hers is a Heaven that affords us "Heavenly Hurt" (Poem 258), "piercing Comfort" (Poem 561), "Niggard Grace" (Poem 247), and "scant Salvation" (Poem 619). The whole truth lies in the doubleness of things:

> The Heaven hath a Hell –
> Itself to signalize –
> And every sign before the Place
> Is Gilt with Sacrifice –
>
> (Poem 459)

Dickinson's pun on "Gilt" is a useful bridge to her religious puns. "Gilt" and its homophone "Guilt" are related by sense as well as by sound: they join in the deadly sin of avarice.[28]

V

In his study of wordplay in medieval Latin hymnody, Walter Ong brilliantly explores the subject of religious puns, particularly where "semantic coincidence penetrates to startling relations in the real order of things." By "the real order of things" is meant "the heart of Christian doctrine, the mysteries distinctive of Christianity."[29] For Herbert, religious puns were a means of condensation, and a number of them "penetrate to startling relations" in Christian doctrine, as does the following couplet from "The Sacrifice." Christ speaks:

> Some said, that I the Temple to the floor
> In three dayes razed, and raised as before.
>
> (65–66)

The "Temple" is an image for Christ's body (see John 2:21). A common meaning of "raze" in Herbert's day was to cut, to slit, to wound the skin or any part of the body (as in "razor"). We are dealing, then, with a triple pun which has a doctrinal, not only a phonetic relation – "razed" (destroyed), "razed" (wounded), and "raised" illustrate the mystery of the Crucifixion and the Resurrection. In the following lines from "The Church-Porch," the pun is implied:

> O what were man, might he himself misplace!
> Sure to be cross he would shift feet and face.
>
> (23–24)

Here "cross" means perverse, a condition that anticipates its transformation by the Cross. And of course we note the omnipresent pun on Son/Sun in the poetry of Herbert, Donne, and Vaughan.[30]

Dickinson, on the other hand, may use religious puns to *discredit* religious decorum by pointing to startling relations in what she considers to be the real order of things:

> Some keep the Sabbath going to Church –
> I keep it, staying at Home –
> With a Bobolink for a Chorister –
> And an Orchard, for a Dome –
>
> Some keep the Sabbath in Surplice –
> I just wear my Wings –
> And instead of tolling the Bell, for Church,
> Our little Sexton – sings.
>
> God preaches, a noted Clergyman –
> And the sermon is never long,
> So instead of getting to Heaven, at last –
> I'm going, all along.
>
> (Poem 324)

Dickinson establishes the pattern of doubleness in the opening lines: some go to Church, the poet stays Home. Her Chorister is a North American songbird (dressed appropriately in black and white); the choristers in the Church are probably singing Isaac Watts. (Compare Emerson's statement in "Self Reliance": "If, therefore, a man claims to know and speak of God, and carries you backward to the phraseology of some old mouldered nation in another country, in another world, believe him not" [270].) Dickinson brings the Sabbath into the orchard just as Emerson has brought the catechism into the pond, the pastures, and the woods.

The poem turns on the homophonic pun on "Surplice," a word whose relation to "Surplus" is both phonetic and historical.[31] In fact the Surplus/Surplice grievance is an old one in Christianity; its dialectic might be the Reformation seen through a microscope. Chaucer's Monk, for example, is dressed in Surplus:

> I seigh his sleeves purfiled at the hond
> With grys, and that the fyneste of a lond.
> (General Prologue 193–94)[32]

And so is his Friar:

> For ther he was nat lyk a cloysterer
> With a thredbare cope, as is a povre scoler,
> But he was lyk a maister or a pope.
> Of double worstede was his semycope,
> That rounded as a belle out of the presse.
> (259–63)

Absalom, the parish priest of *The Miller's Tale*, combines his Surplus with Surplice to personify Dickinson's pun most elegantly:

> With Poules wyndow corven on his shoos,
> In hoses rede he wente fetisly.
> . . . . . .
> *And thereupon he hadde a gay surplys*
> As whit as is the blosme upon the rys.
> (3318–24; italics added)

In the seventh line of Dickinson's poem, "tolling the Bell, for Church," has its own doubleness: Will the bell toll to mark the death of the Church? Will the bell toll to summon worshippers to Church? Neither, I think, and that may reflect the poet's own ambivalence. Instead, the Sexton sings, and he sings because he has the key, naturally – the poet connected sextons with keys just as others do (see Poem 640: "Life is over there –/ Behind the Shelf / The Sexton keeps the Key to"). Moreover God is a *noted* clergyman – but the puns should no longer surprise.

Dickinson has effectively attacked the "set apart" Sabbath with wordplay. The elevated tone of a religious sermon is undercut by bird songs ("never long") and by puns; both serve to undo the decorum of orthodoxy. Although on this occasion the Sexton only sings, he metonymy for all the fittings, trappings, ornaments of worship of the established Church. To bring God into nature by, first, making him a clergyman, then punning on his epithet, is to make the clergyman, not God, absurd. As soon as we can hear the voice of God "without mediator or veil" the clergy is redundant – all Surplice becomes Surplus. In Emerson's words, "the relations of the soul to the divine spirit are so pure that it is profane to seek to interpose helps" (269).[33]

VI

In *The Figure of Echo*, John Hollander discusses all too briefly the "substitution of a like-sounding word for an expected one."[34] Here I shall use the term "substitution" to refer to the kind of wordplay whereby the reader's expectations are thwarted by the ingenuity of the author. (I avoid the term "displacement" because it is so often used to describe an unconscious process in dream language.) Such wordplay depends for its effect on the company it keeps – a homonym is self-contained and independent of context; whereas substitution does not work when taken out of context. When the Mock Turtle says that the classical master "taught Laughing and Grief," the wit depends on our association with "classical" (Latin and Greek), and the phonetic relation between "Grief" and "Greek" is secondary. Pope's *Dunciad* gives us the following examples of substitution; all three depend on changes within an idiomatic phrase that must stay in place:

> Taylor, their better Charon, lends an oar,
> (Once swan of Thames, tho' now he sings no more.)
> (III, 19–20)

Of course the reader expects "lends an ear," an expression set in common speech since the fourteenth-century.

> Wond'ring he gazed: When lo! a Sage appears,
> By his broad shoulders known, and length of ears.
> (III, 35–36)

With the omission of one letter, Pope turns the Sage into an Ass. I hesitate to give the third example:

> Fierce champion Fortitude, that knows no fears
> Of hisses, blows, or want, or loss of ears.
> (I, 47–48)

Surely no one would dispute Pope's substitutions, particularly in the context of a satire, where the underlying paradigm is the reversal from art to ignorance, order to chaos, and where the poet ends with a reverse fiat that unsays the first chapter of Genesis. Other examples of substitution, however, are often overlooked. Browning, for example, in "The Bishop Orders His Tomb at Saint Praxed's Church," gives us an excellent model of religious substitution. The Bishop speaks:

> And then how I shall lie through centuries,
> And hear the blessed mutter of the mass.
>
> (81–82)

We expect a Bishop to address "the blessed Mother." Browning's substitute, "mutter," only confirms that the Bishop understands nothing about Sacrament: the "mass" he refers to undoubtedly stems from *massa*, not *missa*. All this we know from the text. Browning's wordplay serves to reinforce his illustration of the Renaissance Surplice/Surplus dialectic.

Although substitution as wordplay is one of Dickinson's favourite tricks, it has received no critical attention. The following example illustrates one aspect of this technique:

> He put the Belt around my life –
> I heard the Buckle snap –
> And turned away, imperial,
> My Lifetime folding up –
> Deliberate, as a Duke would do
> A Kingdom's Title Deed –
> Henceforth, a Dedicated sort –
> A Member of the Cloud.
>
> (Poem 273, stanza 1)

I agree with Adrienne Rich's reading of this poem: it is "about the poet's relationship to her own power, which is exteriorized in masculine form."[35] Here, in a ceremony of investiture, the poet becomes "A Member of the Cloud," a phrase that has confused any number of readers. Members of such an order (and there is an unspoken pun on "order" throughout stanza 1) are distinguished persons who, when they are honoured, are given particular insignia. Clearly the sovereign, or "Duke" (the personified power) has conferred the title of "poet" on Dickinson, and one of the insignia of her new order is a "Belt" with a "Buckle." (The principal order of knighthood in Dickinson's time was the Order of the Garter, and the garter itself is composed of an embroidered velvet belt and a gold buckle.) The moment this order (to devote herself to poetry, to serve this poetic power, to sublimate her creative energies) is conferred, Dickinson is no longer an ordinary member of the *Crowd* – the phrase is a common one; instead, elevated to a higher, nobler, plane of existence, she becomes "A Member of the Cloud," for clouds move high above the general level of the ground, just as nobility moves above the general level of the crowd. As a "Member of the Cloud" Dickinson may join such inspired poets as Elijah who, in Poem 1235, rides off "Upon a Wheel of Cloud." "He put the Belt around my Life" is about poetic election (or poetic possession, as Rich says), and the Crowd/Cloud substitution, a dual model of transformation and sublimation (I use the term in a number of senses), is crucial to a reading of the poem. With her brilliant model of wordplay, Dickinson manages to pack two time frames – past and present, before and after – into one phrase.

This tightly compressed quatrain turns on the substitution of "Expanse" for "Expense":

> Obtaining but our own Extent
> In whatsoever Realm –
> 'Twas Christ's own personal Expanse
> That bore him from the Tomb –
>
> (Poem 1543)

We normally speak of someone's *personal Expense*, but Dickinson's wordplay (taking over Walter Ong's phrase again) "penetrates to startling relations in the real order of things," for in the Gospels, Christ's Expanse was obtained at the Expense of the Crucifixion.

These examples of substitution serve to underpin my reading of "I measure every Grief," a poem that, despite its complexity, has elicited surprisingly little critical ingenuity.

> I measure every Grief I meet
> With narrow, probing, Eyes –
> I wonder if It weighs like Mine –
> Or has an Easier size.

I wonder if They bore it long –
Or did it just begin –
I could not tell the Date of Mine –
It feels so old a pain –

I wonder if it hurts to live –
And if They have to try –
And whether – could They choose between –
It would not be – to die –

I note that Some – gone patient long –
At length, renew their smile –
An imitation of a Light
That has so little Oil –

I wonder if when Years have piled –
Some Thousands – on the Harm –
That hurt them early – such a lapse
Could give them any Balm –

Or would they go on aching still
Through Centuries of Nerve –
Enlightened to a larger Pain –
In Contrast with the Love –

The Grieved – are many – I am told –
There is the various Cause –
Death – is but one – and comes but once –
And only nails the eyes –

There's Grief of Want – and Grief of Cold –
A sort they call "Despair" –
There's Banishment from native Eyes –
In sight of Native Air –

And though I may not guess the kind –
Correctly – yet to me
A piercing Comfort it affords
In passing Calvary –

To note the fashions – of the Cross –
And how they're mostly worn –
Still fascinated to presume
That Some – are like My Own –

(Poem 561)

Until the first part of the eighteenth century, "grief" could signify a bodily injury or ailment; a sore, or wound. The root of "grief" is the Latin *gravis*, "heavy." Apparently the kinds of grief that Dickinson sets out to "measure" throughout the poem may be wounds, sorrows, and weights. The Cross stands for all physical and emotional afflictions. The wonder is that she can sustain a pattern of imagery that accommodates such a number of categories: abstract, concrete, literal, figurative. For example, the verb "measure" in stanza 1 has diverse meanings: one can measure the size of a wound, or gauge someone's sorrow, or weigh a literal burden, and so on.

On first reading, the poem appears to be straightforward. The poet meets those who grieve; each person's grief is a synecdoche for "Calvary"; she watches "the passing Calvary" as one might watch a fashion show, in this case a literal display of emotions; she compares the suffering she meets with her own. But such a tidy closure only manages to trivialize the kinds of suffering that the poet observes. In fact the poem itself, Dickinson's effort to interpret human suffering in terms of the Crucifixion, its archetype, is a model of religious doubt. With her "narrow, probing Eyes" the poet examines "Grief" from every angle, but she cannot reach conclusion: "I wonder . . . or . . . I wonder . . . or . . . I could not tell . . . .I wonder if . . . And whether . . . could They . . . I wonder . . . or would they . . . I am told." In the final two stanzas she transforms this doubt into a mass of entangled language where meanings are unfixed.

As a paradoxical image for the Crucifixion or, more specifically, for the spear that pierced Christ's side (John 19:34), "piercing Comfort" in the penultimate stanza is a paradigm of the sort of doubleness that runs beneath the text. Noting the multifaceted "fashions – of the Cross," for example, Dickinson may note the pattern grief takes; she may note how people bear their grief; she may note how others cover or mask sorrow; she may note the customs of mourning; she may note the fabric of grief; she may note the length of sorrow or the period of mourning; she may note how the grief is fashioned. This catalogue can be extended with the least ingenuity.

Awash in plurisignation *we* note that "worn," in the final stanza, may be either a verb or an adjective; so that "fashions – of the Cross" may be worn (put on) or worn away, worn down, worn out. The adverb/adjective "mostly" accommodates itself. To combine variously the slippery "fashions" with the equally slippery "worn," and then to take "Cross" literally (Medieval Crosses are mostly worn, gold Crosses are mostly worn on chains), is to drown in Babel.[36] And then, "In passing Calvary" is problematic. Is the poet passing Calvary? Is Calvary passing her as a fashion show? (Compare Whitman's "Agonies are one of my changes of garments.")[37] If *she* is passing Calvary, she may see the place where Christ was crucified; or she may see "a series of representations, in a church or a chapel, of the scenes of the Passion" ("Calvary," *OED* 2). The kinds of grief that she observes are indeed "a series of representations . . . of the Passion."

I suggest that Dickinson has substituted "fashions – of the Cross" for the more likely "passions of the Cross"; and further, that she has substituted "And how they're mostly worn" for the more likely "And how they're mostly borne." "Passion," formerly also in the plural, refers to the sufferings of Christ on the Cross, often also including the Agony in Gethsemane. "Passion Play" is a familiar term, but other phrases given in the *OED* include "Passion Cross," "Cross of the Passion," "Cross of Passion." The Cross, like the nails in Dickinson's seventh stanza, is one of the instruments of the Passion. Even "passions" (plural and lower case) is used in reference to the Crucifixion; witness these lines addressing Christ in Vaughan's "The Nativity": "Great *type* of passions come what will,/Thy grief exceeds all *copies* still." Stated otherwise, Christ's Passion is the archetype of all passions, and no copy can equal it: an *imitatio Christi* cannot be other than an imitation. The kinds of grief that fascinate Dickinson are, in Vaughan's terms, "passions," or imitations of Christ's suffering; and such passions are normally "borne," as they are in the famous chapter of Isaiah that Dickinson knew well: "surely he hath borne our griefs, and carried our sorrows . . . . But he was wounded for our transgressions, he was bruised for our iniquities . . . and with his stripes we are healed" (Isa. 53:4,5; compare 1 Peter 2:21–25). If indeed the final stanza of Poem 561 centers on the religious substitutions I propose (and Dickinson's model should be compared to Browning's "blessed mutter of the mass"/blessed Mother of the Mass), then the unspoken, underlying text moving in counterpoint to hers might read,

> To note the passions – of the Cross –
> And how they're mostly borne –
> Still fascinated to presume
> That Some – are like My Own –

Such cunning wordplay, whereby one rhyming or like-sounding word is substituted for another, again alludes to and parallels Christian belief: the word "substitution" itself is used "to designate a doctrine of the Atonement according to which Jesus Christ suffered punishment vicariously for man" (*OED* 2b). In Christian typology, just as Abraham sacrificed the ram in place of Isaac, so Christ sacrificed himself on behalf of man; both type and antitype include the act of substitution. But it should be noted that the model of the Atonement, like many religious models, lends itself to parody, itself a kind of substitution: Milton's demonic trio of Satan, Death, and Sin, for example, parodies the Trinity; and Sin's language parodies grotesquely the Nicene creed (*PL* II, 870). Similarly, the two lines that concern us in this discussion of Dickinson's poem apparently pervert and parody her own religious subtext with its overtones of Isaiah 53: "To note the passions – of the Cross / And how they're mostly borne."[38]

Already I have noted the unstable word "fashions," whose plurisignation mimics its own inconstancy. Revivalism was the latest fashion of the Cross in Dickinson's time, and one that caused her "anguish," as Richard Sewall observes;[39] and I propose that the passions/fashions, worn/borne substitutions parody the whole revival movement of the Connecticut Valley with its gaudiness, professions of faith, and evangelical clichés. That "the letter killeth, but the spirit giveth life" (2 Cor. 3:6) was as true for Dickinson as it was for Emerson, Thoreau, and Whitman; and in Poem 561 she may be subverting and parodying through wordplay *all* fashionable cults, especially those that are constantly being re-formed. When such untrustworthy language as the poet uses in the final stanzas of the poem centers on the Cross, the still point of Dickinson's turning world, it points to a radical disjunction between her own beliefs and those of the fashionable religious movements of her day.

VII

Roberta Frank, in her study of paronomasia in Anglo-Saxon scriptural verse, observes that multiple puns on "word" are common: the Old English *Genesis* poet, for example, "opens his work not with the first verse of the Book of Genesis but with a threefold play on 'word'"; his triple pun "seems to be trying to persuade us that the poet's literary and Christian purposes are one, that nothing could be more natural or right in English than that the *weard*, king of *weroda*, should be praised in *wordum*."[40]

Both Emerson and Dickinson adapt the language of the fourth Gospel to the creation of poetry: "In the beginning was the Word, and the Word was with God, and the Word was God" (John 1:1); verse 14 reads, " And the Word was made flesh, and dwelt among us . . . . " Emerson maintains in "The Poet" that "thought may be ejaculated as Logos, or Word" (466); in "Self Reliance" he insists that "a man is the word made flesh" (275). And "Bacchus," a poem about poetic inspiration, centers on "Wine which is already man."[41] As late as 1872 Emerson is still redefining "transubstantiation": "American life storms about us daily and is slow to find a tongue. This contemporary insight is transubstantiation, the conversion of daily bread into the holiest symbols; and every man would be a poet if his intellectual digestion were perfect."[42]

Simply by employing the language of the fourth Gospel to describe the poetic process, Dickinson reclaims the rhetoric of religion for secular use. In Poem 1126, for example, the poet is inter-viewing (in its radical sense of *entrevoir*) words from her lexicon as they apply for a vacant position in her poem – again, the unspoken pun on "position" is crucial.

> Shall I take thee, the Poet said
> To the propounded word?
> Be stationed with the Candidates
> Till I have finer tried –
>
> The Poet searched Philology
> And was about to ring
> for the suspended Candidate
> There came unsummoned in –
>
> That portion of the Vision
> The Word applied to fill
> Not unto nomination
> The Cherubim reveal –

The "Candidate" of the first two stanzas has been "suspended"; that is, he or she is temporarily deferred (left up in the air) until the poet has considered other words for the position. (In practice, when Dickinson "suspended" words she noted them down as variants in her worksheet drafts and often in the fair copy also.) Here, as she is about to fill the vacancy, another word miraculously appears. In terms of biblical typology, just the Word filled the Messianic vision of the Old Testament, so, in a moment of poetic grace, the "Word" fills Dickinson's poetic "Vision." Each word of every poem is, finally, spirit incarnate; the creation of poetry is analogous to a religious sacrament:

> Your thoughts dont have words every day
> They come a single time
> Like signal esoteric sips
> Of the communion Wine
> Which while you taste so native seems
> So easy so to be
> You cannot comprehend its price
> Nor it's infrequency
>
> (Poem 1452)

In other words, as in Poem 1651, "A Word made Flesh is seldom/And tremblingly partook." But it is not the Eucharistic bread and wine that are converted into "A Word made flesh." Instead, words from Dickinson's lexicon (she never calls it a "dictionary") are transformed into poems made up of words that breathe and have "not the power to die."[43] The "Book" she refers to in Poem 1587 is certainly her lexicon:

> He ate and drank the precious Words –
> His Spirit grew robust –
> He knew no more that he was poor,
> Nor that his frame was Dust –
>
> He danced along the dingy Days
> And this bequest of Wings
> Was but a Book – What Liberty
> A loosened spirit brings –

Again, in a quatrain from Poem 728, the poet is eating and drinking words from the same "Book"; it would be hard to find a more cunning example of etymological wordplay:

> Easing my famine
> At my Lexicon –

Logarithm – had I – for Drink –
'Twas a dry Wine –

The root of "Logarithm" is *logos*. Dickinson's "Wine" – metonymy for the Lord's Supper – may be "dry" (as it was for Emerson) in a number of senses. First, it is not sweet; second, it may be stiff and solid; third, it yields no moisture, and therefore no nourishment. Apparently "dry Wine" cannot sustain the poet; to ease her spiritual "famine," she drinks "precious Words" from her "Lexicon" (Gr. *lexis* "word") and transforms them into the completed lyric.

This chapter began with a discussion of Emerson's attitude to the rhetoric of religion. To believe that language can be redeemed and purified, that it can be re-turned, trope upon trope, to its poetic origins, is to assume that the Fall of man and the perversion of language are, in some radical sense, parallel.[44] By suggesting that fallen theological language can slough off its encrusted layers of metaphor, Emerson is really saying that the poet, as redeemer, can cleanse words of their inherited meaning – the sins of language – and direct them back to their prelapsarian nakedness. Wordplay is one way back to the garden of primary meanings. If words can indeed be directed back to their source, and if that source – to follow Emerson – is the mind of God, then etymology would be a sacred exercise, and so would religious wordplay, which is normally based on etymologies, real or imagined.[45] In theory, then, lexicons, as images or types of God's mind, are sacred texts. And what Dickinson called "this consent of language/This loved Philology" (Poem 1651) was, for her, a way to see God and live.

5
Robert Frost: The Design of Violence

William Paley's *Natural Theology* (1802) is dedicated "To the Honourable and Right Rev. Shute Barrington, LL D, Lord Bishop of Durham" – the last but one of the Counts Palatine: "The following Work [Paley writes] was undertaken at your Lordship's recommendation, and amongst other motives, for the purpose of making the most acceptable return that I could, for a great and important benefit conferred on me."[1] My motives are not unrelated to Paley's: given first as a public lecture, the present study was undertaken for the purpose of making an acceptable return for a benefit conferred on me – the Macmillan Fellowship at the University of Durham.

Paley's phrase "acceptable return" suggests the closing prayer of Psalm 19: "Let the words of my mouth, and the meditations of my heart, be acceptable in thy sight, O Lord, my strength and my redeemer." The first verse reads: "The heavens declare the glory of God; and the firmament sheweth his handywork." In essence, Paley's *Natural Theology*, like the Argument from Design in general, is an elaborate and extended exegesis of Psalm 19:1. For Paley, as for Kirby and Spence, among other natural theologians, the universe with its plants, insects, and birds – God's "handywork" – manifests Divine intention and testifies to an intelligent and benevolent Creator.

"Suppose," Paley argues in his opening chapter, "I had found a *watch* upon the ground, and it should be inquired how the watch happened to be in that place." That watch, he reasons, "must have had a maker, . . . there must have existed, at some time, and at some place or other, an artificer, who formed it for the purpose which we find it actually to answer; who comprehended its construction, and designed its use." Furthermore, it would not "invalidate our conclusion, that the watch sometimes went wrong, or that it seldom went exactly right. The purpose of the machinery, the design and the designer," would be evident in any case. "It is not necessary that a machine be perfect in order to show with what design it was made; still less necessary, where the only question is, whether it were made with any design at all." In Paley's view, then, "there cannot be a design without a designer; contrivance without a contriver."[2]

The word *design* normally refers to a plan, a scheme, a project, a purpose, an intention. Nevertheless, like *artifice* or *craft*, *design* may, without qualifying adjectives, occur in what the *OED* terms a "bad sense"; thus *design* may signify "crafty contrivance, hypocritical scheming." Likewise *designer*: while it may simply refer to anyone who designs or plans (a building, a can-opener, a watch), *designer* in its "bad sense" refers us to "one who cherishes evil designs" – that is, to a *designing* intriguer with dark intent.

The arch-designer in a bad sense is Satan, Milton's "Artificer of fraud" (*PL* IV, 121), who, we are told, "designs" in Adam and Eve "to ruin all mankind" (V, 227–28).[3] The word *ruin* is cognate with the Latin *ruere*, to fall; and one implication of mankind's ruin or Fall is the fall of language into doubleness, and also into *duplicity* – the bad sense of *doubleness*. Emerson once remarked, "There is a crack in every thing God has made."[4] If that is so, then the cracks in everything, including language, are the result of the Fall. Cracked words, hinged words with detachable parts, may be fractured, their parts cohering through sound but not sense, like the cracked Humpty-Dumpty, joined by assonance, separated forever by a hyphen. Or like *design*, which in one sense declares God's handywork, and, in its "bad sense", declares the artifice or craft of God's "adversary" (1 Pet. 5:8) – the "Prince of this world" (John 12:31).

Cast out from Heaven, Satan is "Left at large to his own dark designs" (I, 213). Whereupon he advises the rebel angels "To work in close design, by fraud or guile/What force effected not" (I, 645 ff.). What Milton calls Satan's "bold design" (II, 386) – to invade Paradise, to seduce mankind, to ruin the handywork of God – is *bold* in its "bad sense" ("audacious, presumptuous; opp. to 'modest'" [*OED* 3]). Whence, asks Milton, "But from the author of ill could spring/So deep a malice?" (II, 381). The author of ill – the "genius of misfortune," Stevens calls him – is the author of duplicity and also of the "bad sense" of things: entering "into the fold" (IV, 187) of the Garden of Eden, Satan implicates mankind in a twofold and duplex sense of language not unrelated to the "mazy folds" of the subtle serpent: "hap may find/The serpent sleeping, in whose mazy folds / To hide me, and the dark intent I bring" (IX, 159ff.). Appropriately, Satan enters the double-tongued and insinuating serpent "in at his mouth" (IX, 186).

"In the beginning was the pun," says Samuel Beckett. Michael Edwards disagrees: "a truer formula," he writes, "would be 'since the Fall is the pun' (or even: 'Adam was *pun*ished')." According to Edwards (in *Towards a Christian Poetics*), the pun "mocks everything that it *lights on* . . . most particularly the apartness of sound and sense" (italics added).[5] Mockery includes imitation, mimicry, parody, repetition, doubling, counterfeit, simulation. In *Paradise Lost*, Satan enters into the garden of Eden – lights on the garden of Eden – with a wicked string of puns:

> Due entrance he disdained, and in contempt,
> At one slight bound high overleaped all bound
> Of hill or highest wall, and sheer within
> *Lights on* his feet . . . .
>
> (IV, 180ff.; italics added)

At first, apart from picking up the slight Miltonic echo in Edwards's definition of puns, one notices the pun on *Due* with its unanchored and uncertain referent. If *Due* is an adjective describing *entrance*, it describes the proper or rightful entrance to Eden, the one gate. Whereas if *Due* is a passive verb (i.e. "owed or entitled to"), and *entrance* its object (a reading that would be compelled by a comma – "due entrance, he disdained"), the sense changes radically: Satan was due entrance – he had the right of admission; nevertheless, he disdained to enter the garden by the proper gate. And who or what is the subject/object of "in contempt"? One notes also the triple pun on the doubled word *bound*: with an upward spring, a "slight *bound*," Satan leaps over the wall, limits, *bound* of Paradise, *bound* to ruin mankind. Further, to give the Devil his due, one notices the satanic ingenuity of the word *slight*: the adjective can mean smooth, performed with little exertion. On the other hand, its homophonic double, *sleight*, means artful, crafty, deceptive, as in the phrase "sleight-of-hand." (Satan, of course, is the trickster *par excellence*.) Moreover both *slight* (and *sleight*) may be nouns, in which case a comma after the word *slight* brings yet another sense into focus. And just who has been slighted by such sheer nonsense?

At this overcrowded juncture, a passing remark of Christopher Ricks's is apposite: "*in a pun there are two senses which either get along or quarrel*" (italics added).⁶ Apparently, then, there are at least two sorts of homophones – doubles that quarrel, and doubles that get along. And this chapter is concerned with the former, that is, with words like *design*, whose senses have had a falling out, or whose one sense mocks the other. Thus I turn to René Girard and his theory of mimetic doubling or "conflictual mimesis."⁷ The following points attempt to summarize Girard's model of imitative violence; the terminology and phrasing of his translators are used throughout:

1. The model begins with two rivals, or warring doubles, or enemy twins.
2. Their rivalry – the conflict between the doubles – may be provoked by an object that both desire; this Girard calls "acquisitive mimesis," or "mimetic desire," or "acquisitive imitation."
3. A "mimetic crisis" occurs; "conflictual mimesis" invariably leads to physical violence.
4. The *absence* of difference, not its presence, is always perceived as "terrifying" (14). *Any* mimetic reproduction – twins, doubles, look-alikes, *repeated words* (10) – suggests violence.
5. To end the mimetic crisis, to prevent violence, and to restore peace in the community, "violence seeks and always finds a surrogate victim" – a scapegoat, substituted for the warring doubles, and then in some way expelled from the community.
6. Originally, the sacrifice of the scapegoat – a ritual act of violence – unified and brought renewed peace to the community, putting an end to the mimetic crisis.
7. Although one may distinguish between "legitimate and illegitimate violence" (399), violence is always the true subject of ritual, and ritual always takes the form of violence. For ritual is "nothing more than the regular exercise of "good" violence."⁸

In Girard's imagination, violence has all the characteristics of a subjective agency stalking its prey. "When unappeased [he writes], violence seeks and always finds a surrogate victim. The creature that excited its fury is abruptly replaced by another, chosen only because it is vulnerable and close at hand."⁹ Behind Girard's text lurks the first epistle of Peter: "Be sober, be vigilant; because your adversary the devil, as a roaring lion, walketh about, seeking whom he may devour" (5:8). Further, for Girard, "*Satan is the name of the mimetic process* seen as a whole; that is why he is the *source* not merely *of rivalry* and disorder but of all the forms of lying order inside which mankind lives" (162; italics added); here the subtext is John 8:44, wherein Satan is called "a murderer from the beginning" and "a liar and the father of lies." In Girard's view, then, the terms *Satan* and *Violence* are interchangeable, as are *Violence* and *mimetic desire, Satan* and *conflictual mimesis*.[10] This is central to the Design of Violence. Adhering to the logic of Girard's argument, one suspects, or at least intuits, that Satan may be radically entangled with words whose senses quarrel – that is, with puns that mock everything they light on, including their own doubles.

Let us now take a proof-text to Girard's theory of the "victimage mechanism" and its possible relation to mimetic rivalry and "warring doubles" in language – Robert Frost's apparently slight sonnet, "Design," first published in 1922, the year of *The Waste Land*. As well, we will consider several details of its early draft, "In White" (of c. 1912), a poem that ends by questioning the sense of the word *design*: "Design, design! Do I use the word aright?"[11] Which is to say, do I use the word in its good sense or "bad sense"? Does *design* signify God's handywork, or does it perhaps signify the malice of his designing adversary? Here is the final version of "Design":[12]

> I found a dimpled spider, fat and white,
> On a white heal-all, holding up a moth
> Like a white piece of rigid satin cloth –
> Assorted characters of death and blight
> Mixed ready to begin the morning right,
> Like the ingredients of a witches' broth –
> A snow-drop spider, a flower like a froth,
> And dead wings carried like a paper kite.
>
> What had that flower to do with being white,
> The wayside blue and innocent heal-all?
> What brought the kindred spider to that height,
> Then steered the white moth thither in the night?
> What but design of darkness to appall? –
> If design govern in a thing so small.

As a term in biology, the word *mimicry* (like *mocker*) refers to a close external resemblance in form and/or colour which one creature bears to another or to some inanimate object, often for the purpose of camouflage. In Frost's sonnet several phenomena – words, insects, flowers, sounds – have reproduced themselves mimetically, and according to Girard, all mimetic doubling with its lack of difference suggests violence or may be interpreted as a possible cause of violence, which, as we shall see, is anyway its own cause. Consequently, for Girard all mimetic doubling – mockery, imitation, simulation, lies, repetition – is inherently "terrifying," a word that may gloss Lionel Trilling's notorious description of Frost as a "terrifying" poet: "I think of Robert Frost as a terrifying poet .... The universe that he conceives is a terrifying universe. Read the poem called 'Design' and see if you sleep the better for it."[13]

To read "Design" as a parable of mimetic violence is not only to decipher the assorted characters mixed on the white page, but also to guess at the rôles played by Frost's "characters of death and blight." "All violence," says Girard, "has a mimetic character" (198). Adapting his model of ritual mimesis to Frost's poem, one suspects that the heal-all (a wild flower, *Prunella vulgaris*) and its look-alike, the spider, may be doubles and thus enemy twins. If so, then the moth would be the sacralized victim and scapegoat of their rivalry. In the sestet, Frost describes the "fat and white" "snow-drop spider" as "kindred" to the "innocent heal-all," a flower that ought to be blue. This one must be an albino, a freak of nature.[14] One aspect of their mimetic doubling, then, is a common but uncommon whiteness. As well, the fat, white spider is equated to the snow-drop, a bulbous plant with a white, bell-shaped flower.

That the flower is specifically a heal-all, a labiate – in fact a bilabiate – is not insignificant: the corolla of the heal-all has "a hooded upper lip and a spreading lower lip," and anything with lips may have a mouth, and may also foam at the mouth. Thus in the penultimate line of the first stanza, the heal-all is "like a froth," an image that runs down the page to meet its visual double, the implicit froth or scum or beads of foam on the surface of the "witches' broth," boiling in its lipped cauldron, and to merge also with the drops of snow of the "snow-drop" spider, described in the first draft of the sonnet as "beady." Like the heal-all, the spider has a mouth, as well as a pair of poison glands used to kill the prey on which it feeds.

When Frost finds the spider, it is "holding up a moth/Like a white piece of rigid satin cloth" – or like a pall. Holding up a piece of white cloth may signify surrender or a peaceful intention, and in Girard's thesis, renewed peace is invariably the aim of ritual violence. But in any case, all satin cloth, like Satan, is markedly two-sided. As for the moth itself, the early version of "Design" includes the phrase, "the miller's plight." Whereas the female miller-moth (*hepialus humuli*) is brown, the wings of the male are pure white, "rendering him conspicuous in the evening when pairing takes place" (according to the 13th edition of the *Encyclopedia Britannica*). During the moth's ritual dismemberment or *sparagmos*, a particularly sinister type of pairing takes place when the moth's wings are detached from its body: "And dead wings carried like a paper kite." Paper kites, of course, take their name from the hovering bird of prey.

Girard argues that "any part of the body that can be detached ... is a potential double and therefore a threat of violence" (14). And here I am concerned with the detached signification of line 5 – "Mixed ready to begin the morning right." After all, how *should* one begin the "morning right" except to eliminate and to pray? Coincidentally, as the moth is being eliminated – expelled outside the limen or pale (as it were), and dis-membered – the fat, white spider is preying, relying on its subtly-designed web as a preyer text. (That Frost describes the spider as "beady" in the early draft is surely *no* coincidence: "prayer" is cognate with "bead"; in fact, as in "bidding prayer," or even "beads-bidding," the etymons of *prayer* and *bead* are synonyms.) Clearly the unnatural phrase "morning right" cries out for its mimetic double: to substitute *mourning* for *morning*, and then *rite* for *right*, is to come upon a mourning rite (a wake or funeral), even a morning rite, but in any case, upon a scene of ritual violence that includes a chorus keening "ai, ai, ai . . . " fifteen times in fourteen lines of poetry.

With the phrase "witches' broth" in line 6, Frost makes a pointed allusion to the boiling and bubbling "hell-broth" (I.vi.19) mixed by the witches in *Macbeth*, the play within the play of "Design." And here one recalls that the language of the three Weird Sisters is inseparable from their duplicity; that their temptation of Macbeth, not unlike Satan's temptation of Eve, depends on the linguistic doubleness of their prophecies. Lady Macbeth's phrase, "In every point twice done, and then done double" (I.vi.15), echoes the witches' language, and serves also as the mimetic model and portent of the physical violence unleashed on Duncan by Macbeth, his enemy twin. But this is matter for another study; here I am concerned only with the following lines spoken at the banquet where Banquo's ghost appears:

> Lady Macbeth: Are you a man?
> Macbeth: Ay, and a bold one, that dare look on that
>   Which might appall the devil.
>
> (III.iv.58ff.)

Macbeth's startling use of *appall* should be compared with the penultimate line of Frost's "Design," whose sestet poses a series of unsettling and unsettled questions about the convergence of the twin enemies – the heal-all and the spider – and the moth. What brought the flower and the so-called "kindred" spider together in the first place, Frost asks. And what "Then steered the white moth thither in the night?" His uneasy and conditional answer is, "What but design of darkness to appall?" At first reading, the sense and syntax appear straightforward, more or less: "some subjective agency or designer no doubt designed this dark scene to appall us, dismay us, frighten us." At the same time, though, the phrase "design of darkness" may be a syntactical crux: is the design characterized by, composed of, darkness; or does the noun "darkness" refer to and personify someone with dark designs who is bound up with the "prynce of derknes . . . our goostly ennemy the devyll" (*OED* 4a; cf. *King Lear* III.iv.147)?[15]

Such confusion serves to concentrate and focus our critical attention on the phrase, "design of darkness," and also on the first draft of "Design," whose penultimate line reads: "What but design of darkness and of night?" Reading that aloud, one overhears snatches of Paul in I Thessalonians: "we are not of the night, nor of darkness" (5:5); and in Romans 13:12: "let us therefore cast off the works of darkness," which as we know are cunningly and designedly wrought. Likewise, when Banquo refers to the witches as "instruments of darkness" (I.iii.124), we infer that their two-part language is in-spired by that agency Paul names, "the prince of the power of the air" (Eph. 2:2), who may also control Mr. Kurtz's "heart of darkness." In a close reading of "Design," the most revealing example of Frost's linguistic intent (if intent matter in a thing so small) may be his sonnet "Once by the Pacific" with its bold Miltonic allusion: "It looked as if *a night of dark intent* / Was coming, and not only a night, an age" (italics added). And as we have seen, the words "dark intent" are spoken by Satan, who enters the serpent's folds "To hide me, and the *dark intent* I bring" (IX, 159ff.).

Suddenly one is in a critical quandary: does the so-called "design of darkness" intend to appall *us* with this ritual drama of heal-all, spider and moth? Or is the mimetic ritual in and of Frost's "small" poem – its design – intended to appall the "design of darkness" (and the knight of dark intent)? In other words, does the word "design" "govern" the syntax of the penultimate line of the poem? Posed differently, does the phrase "design of darkness" govern the verb "to appall"? Or, inversely, is the phrase "design of darkness" governed *by* the verb *appall*? Here one is really asking whether "design of darkness" is the subject or the object of *appall*, and thus whether or not "design of darkness" is in the accusative, which anyway is Satan's accustomed rôle. If so, then the sense of Frost's penultimate line would go something like this: "the white heal-all, the white spider and the white moth have converged in this poem of ritual mimesis in order to appall the design of darkness."

Authority for such an extravagant and seemingly far-fetched sense of *appall* comes first of all from Macbeth, an authority on evil, who imagines, in lines cited above, that Satan can somehow be appalled. Frost's authority for the contrived inversion of his syntax may be Blake: "How the Chimney-sweeper's cry / Every black'ning Church appalls." Is it that the cry of the pale Chimney-sweep appalls the black'ning Church; that is, do the tears of the Chimney-sweep's weeping (his "weep! weep!") appall (whiten or horrify) the black'ning Church? Or does the black'ning Church appall the cry of the chimney-sweep? Perhaps the most extended conjunction of whiteness and *appall*, along with its doubles and incipient doubles, is found in Chapter 42 of *Moby-Dick*: "It was the whiteness of the whale that above all things appalled me," says Ishmael, who adds: "the one visible quality in the aspect of the dead which most appals the gazer, is the marble pallor lingering there . . . . And from that pallor of the dead, we borrow the expressive hue of the shroud in which we wrap them [a pall; Melville puns obliquely on the Latin *pallium* or cloak"] . . . . Yea, while these terrors seize us, let us add, that even the king of terrors, when personified by the evangelist, rides on his pallid horse."[16]

Let us return to the matter of cracked and quarrelling and fractured homophones, of "warring doubles" like *design/design*, for example, and *prey/pray*, whose sound and sense no longer cohere. In Girard's scheme of mimetic violence, there are two sorts of imitation: "non-violent imitation" and "violent imitation" (430), corresponding to "legitimate and illegitimate violence" (399). And I suggest that words whose senses quarrel participate in violent imitation (the only kind of imitation left once "good" or "ritual violence" has disappeared); and that *the scapegoat and sacrifice in their rivalry is meaning itself*. If all mimetic doubling leads to mimetic rivalry, then anything and everything that mimics and mocks its double constitutes a threat of violence. Consider the Tweedle twins, for example, the self-reflexive Tweedledum and Tweedledee, whose mimetic rivalry and antagonism is apparently caused by their desire for the same object – a rattle – and who then get all dressed up for a mock-battle that was anyway, from the beginning, inherent in their doubled names. Whether we point to the Tweedle twins, or to *their* warring doubles, or to warring doubles in language like *design / design*, "Satan is the mimetic model . . . *par excellence*" (419).

To conceive of Satan as *the* "mimetic model," as Girard does, is in effect to evoke Satan's original envy of and mimetic rivalry with God – his designs upon the throne of the Deity: "through envy of the devil [*diabolus*] came death into the world: and they that do hold of his side do find it" (Wisdom 2:24). And this envy I take to be the ur-model of *all* violent imitation and duplicity in language. In Genesis 3, for example, as Edwards notes, the subtle serpent "aggresses specifically the language of God by questioning it: 'Yea, hath God said, ye shall not eat of every tree of the garden?', and . . . by contradicting it: 'Ye shall not surely die.'"[17] To *aggress* God's language rather than address it is typical of Satan's arrogance and of his punningly bad sense: the verb *aggress* means to "begin a quarrel" with or "assault" (*OED* 3). Hence, with a "bold design" (Milton's phrase) that relies wholly on beguiling and duplex speech, Satan sets out to deny the priority of the creating Word by mocking and reversing and negating the sense of divine words.

We have arrived at a final crux. Girard contends that "*Satan is the name of the mimetic process* seen as a whole; that is why *he is the source* not merely of rivalry and disorder, but *of all the forms of lying order inside which mankind lives*" (162; italics added). That Satan should be called the source of anything at all is disturbing, that is, until one somehow grasps the elusive substance of Girard's model: *all Satan can do is imitate*; he originates nothing at all except mimetic rivalry (or violent imitation, or mimetic desire, or sheer envy), which is inseparable from "the false transcendence of violence." Indeed "Satan could be said to incarnate mimetic desire were that desire not, by definition, disincarnate. It empties all people, all things, and all texts of their substance."[18]

Violence is always, says Girard, "the true *subject* of every ritual," since the purpose of ritual is to contain and control and to rechannel violence. Just as there are two sorts of imitation – violent and non-violent imitation – there are, for Girard, two sorts of violence: the "organized violence of ritual," and "spontaneous collective violence" (133). As long as the "sacrificial order" is stable and secure, violence is not loosed. But once "the sacrificial order begins to come apart, this subject [of ritual] can no longer be anything but the *adversary par excellence*, which combats the installation of the Kingdom of God. This is the devil known to us from tradition – Satan himself . . . " (210).

In Girard's terms, violence unrestrained by ritual is metonymy for Satan. Yet violence or Satan, even when it is without restraint, is never free, for Satan is his own constraint:

> And like a devilish engine back recoils
> Upon himself . . .
>   . . . and from the bottom stir
> The hell within him, for within him hell.
>
> (IV, 17ff.)

Milton's chiasmic and recoiling lines point to circularity and self-entrapment. To quote Girard, who might be glossing Milton, "Satan is absolutely identified with the circular mechanisms of violence" (162). Furthermore, violence or Satan forms "a *closed kingdom*" (197; italics added), apprehended in popular idiom as the vicious circle or *Teufels Kreis*.[19] Violence is the subject of violence, just as Satan is the subject of his own closed kingdom: "Which way I fly is hell; myself am hell" (IV, 75).

There are puns that quarrel and puns that get along. The brilliance of Ricks's point is that quarrelling puns draw attention to the pun qua pun, that is, as a sound that stops short of sense by its failure to refer outside itself. Puns whose senses get along, on the other hand, refer beyond themselves, and may even penetrate "to startling relations in the real order of things" (to quote Walter Ong's study of religious word-play.)[20] Put simply, the non-violent pun refers us to the order underwritten by the creating Word of God, thereby escaping from self-involvement into meaning. Whereas the signifiers of the quarrelling pun are only specular, reflecting not even each other but, like Narcissus, the enclosed and mirrored self or ego mistaken for other.

The Design of Violence is primarily to obscure the dark intent it brings through verbal sleight-of-hand. And one of its mimetic tricks is to insinuate that there is or even can be any other closed system but its own – the closed system of violence. Among those for whom the sacrificial order has collapsed, language is the fashionable closed system; mirror-wise, the fashionable closed system is language. In a world of self-referentiality, one quickly gets over the nostalgia for presence, finding satisfaction in the limitless possibilities afforded by chaos. But the semantic chaos produced by self-reflexive signifiers conceals an underlying order: the order of the closed system of violence, or the closed kingdom of the ego, preying to and on itself.[21]

6

Understanding Understatement: Biblical Typology and "The Displaced Person"

> The Southern writer can outwrite anybody in the country because he has the Bible and a little history.
>
> Flannery O'Connor

Typology is a "neglected subject, even in theology," Northrop Frye contends, "and it is neglected elsewhere because it is assumed to be bound up with a doctrinaire adherence to Christianity."[1] By "typology" Frye means a two-part figure of speech comprising type and antitype: "Everything that happens in the Old Testament is a 'type' or adumbration of something that happens in the New Testament, and the whole subject is therefore called typology . . . . What happens in the New Testament constitutes an 'antitype,' a realized form, of something foreshadowed in the Old Testament."[2]

Instead of the terms "type" and "antitype" (from the Greek *typos*), Erich Auerbach in his seminal essay "Figura" uses the Latinate "figure" and "fulfillment"; the aim of figural interpretation is "to show that the persons and events of the Old Testament were prefigurations of the New Testament and its history of salvation."[3] Insisting on the actuality/thingness of types, Joseph Galdon defines typology as "the method of interpreting scripture in which the persons and events, incidents and narratives of the Old Testament, the Old Testament *res ipsae*, are viewed as realities which are also at one and the same time prophetic signs and foreshadowing of the persons and events in God's redemptive plan as it is fulfilled and revealed in the New Testament."[4] Stated otherwise by Auerbach, "*figura* is something real and historical which announces something else that is also real and historical. The relation between the two events is revealed by an accord or similarity."[5] The argument of the present chapter is that the typological method of biblical exegesis is the implicit structural principle of Flannery O'Connor's short story "The Displaced Person."

In a letter of November 25, 1955, O'Connor wrote: "The displaced person did accomplish a kind of redemption in that he destroyed the place, which was evil, and set Mrs. McIntyre on the road to a new kind of suffering.... None of this was adequately shown and to make the story complete it would have had to be – so I did fail myself. Understatement was not enough."[6] In fact all this is more than adequately shown: anyone who discerns even faintly the typological pattern – the "under-statement" – hidden beneath the story knows that Mr. Guizac is a redemptive figure, that the McIntyre farm is related to the biblical cities of the plain. A reading of "The Displaced Person" must draw on typology as a mode of thought. Typology, however, depends on a firm grasp of the Old and New Testaments and of the figurative method of exegesis; and O'Connor knew that most of her readers would be without these. What Sr. Mariella Gable calls O'Connor's "Scripture-anchored fiction"[7] is, in the words of Paul, "the wisdom of God in a mystery" (1 Cor. 2:7). And whether or not readers could unravel that mystery was, for O'Connor, irrelevant:

> The fact that Catholics don't see religion through the Bible is a deficiency in Catholics. And I don't think the novelist can discard the instruments he has to plumb meaning just because Catholics aren't used to them. You don't write only for now. The biblical revival is going to mean a great deal to Catholic fiction in the future. Maybe in fifty years or a hundred Catholics will be reading the Bible the way they should have been reading it all along. I can wait that long to have my fiction understood. The Bible is what we share with all Christians, and the Old Testament we share with all Jews. This is sacred history and our mythic background. If we are going to discard this we had better quit writing at all.[8]

For O'Connor, what is central is not meaning, but mystery.

I

Frye's visual metaphor for biblical typology is a double mirror: "the two testaments form a double mirror each reflecting the other but neither the world outside."[9] His model is useful, first because it insists on the reflective back and forth movement of type and antitype, and second, because it differentiates between typology and allegory. As I will show, historically-based typology works as a pattern of identification and metonymic equivalents, while in allegory one narrative normally defers temporally to the other, or to a "true," usually moralistic, system extrinsic to the Bible. Jean Daniélou declares: "Allegory is not a sense of scripture at all; it is the presentation of philosophy and Christian morality under biblical images."[10] To follow Auerbach, "figurative interpretation establishes a relationship between two happenings, *both of which are historical* . . . . In the classical examples, the second is always the incarnation of Christ and the happenings connected with it . . . and the whole is a synthetic interpretation of pre-Christian world history in view of the incarnation of Christ" (italics added).[11] A figural schema "permits both its poles – the figure and the fulfillment – to retain the characteristics of concrete historical reality . . . . An event taken as a figure preserves its literal and historical meaning."[12] Or as Beryl Smalley explains:

> Origen inherited the Christian teaching that the Old Testament prefigures or foreshadows the New: *omnia in figura contingebant illis*. This conception of allegory differs from Philo's in that *both the sign and the thing signified are conceived as historical* and would have no signification if they were not. Today it is sometimes distinguished from allegory and called typology.[13] (italics added)

Thus Israel in the wilderness is a type, not an allegory of Christ in the wilderness, just as the Jonah story is a type, not an allegory of the Passion.

According to Frye "every text is the type of its own reading";[14] thus every reading is an antitype of the text. The double mirror of Old and New Testaments, although not reflecting the world outside, will be reflected by other texts/mirrors of which the Bible is a type. Frye's approach to figural exegesis – following Auerbach – takes typology in its strictest sense outside the relationship between the two biblical testaments into the secular world. Typology is fluid and moves through time: "the type exists in the past and the antitype in the present, or the type exists in the present and the antitype in the future."[15] Adapting this model of forward-movingness to Frye's image of the double mirror, we might add to it a series of folding mirrors leading off to the right of the two-part Christian Bible. The various panels would represent texts – biblical exegeses, writings of the Church Fathers, Christian doctrine, *The Divine Comedy*, *Paradise Lost*, all of them readings, thus antitypes of the Bible. Further panels would reflect both the Bible and its textual/exegetic reflections, including modern hermeneutics, and so on. The difficulty with this intertextual model, however, is the placing of pre-biblical or extra-biblical texts, since according to Frye, the double mirror of Old and New Testaments does not reflect the world without. In *The Great Code*, Frye dissolves this problem arbitrarily but usefully by taking "the Bible as a key to mythology, instead of taking mythology in general as a key to the Bible."[16] He can thus classify what might otherwise be taken for pre- or extra-biblical types as parodies or "demonic perversions" of Judaeo-Christian persons and events.

II

"'As far as I'm concerned,'" says O'Connor's Mrs. McIntyre, "'Christ was just another D.P.'" (229).[17] Typologically this is so: the archtype, or ur-type, of Biblical displacement is the Fall. Adam and Eve prefigure Israel, displaced during the Exodus and wandering in the desert for forty years. Between the Fall and the Exodus the Pentateuch contains a number of displacements: Ishmael displaced by Isaac; Isaac displaced by the ram as sacrifice; Esau displaced by Jacob; Moses displaced by Joshua. In Christian thought, the antitype of displacement, and the typological focus towards which all Old Testament figures of displacement move, is the Incarnation. Above I have cited Auerbach's remark that in the "classical" examples of figural interpretation, the fulfillment or antitype "is always the incarnation of Christ and the happenings connected with it." This concept is central to "The Displaced Person": "One of the awful things about writing when you are a Christian," O'Connor explains, "is that for you the ultimate reality is the Incarnation, the present reality is the Incarnation, and nobody believes in the Incarnation; that is, nobody in your audience."[18] Metonymically, all Old Testament figures of displacement point to the Incarnation – the divine displacement – and in turn, those figures are evoked by Mr. Guizac, the Displaced Person of O'Connor's text.[19]

The Incarnation, in O'Connor's words, was "a unique intervention in history.... It is the fact of the Word made flesh."[20] In Paul's letter to the Philippians, the Incarnation is explicated:

> Have this in mind among yourselves, which you have in Christ Jesus, who, though he was in the form of God, did not count equality with God a thing to be grasped, but emptied himself, taking the form of a servant [or slave], being born in the likeness of men. And being found in human form he humbled himself and became obedient unto death, even death on the Cross. (1 Phil. 2:5–8; RSV) [21]

At that moment, according to Paul, the Hebrew Bible becomes "merely a shadow of things to come" – I am quoting Auerbach – for its Messianic vision had been fulfilled: "As a whole it ceased for him [Paul] to be a book of the law and history of Israel and became from beginning to end a promise and prefiguration of Christ."[22] In the Pauline Epistles, Jewish Law is said to be displaced by Faith; thus Augustine could write that a Christian should hold "not the works of the law, by which no man is justified, but to the law of faith, by which the just man lives."[23] Milton's well-known text reads, "From shadowy types to truth, from flesh to spirit,/From imposition of strict laws, to free / Acceptance of large grace ... " (*Paradise Lost* XII, 303 ff.). For many Christian exegetes, the Letter of the "Old Testament" or the "Old Covenant," both typological terms, was displaced by the New Testament or Spirit, the Incarnation of the Word becoming the central referent and focus of all typological schemata. Robert Fitgerald, placing Mrs. Shortley among O'Connor's visionaries, says: "A page of prophecy in the Old Testament is hardly more eloquent than some of them, and I can think of nothing in literature that teaches better than they do why the Old Testament had to be completed by the New."[24]

Whether or not the reader agrees with Fitzgerald's or with Frye's understanding of the relation between the Hebrew Bible and the Christian Bible does not matter in a study of "The Displaced Person." We are dealing with methodology, not claim.[25] The text assumes the conventions of and anticipates a typological reading; its informing structure is a Christian orthodoxy that for O'Connor would have included the figural method of biblical exegesis with its radical premise that the New Testament fulfils the Old, that the Incarnation is the divine fulfillment of Old Testament prophecies. To Mrs. McIntyre, Mr. Guizac's face "looked as if it might have been patched together out of several others" (222). Extending O'Connor's metaphor, one might say that in figural thinking, the person of Christ is patched together out of all Old Testament types – that is the metonymic paradigm that informs typology as a mode of thought and as a figure of discourse. Furthermore, just as all biblical types move towards and are finally identified with the person of Christ, so the narrative and figurative structures of "The Displaced Person" depend on clusters of recurring typic images, all pointing metonymically to Christ. Or else they point towards the Devil, Christ's insinuating adversary, which is to approach Christ through the labyrinth of indirection as Mrs. Shortley does. What figural thinking assumes – and this is implicit in O'Connor's text – is that "in God there is no distinction of times since for him everything is a simultaneous present, so that – as Augustine once put it – he does not possess foreknowledge but simply knowledge." Like the mystery plays of the Middle Ages, the context of "The Displaced Person" is part of what Auerbach calls "one great drama whose beginning is God's creation of the world, whose climax is Christ's Incarnation and Passion, and whose expected conclusion will be Christ's second coming and the Last Judgment."[26]

III

"The Displaced Person" opens with a "ragged wall of cloud," with a highway ("Mrs. Shortley was watching a black car turn through the gate from the highway"), and with the "red clay road" that links it to the McIntyre farm (194). What Frye calls "the miraculous highway, the path opened through the Red Sea,"[27] is the type of all paths of salvation and redemption including Isaiah's highway: "Prepare ye the way of the Lord, make straight in the desert a highway for our God" (Isa. 40:3). In a complex montage of biblical type and antitype, the crossing of the Red Sea by the children of Israel stands for salvation/redemption by water: "our fathers were under the cloud, and all passed through the sea; And all were baptized unto Moses in the cloud and in the sea" (1 Cor. 10:1–2). Its type is Noah's flood, one of the many Old Testament events with a double meaning: Daniélou observes that "the divine action in the

Flood is at once a condemnation and a forgiveness, and we shall find this so in all events which are the antitypes of the Flood."[28] The New Testament antitype of every figure of redemption by water is traditionally taken to be Christ's baptism and thus the sacrament of baptism in general. Included in St. Ambrose's series of baptismal types, Daniélou tells us, is the Spirit born over the waters of Genesis 1:2, the Flood, and the crossing of the Red Sea.

Having come "from over the water" (199), like Noah's family and like the children of Israel, the Guizacs arrive at the McIntyre farm in a black car. Some weeks later, "as it began to drizzle rain," and "Just before dawn" (this sets up a nice parallel with the Guizacs' forced exodus from their house in Poland: " . . . in Poland they lived in a brick house and one night a man come and told them to get out of it before daylight" [207]), the Shortleys' "square black automobile" leaves the farm loaded down with two iron beds, two rocking chairs, two mattresses, Mr. and Mrs. Shortley, "two long bony yellow-haired girls," a cat with two kittens, a crate of chickens (213–214). What O'Connor calls their "loaded car" is theologically loaded: "The car moved slowly like some overfreighted leaking ark" (as did Mrs. Shortley herself who "had an immense weight to carry around," and who "would go about like a large hull of herself" [210]). Their unreliable vessel, like Bosch's Ship of Fools, is a demonic inversion of Noah's ark of salvation, whose New Testament antitype is the Church. St. John Chrysostom writes: "The story of the flood is a mystery and the details are types of the future. The ark is the Church, Noah is Christ; the dove the Holy Spirit."[29] For Augustine too, Noah's ark was *praefiguratio ecclesiae,* and Christian iconography often depicts Noah, his family, and the animals in a floating structure that is part ark, part church.

The Shortleys' "square" automobile/ark makes "more than its customary grinding noises as if it were protesting the load" (212). O'Connor's adjectives for that ark, "square" and "overfreighted" (it was "rectangular" in the first version of the story),[30] recall freight trains of World War II, their boxcars jammed full with Displaced Persons and their boxes and bundles. In Mrs. McIntyre's dream, the Priest says to her, and to the reader: "'Think of the thousands of them, think of the ovens and the boxcars and the camps and the sick children and Christ our Lord'" (231). Brilliantly O'Connor's language evokes at least four historical events: Noah's flood, the Exodus from Egypt, the Massacre of the Innocents, the Holocaust.[31] Nazi ovens stand metonymically for all demonic machinery: for the

Shortleys' so-called "ark," and for the Egyptian "furnace of iron" (1 Kings 8:51), itself a type of Nebuchadnezzar's "burning fiery furnace" (Dan. 3:21).[32] Mrs. Shortley sits in all these ovens at once, her knee "pushed into her stomach," her leg "twisted under her" (as the Grandmother's is in "A Good Man is Hard to Find"): "Fierce heat seemed to be swelling slowly and fully into her face as if it were welling up now for a final assault." Suddenly, gratuitously, the fire of destruction becomes the refining fire of the Holy Spirit. Just as the Israelites were brought "forth out of Egypt, from the midst of the furnace of iron," and just as the three Jews, Shadrach, Meshach and Abed-nego, remained whole while in the "midst of the burning fiery furnace," Mrs. Shortley is saved, the dove of the Holy Spirit represented absurdly by the "crate of chickens" on top of the automobile. In Christian iconography the dove is often shown perched on top of Noah's ark. Karl Barth observes in a passage marked by O'Connor that a "quite specific astonishment stands at the beginning of every theological perception . . . ."[33] At Mrs. Shortley's moment of revelation, "her fierce expression faded into a look of astonishment and her grip on what she had loosened. One of her eyes drew near to the other and seemed to collapse quietly and she was still" (213–14).

> The two girls, who didn't know what had happened to her, began to say, "Where we goin, Ma? Where we goin?" They thought she was playing a joke and that their father, staring straight ahead at her, was imitating a dead man. They didn't know that she had had a great experience or *ever been displaced in the world from all that belonged to her.* They were frightened by the gray slick road before them and they kept repeating in higher and higher voices, "Where we goin, Ma? Where we goin?" while their mother, her huge body rolled back against the seat and her eyes like blue-painted glass, seemed to contemplate for the first time the tremendous frontiers of her true country. (italics added)

The Fall from Eden is the type of displacement; its New Testament antitype is the Incarnation. Inversely the demonic counterpart of the Incarnation would be Satan's fall from heaven: "I beheld Satan as lightning falling from heaven" (Luke 10:18). Frye tells us that "each apocalyptic or idealized image in the Bible has a demonic counterpart . . . there are two varieties of demonic imagery: the parody demonic associated with the temporary prosperity of heathen kingdoms, and the manifest demonic, the wasteland of drought that lies in wait for them."[34] In "The Displaced Person," O'Connor sets up an opposition between two countries: the heathen kingdom of Tyre (and thus of Mrs. McIn*tyre*), whose destruction is prophecied by Ezekiel; and the "true country," represented by the Priest, the Peacock, and the Displaced Persons. The best known of wicked kingdoms are Sodom and Gomorrah. By placing Mrs. Shortley "next to the block of salt" (205), then, O'Connor evokes Lot's wife who became a "pillar of salt" while looking back to Sodom (Gen. 19:26). This detail fuses with other images of petrification related to Mrs. Shortley, and with ruined biblical cities also – her imagined "war of words" (209) recalls the Tower of Babel. That Mrs. Shortley is shown with the "block of salt" should warn the reader that her point of view is backward in many senses, that her so-called "vision" of the "gigantic figure" with "fiery wheels" is an egocentric and perverse misreading of Ezekiel's great epiphany, itself a figure/type of the four Evangelists (1:10; cf. 10:12–14), and thus of the Gospels and of Salvation.[35] To Mrs. Shortley, who "was not able to tell if the figure was going forward or backward," and who anyway views it with her eyes "shut tight," it prophesies destruction (210). In brief, her religion is parodic-demonic: she considers "the devil the head of it and God the hanger-on" (with a pun on "hanger-on" that evokes the Crucifixion from her demonic point of view [203–204]).

In Mrs. Shortley's view, Europeans "never have advanced or reformed. They got the same religion as a thousand years ago" (206). Unless we identify this "giant wife of the countryside" (194), or "Big Belly" (206), as an antitype of the Great Mother and her pre-biblical fertility cults (and thus as a type of the Gentiles), Mrs. Shortley's observations are wrong-headed only. What is notable here – and this is O'Connor's joke – is that "the giant wife" is literally married to "the countryside," and that *she* "got the same religion" as at least three thousand years ago. And that is why, in the first section of the story at least, her subordinate husband/consort/lover, Mr. Shortley, like Adonis and Tammuz and Attis and Osiris, is a dying vegetation god ("If everybody was as dead as I am, nobody would have no trouble"), who is identified grotesquely with corpses and paralysis: "Mr. Shortley folded his hands on his bony chest and pretended he was a corpse" (206). Without these typic and mythic underpinnings, O'Connor's characterization of Mr. Shortley lacks context. Considered as a vegetation deity, however, Mr. Shortley, "a paralysed man propped up to enjoy a cigarette" (200), evokes the derisive but common appelations "vegetable" or "human vegetable," terms not infrequently used for people hooked up to life-support systems. True to the typological method, O'Connor's mythic imagination is appropriately concrete. Examples of death-in-life imagery accumulate meaning throughout the text, so that when she finally writes, "Mr. Shortley had risen straight up in bed like Lazarus from the tomb" (208), she recalls both the resurrected vegetation gods of pre-biblical cults and Lazarus, who is a type of the Resurrection. Moreover the reader learns that Mr. Shortley's feat of drawing the cigarette stub into his mouth, pretending to swallow it, then spitting "the smoldering butt into the grass," was "actually his way of making love" to Mrs. Shortley: "It nearly drove her wild and every time he did it, she wanted to pull his hat down over his eyes and hug him to death" (200–201). Their love/death ritual hints at any number of displaced fertility rites. Presumably what Mr. Shortley spits into the grass represents semen, even the phallus of a dismembered god. And that might explain why Mrs. Shortley, in an act of sympathetic magic, "dug a little hole for it with her toe and covered it up."

IV

"After Mrs. Shortley's death," as Robert Fitzgerald notes, "her role as the giant wife of the countryside devolves upon Mrs. McIntyre."[36] Clearly Mrs. Shortley and Mrs. McIntyre are related ("anyone would have thought they were kin" [227]). And typologically they are related to the Great Whore of Babylon, mistress of the Antichrist/Tempter, whose role Mr. Shortley takes on in the third section of the story. According to Mrs. Shortley, the Priest intends "to plant the Whore of Babylon in the midst of the righteous!" (209); unless we know she is there already, we miss O'Connor's point (and we miss also the sexual undercurrent of Mrs. McIntyre's relation with Mr. Shortley). In place of the cup full of the blood of saints and martyrs held by the Great Whore (Rev. 17), Mrs. McIntyre, in order to "endure" the Priest's talk about Purgatory, "put at least a finger of whiskey in her own ginger ale" (225). With her "red bangs that came almost down to two high orange-colored penciled eyebrows," and her "little doll's mouth" (197), Mrs. McIntyre, like the Great Whore, is interchangeable with a wicked city – Tyre – and is linked typologically to the forgiven harlots of the Old and New Testaments, especially to Rahab, a Gentile type of Mary Magdalene. Married three times, the first time for money, and divorced twice ("Mr. Crooms, her second, was forty miles away in the state asylum and Mr. McIntyre, her last, was intoxicated, she supposed, in some hotel room in Florida" [218]), at the end of "The Displaced Person" Mrs. McIntyre is being instructed in the doctrines of the Church by the old Priest.

At the beginning of this study I quoted O'Connor's remark, "The displaced person did accomplish a kind of redemption in that he destroyed the place, which was evil, and set Mrs. McIntyre on the road to a new kind of suffering." According to Daniélou, the episode of Rahab, together with the Flood and the Passover – both events are evoked in "The Displaced Person" – "forms one of the three great mysteries which enshrine the biblical theology of the Redemption."[37] In his analysis of the typology of Rahab, Daniélou describes her as "a type of sinful humanity, and particularly of the Gentiles, shut out of the covenant and saved by the mercy of Christ, since Rahab does not belong to Israel."[38] Most significant in Mrs. McIntyre's relation to Rahab is Rahab's hospitality to Joshua's spies and its ironic reverberations in O'Connor's text: the Letter to the Hebrews reads, "By faith Rahab the harlot did not perish . . . because she had given friendly welcome to the spies" (11:31; RSV). At the beginning of "The Displaced Person" we read: "Mrs. McIntyre was coming down the steps of her house to meet the car. She had on her largest smile . . . . here was the owner of the place out to welcome them" (194). As far as Mrs. Shortley is concerned, the Guizacs are spies: "The Negroes knew about his [Mr. Shortley's] still . . . . But with foreigners on the place, with people who were all eyes and no understanding . . . with this kind of people, you had to be on the lookout every minute." To Mr. Shortley, she says, "'That man [Mr. Guizac] prowls . . . Who's to say if he found it he wouldn't go right to her and tell? . . . I wouldn't be a tall [sic] surprised if he don't know everything you say, whether it be in English or not'" (204–205). Mrs. Shortley's rhetoric moves into the second part of the text: "Mrs. McIntyre remembered Mrs. Shortley's words: 'He understands everything, he only pretends he don't . . . '" (223).

Rahab's figural attribute is the scarlet thread or cord. St. Justin writes: "For the sign of the scarlet thread, which the spies sent to Jericho by Joshua, son of Nave, gave to Rahab the harlot, telling her to bind it to the window through which she let them down to escape from their enemies, also manifested the symbol of the blood of Christ, by which those who were at one time harlots and evil persons out of all nations are saved, receiving remission of sins, and continuing to sin no longer."[39] Although Mrs. McIntyre is sliding straight towards the depths of hell – see, for example, the "deep vertical pit" in her face that gets even deeper when she discovers the photograph of the Displaced Person's cousin (217, 222) – her "red head-kerchief" or protective covering may stand for Rahab's scarlet cord, thus for the saving blood of Christ and its type, the blood of the Passover (Exod. 12:13). On the day of the murder, Mrs. McIntyre "had on a heavy black coat and a red head-kerchief with her black hat pulled down on top of it to keep the glare out of her eyes" (234). In the stark, Breugelesque landscape of Mr. Guizac's passion, the red textile is echoed by one textual detail only, the "bloody pants legs" of the Priest (235). They in turn echo a telling detail included at the beginning of the short version of "The Displaced Person," published in *The Sewanee Review*: Mrs. Shortley "had on a pair of red rubber boots spattered with clay."[40] I think that the red head-kerchief and the red boots stand for the blood of the Lamb, and thus for the sign of the Passover and of the women's salvation. Neither Mrs. Shortley nor Mrs. McIntyre "deserves" to be saved; and surely this is O'Connor's point: Redemption is purely gratuitous; we are saved by Grace.

Mrs. McIntyre's first husband the Judge, a "dirty snuff-dipping Court House figure" (a type of the Law), is a parody of Solomon (a type of Christ), who not only had peacocks (1 Kings 10:22) but was rich and wise. Witness his visitor the Queen of Sheba: "behold, the half was not told me: thy wisdom and prosperity exceedeth the fame which I heard" (1 Kings 10:7). O'Connor's "snuff-dipping" Judge was also "famous all over the country for being rich"; except "he didn't have a nickel" (218). And his wisdom, cited in a "reverent way" by Mrs. McIntyre, includes the following: "One fellow's misery is another fellow's gain"; "You can always tell a nigger what to do and stand by until he does it"; "The devil you know is better than the devil you don't." Moreover, just as the "porch" on which Mrs. McIntyre and the priest converse is a demonic parody of Solomon's "porch of judgment" (1 Kings 7:7), so the Judge's office is a perversion of Solomon's temple, and that is where Mrs. McIntyre goes to seek comfort:

When she had cried all she could, she got up and went into the back hall, a closet-like space that was dark and quiet as a chapel and sat down on the edge of the Judge's black mechanical chair with her elbow on his desk. This was a giant roll-top piece of furniture pocked with pigeon holes full of dusty papers. Old bankbooks and ledgers were stacked in the half-open drawers and there was a small safe, empty but locked, set like a tabernacle in the center of it. She had left this part of the house unchanged since the old man's time. It was a kind of memorial to him, sacred because he had conducted his business here. (221)

Again O'Connor's language is theologically loaded. Solomon's remarkable temple (built with logs supplied by the King of Tyre) prefigures not only the Temple at Jerusalem, but also Christ, "who spake of the temple of his body" (John 2:19–21). To work backwards historically from the doubled "temple" of the New Testament, through Old Testament types and antitypes, is to arrive at "tabernacle," the word used for the portable tent of worship carried in the wilderness: "And Moses took the tabernacle, and pitched it without the camp . . . and called it the Tabernacle of the congregation" (Exod. 33:7). The Judge's safe, "set like a tabernacle in the center" of the desk, makes dark reference to the Holy of Holies, the *temenos* or sacred space representing God's invisible presence. That it was entered once a year by the High Priest, parodied here by Mrs. McIntyre, makes the scene especially jarring; moreover in Solomon's temple the ark of the covenant is covered and protected by cherubs' wings (2 Chron. 6: 8), and Mrs. McIntyre (who has "her elbow on his desk"), with her "aging cherubic face" (224), is metonymically the "naked granite cherub" bought by her first husband the Judge "partly because its face reminded him of his wife and partly because he wanted a genuine work of art over his grave" (221). Instead of protecting the ark of the covenant, Mrs. McIntyre is protecting a "safe" that is "empty but locked"; and the Judge's desk contains bankbooks and ledgers, all testifying to bankruptcy. Had the "safe" simply been locked to Christianity, it might have contained the Old Testament but not the New. That it is both locked and empty, however, suggests again that Mrs. McIntyre, like Rahab and like the Queen of Sheba, is Gentile, that she is prostituted to the worship of idols that we know to be the conflated Mammon-imago of the Judge and money. This is a bold typological leap. The Vulgate uses the word *arca* for both Noah's ark and the ark of the covenant, although the Hebrew words are not the same: based on this semantic coincidence, O'Connor makes the Judge's so-called "safe"/"chapel"/"tabernacle" a parody of Noah's ark, of the Church, and of Salvation. The sinister "black mechanical chair" in which the cherubic Mrs. McIntyre sits represents all demonic machinery. With her description of the "pigeon holes full of dusty papers," O'Connor evokes the absent presence of Noah's dove and of its antitype, the Holy Spirit. A letter of 1956 directs us to O'Connor's arcana: "It may be a matter of recognizing the Holy Ghost in fiction by the way He chooses to conceal himself."[41]

V

Most interpreters try to explain the Displaced Person's Christ-like nature allegorically, because they do not recognize his typological derivation. At the Incarnation (the divine displacement) Christ took "the form of a servant." That Mr. Guizak, the Displaced Person, arrives at the McIntyre farm in the role of a suffering servant establishes an obvious parallel with Christ's human nature, and because of this, Mr. Guizac's story is often read as an *imitatio Christi*. Which in part it is, just as all persecution and suffering is an *imitatio Christi*. Astor, the old Negro on the McIntyre farm, is a suffering servant also: "Bars of sunlight fell from the cracked ceiling across his back and cut him in three distinct parts" (214). Typologically the stripes on Astor's back evoke the suffering servant passage in Isaiah, a type of the Crucifixion: "But he was wounded for our transgressions, he was bruised for our iniquities . . . and with his stripes we are healed" (53:5; cf. 1 Pet. 2:24). Both Mr. Guizac and Astor, who is noticeably absent at the murder, are antitypes of the suffering servant of Isaiah ("'Black and white,' he said, 'is the same'" [215]). But the two men are not and cannot be "Christ figures," however unhistorically and loosely that term is used in O'Connor criticism. Even when the typological method of Biblical exegesis is applied to secular texts, and especially to O'Connor's, the only possible antitype of Christ is the Second Coming, adumbrated in "The Displaced Person" by the Peacock. This O'Connor knew: at Mr. Guizac's murder, Mrs. McIntyre "had heard the litle noise the Pole made as the tractor wheel broke his backbone" (234). The fourth Gospel, stressing the typology of the Crucifixion, tells us specifically that the soldiers did not break Christ's legs so "that the

Scripture should be fulfilled, A bone of him shall not be broken" (19: 33–36; cf. Psalm 34:20, "He keepeth all his bones: not one of them is broken").[42]

At the same time, Mr. Guizac is clearly a redemptive figure: as the Priest explains to Mrs. McIntyre, conflating Christ (who came in the guise of a servant) and the Displaced Person, "He came to redeem us" (226). What no one has remarked is the fact that the name "izac" or Isaac is hidden/disguised within Mr. G*uizac*'s name. As *Saul* is to St. *Paul*, Izak is to Guizak: in both cases the Christian antitype includes and fulfils its figural counterpart. (That names and their anagogic meaning are crucial to typological thinking is apparent in the elaborate typological exegesis surrounding the names Joshua/Jesus.) O'Connor's strategies of naming, and of concealment, parallel typology as a model of thought: the Old Testament conceals the New, the New Testament reveals the Old. The name "Guizac" alone should indicate a figurative pattern hidden and disguised within "The Displaced Person."[43] As whole for the part (his face "looked as if it might have been patched together out of several others"), Guizac is an antitype of Isaac, an Old Testament type of Christ.[44]

I have called Mrs. McIntyre an antitype of Rahab, thus of the Gentiles, and have identified the Shortleys with pre-biblical cults. As an antitype of Isaac, Mr. Guizac presumably stands for both the Children of Israel and for the early Christians; in short, for the seed of Abraham. (That may explain why the first time we glimpse Mrs. Guizac – the second is at the lamentation – she is "a woman in brown, shaped like a peanut" [195]: nuts of course are both seed and fruit.) The following is Daniélou's brief review of the story of Isaac in relation to the life of Christ:

> The miraculous birth of Isaac was the consequence of Yahweh's promise (21:2). Laughter and rejoicing are signified by his name (21:6) . . . . He carries the wood of sacrifice (22:6). But equally with the parallelism [with Christ], the narrative brings out the differences, the essential differences between type and reality: Isaac was born miraculously, but not of a virgin, simply of a barren woman; the sacrifice is *staged* but not *accomplished*.[45] (italics added)

In early Christian literature, Isaac carrying the wood for his sacrifice is considered a type of Christ carrying the Cross; however the sacrifice of Isaac is considered an *unfulfilled* type of the Passion. Chrysostom writes: "And now they laid the cross upon him as a malefactor. For even the wood they abominated and endured not even to touch it. This was also the case in the type; for Isaac bore the wood. But then the matter [God's purpose] stopped, at the will of his father, for it was the type; while here it proceeded to action, for it was the reality."[46] For many exegetes the actual type of the Crucifixion is the animal that displaced Isaac – the ram "caught in a thicket by his horns" (Gen. 22:13), an image taken by Tertullian and by Augustine as a type of Christ's crown of thorns. In other words, Isaac and the ram are *a double type of the double-natured Christ*. One of the doctrines that underpin "The Displaced Person" and inform its typological pattern is the double nature of Christ: as lamb and as spiritual lamb (St. John Chrysostom); as the only son and the lamb at his side (St. Gregory of Nyssa); as Word and as flesh; as human and divine. As cited by Daniélou, Theodoret writes: "The Father offered his well-beloved Son for the world: Isaac typified the divinity, the ram the humanity."[47] In O'Connor's words: "The Church has always been mindful of the relation between spirit and flesh; this has shown up in her definitions of the double nature of Christ . . . ."[48]

If Mr. Guizac is Isaac's figural counterpart – and O'Connor's naming, once deciphered, couldn't be more overt – and further, if he is the human rather than the divine side of the figural equation as I suggest, then the ram that in the Old Testament displaces Isaac and stands typologically for Christ's humanity should be caught/concealed somewhere in the density of O'Connor's text. Throughout the story, Mr. Guizac is associated with water, with cleanliness ("he was scrupulously clean" [201]), and with "the wet spotless concrete floor" (231, 219; cf. "immaculate"), phrases that suggest he is without blemish, and thus an acceptable sacrificial figure. (Shortly before the murder, Mrs. McIntyre observes that the Guizacs "were getting fat" [230]). And indeed, Isaac's ram (which in the Pentateuch modulates to the Paschal lamb and the sacrificial "ram without blemish") surfaces in "The Displaced Person" as soon as Mrs. McIntyre discovers the photograph of Mr. Guizac's cousin: "Monster! she said to herself and looked at him as if she were seeing him for the first time. His forehead and skull were white . . . but the rest of his face was red and bristled with short yellow hairs" (222). The word "bristled" is crucial. On the morning of Mr. Guizac's murder, "There was a heavy frost on the ground that made the fields look like the rough backs of sheep; the sun was almost silver and the woods stuck up like dry bristles on the sky line" (233; italics added). The fields Mrs. McIntyre envisions earlier as "stubble" (224) have modulated to fields "like rough backs of sheep." The yellow hairs that "bristled" on Mr. Guizac's "patched face" (223), an image that anyhow recalls fields, have become "woods like dry bristles," or thickets. Lying on his back "on the icy ground," his legs "flat on the ground" (234), the Displaced Person is landscape, altar, farm, woods, and sacrificial ram in one. When the large tractor, fired with the accumulated "heat and strength" of all demonic machinery, crushes him, breaking his backbone, it simultaneously destroys the McIntyre place itself, an antitype of the cities of the plain and of all wicked cities with their false gods. In fulfillment of Ezekiel's prophecies, Tyre is fallen, is fallen:

> And they shall destroy the walls of Tyrus, and break down her towers . . . .
>
> And they shall make a spoil of thy riches, and make a prey of thy merchandise . . . .
>
> For thus saith the Lord God; when I shall make thee a desolate city, like the cities that are not inhabited . . . .
> (Ezekiel 26: 4,12,19)

VI

"What typology really is as a mode of thought," Northrop Frye has observed, "what it both assumes and leads to, is a theory of history, or more accurately of historical process: an assumption that there is some meaning and point to history, and that sooner or later some event or events will occur which will indicate what that meaning or point is . . . . "[49]

7

His Dazzling Absence: The Shekinah in Jonathan Edwards

If we find Jonathan Edwards hard to read, it may be because we have forgotten what he's talking about. I do not mean the Bible and Puritan theology, but the wider context of what was then within the horizon of Christian thinking. What, for example, do we make of Edwards's reference to "the Shechinah" in this passage from *A History of the Work of Redemption* (1739; pub. 1774)?

> Again, by this [the Babylonian] captivity, the glory and magnificence of the temple were taken away, and the temple that was built afterwards was nothing in comparison with it. Thus it was meet, that when the time drew nigh that the glorious antetype of the temple should appear, that the typical temple should have its glory withdrawn.
>
> Moreover they [the Jews] lost by the captivity the two tables of the testimony delivered to Moses, on which God with his own fingers wrote the ten commandments on Mount Sinai. . . .
>
> *Another thing that the ancient Jews say was wanting in the second temple, was the Shechinah, or cloud of glory over the mercy seat.* This was promised to be in the tabernacle: Lev. xvi.2. "For I will appear in the cloud upon the mercy seat." And we read elsewhere of the cloud of glory descending into the tabernacle, Exod. xl.35. and so do we likewise with respect to Solomon's temple. But we have no account that this cloud of glory was in the second temple. And *the ancient accounts of the Jews* say, that there was no such thing in the second temple. This was needless in the second temple, considering that God had promised he would fill this temple with glory another way, *viz.* by Christ's coming into

it; which was afterwards fulfilled. See Haggai ii.7. "I will shake all nations, and the desire of all nations shall come, and I will fill this house with glory, saith the Lord of Hosts." (563; 252–54; italics added)[1]

Nothing in the Bible will help us with the reference to the Shekinah. For Edwards's source, however mediated, is the Rabbinic tradition ("the ancient accounts of the Jews") that five things were absent from the second Temple. These include the Ark, the Mercy Seat, and the Cherubim; the fire from heaven upon the altar; and the visible Presence, or Shekinah.[2] Edwards identifies the Shekinah with the cloud of glory that filled the Tabernacle and Solomon's Temple, interpreting it as a figure or type of Christ.[3]

The root of the post-biblical noun *Shekinah* is the Hebrew verb *shakan* – to tabernacle or to dwell. To follow the *Oxford English Dictionary* (*OED*), *Shekinah* means: "The visible manifestation of the Divine Majesty, esp. when resting between the cherubim over the mercy-seat or in the temple of Solomon; a glory or refulgent light symbolising the Divine Presence." "In the Targums the word is used as a periphrasis to designate God when He is said to dwell among the cherubim, etc., so as to avoid any approach to anthropomorphic expression." The first noted example of English usage is J. Stillingfleet's *Shecinah: or a Demonstration of the Divine Presence in the Places of Religious Worship*, published in 1663. Another example is taken from J. Scott's *Christian Life* (1681–86): "That fiery Schechinah, or visible Glory of the Lord, in which he descended on Mount Sinai." A further citation is a title of 1682: *The Moral Schechinah: or a Discourse on God's Glory*. Isaac Watts takes up *Shekinah* in 1741: "The Schecina, or bright glory, which is a symbol of God's presence." Likewise George Eliot in *Scenes of Clerical Life* (1856): "The golden sunlight beamed through the dripping boughs like a Shechinah, or visible divine presence." In Melville's *Mardi* (1849), the Shekinah is evoked in Babbalanja's vision: "'I, tranced, beheld an awful glory. Sphere in sphere it burned: – the one Shekinah!'"[4] For Disraeli, writing in 1834: "Truth indeed is veiled,/But with a Schekinah of dazzling light."

Jonathan Edwards's understanding of *Shekinah* includes a Christian gloss. From the late seventeenth century (we are told in the *OED*), the term *Shekinah* is applied specifically to Jesus Christ. A sermon of 1684 (on 1 Cor. 1:30) is cited: "The Schechinah, the habitation of the Majesty, is Jesus Christ; there he dwells as between the cherubim over the mercy-seat." Perhaps the best-known instance of the Shekinah-Christ typology, and of the christological reading of the Shekinah idea, is found in Charles Wesley's "Hymn on the Titles of Christ" (1739): "Our Eyes on Earth survey / The Dazzling *Shechinah*! / Bright, in endless Glory bright, / Now in Flesh He stoops to dwell."[5]

What precedes these *OED* citations, and no doubt occasions them, is the publication in 1657 of Brian Walton's Polyglot Bible (*Biblia Sacra Polyglotta*), wherein the Aramaic or Chaldean Targum is printed in parallel with a Latin translation.[6] The word *Shekinah* first appears in the Targum Onqelos, written down between the first and the fourth century A.D. As explicated by John Bowker, the word *targum* "means in general 'translation' or 'interpretation,' but in particular it is most often used to refer to the Aramaic version of the Hebrew Bible."[7]

> The Targums are interpretive translations of the Hebrew text of the Bible. Their interest and fascination lies in the crucial fact that they are not simple or literal translations of the text: they work into their translation an interpretation of what the text means. The reason for this is simple: in origin the Targums were closely connected with the synagogue. From its earliest days (before the fall of Jerusalem in A.D. 70) the synagogue existed primarily for the reading and exposition of scripture, but since many of those present had little or no knowledge of Hebrew, the public reading or reciting of the Hebrew text had to be accompanied by a translation, or *targum*, of it into the vernacular. The written Aramaic Targums are derived from those acompanying translations (*targums*) which were intended to explain the Hebrew text. It is because the purpose of the *targum* was to convey the meaning of the text to the assembled congregation that the *targums* could be so free in their interpretation. They provided a kind of "running commentary" on the text. There was no fear that the sacred text was being altered, or mishandled, because the text had already been read out, The purpose of the *targum* was to expound its meaning.[8]

Wherever the word *Shekinah* is found in the Targums, "it is always in the sense of God's dwelling-house, the abiding of God in a certain spot."[9] The Old Testament speaks of God's dwelling with men. The Targumists, however, use the terms "Shekinah" and "God's

Shekinah" to avoid speaking directly of the Divine Presence. Thus when the Hebrew text states explicitly that God dwells somewhere (on Mount Sinai, in the Tabernacle, in the burning bush, and so on), the Targum substitutes, "cause my Shekinah (or the glory of the Shekinah) to dwell" or "to rest." For example, on Exodus 25:8 ("And let them make me a sanctuary; that I may dwell [*shakan*] among them"), Targum Onqelos reads: "And they shall make a sanctuary before me, and I will cause my Shekinah to dwell among them."[10] Targum Pseudo-Jonathan includes here the divine name: "And let them make for my name the sanctuary, so that I may cause my Shekinah to dwell in their midst." Targum Neofiti goes further: "And they shall build for my name the house of the sanctuary, and I shall cause the glory of my Shekinah to dwell in their midst." When at Bethel Jacob awakens out of his sleep to declare, "Surely the Lord is in this place" (Gen 28:16), the Targum gives: "The glory of the Shekinah of YHWH is in this place." Similarly, the Targum on Haggai 1:8 ("build the house . . . that I may appear in my glory" [RSV]) reads: "build the house . . . that I may cause my Shekinah to dwell in it."

"From meaning the abode of God, the Shekinah gradually came to mean God Himself . . . . Shekinah became coined as a new word signifying the Godhead quite apart from any notion of place": J. Abelson's *The Immanence of God in Rabbinical Literature* (1912) is cited.[11] In the Targums, one does not see God face to face. One may, however, see the glory of his Shekinah – the brilliance or radiance of the Divine Presence. Thus on Isaiah 6:5 ("my eyes have seen the King, the Lord of hosts"), the Targum reads: "My eyes have seen the glory of the Shekinah of the King of this world." In brief, the Targumists interpret the divine glory as "the effulgence of the substantial glory, i.e., of the Shekinah. The Shekinah is used in the Targums as the equivalent for the Divine Being, not for His glory" (Hastings's *Dictionary of the Bible*).

It should be noted that *Shekinah* does not signify a mediator between God and man, nor a separate being or entity, nor an angel, but God himself, "viewed in spatio-temporal terms as a presence."[12] That for the Targumists the Shekinah was not an intermediary is shown most explicitly in their commentary on Exodus 33.16 ("And the tables were the work of God, and the writing was the writing of God, graven upon the tables"), where the term *Shekinah* is used for the Deity.[13] Or to adopt Robert Hayward's explication of *Memra*, a particular way of describing God's active presence in creation and history that in many ways approximates *Shekinah*, it is "not a hypostasis, a being in any way separate from God, or an intermediary between the God of Israel and the creation."[14] Indeed, it would be "difficult" to find in the Targums any passage "in which activity or personality is assigned to the Shekinah."[15]

*   *   *

The Shekinah-Christ typology suggested by Edwards in *A History of the Work of Redemption* depends partly on a remarkable sort of typology based on consonance – that is to say, on the coincidence of sound between the Greek noun *skene* (tent) and the Hebrew verb *shakan*, meaning "to tabernacle" or "to dwell." "And let them make me a sanctuary; that I may dwell [*shakan*] among them" (Exod. 25:8). Likewise, Exodus 29:45: "And I will dwell [*shakan*] among the children of Israel, and will be their God." (Here Onqelos targumises: "and I will cause my Shekinah to dwell in the midst of the sons of Israel.") Compare 1 Kings 6:13: "And I will dwell [*shakan*] among the children of Israel." Similarly Isaiah 57:15:

> For thus saith the high and lofty One that inhabiteth eternity, whose name is Holy; "I dwell [*shakan*] in the high and holy place, with him also that is of a contrite and humble spirit . . . .

In its sense of a sacred dwelling place or tabernacle, the noun *mishkan*, cognate with *shakan*, appears throughout the Hebrew Bible. Psalm 84:1 is typical: "How amiable are thy tabernacles [*mishkan*], O Lord of hosts!" (AV), a verse given thus in the RSV: "How lovely is thy dwelling place [*mishkan*] O Lord of hosts!" As well, God's glory is said to dwell in a *mishkan*: "O Lord I love the habitation of thy house, and the place [*mishkan*] where thy glory [*kavod*] dwells" (Ps. 26:8; RSV).

From the Hebrew words *mishkan* and *shakan*, we turn to the Greek noun *skene*, a word that originally signified a tent. Nevertheless, in the Septuagint (the Greek version of the Hebrew Bible, made by Jews for Jews), *skene* and its word group are normally used to translate the Hebrew *mishkan*. As given in the Septuagint (LXX), Psalm 26:8, cited above, reads: "and the place [*topon*] of the tabernacle [*skenomatos*] of thy glory [*doxes*]." In addition, the "dwelling place" (or "tabernacles") of Psalm 84:1 is rendered *skenomata*, just as the "dwelling places of Jacob" (Ps. 87:2, RSV) become *ta skenomata Iakob*.

The verb form of *skene* (*skeno*) appears in such forms as these in the LXX: "who shall dwell [*kataskenosei*] in thy holy hill?" (Ps. 15:1). In Proverbs Wisdom (*sophia*) is said to "dwell" (*kateskenosa*) with Prudence (8:12).

The practice of translating *mishkan* or "tabernacle" by the Greek *skene* moves from the LXX, through Jewish inter-testamental writings (the so-called Apocrypha), into the New Testament. "And he opened his mouth . . . to blaspheme his name and his tabernacle [*skenen*], and them that dwell [*skenountas*] in heaven" (Rev. 13:6); "I looked, and, behold, the temple of the tabernacle [*skenes*] of the testimony in heaven was opened (Rev. 15:5); "Behold the tabernacle [*skene*] of God is with men, and he will dwell [*skenosei*] with them" (21:3). In this context, the proem to St. John's Gospel is most apposite: "And the Word [*logos*] was made flesh, and dwelt [*eskenosen*] among us" (1:14). In short, a remarkable transition of meaning has taken place, whereby, in the LXX and the New Testament, the Greek noun *skene* and its word group have taken over the connotations of the Hebrew *mishkan* and *shakan*, with their radical sense of "to tabernacle" or "to dwell."[16]

To follow Kittel's *Theological Dictionary of the New Testament*: "If the rendering of *mishkan* by *skene* impressed itself on the translators [of the LXX] as the natural one, this was not because *skene* had of itself the sense of 'dwelling' . . . . Rather it seemed . . . that *skene* was the predestined word for *mishkan* because the two terms contain the same three consonants skn in the same sequence." At the same time, the Hebrew verb *shakan* resonates with the history of God's abiding Presence as recorded in the Hebrew Scriptures and in post-biblical Jewish writings; and "the idea of God's abiding presence was especially connected with the concept of the shekinah in later Judaism."[17]

It is probable that the tents or booths or tabernacles in the transfiguration story may themselves be "an expression of God's gracious and abiding presence": "Master [*rabbi*] . . . let us make three tabernacles [*skenas*]; one for thee, and one for Moses, and one for Elias" (Mark 9:5; cf. Matt. 17:4, Luke 9:33). In Abelson's view, the use of *skene* and its cognates in the New Testament refers to the Rabbinic Shekinah "in some cases but not in all . . . . But the allusion in John 1:14, where the logos is said to 'have dwelt among us' . . . seems a probable reference to Shekinah ideas; and this is borne out when one looks at the usage in that chapter of words like 'light' [and] 'glory,' . . . reminding one of the usage in

Rabbinic literature of *Shekinah, Or* [light], *Kavod* . . . ."[18] According to Hastings's *Dictionary of the Bible*:

> There can be no reasonable doubt that the Greek word *skene* (= "tabernacle") was from its resemblance in sound and meaning used by bilingual Jews for the Heb. *Shekinah*.

*   *   *

In Edwards's *Work of Redemption*, as we have seen above, the biblical "cloud of glory" is conflated with the Shekinah. As proof-text Edwards directs us to Exodus 40:35:

> Then a cloud covered the tent of the congregation, and the glory of the LORD [*kavod* YHWH] filled the tabernacle [*mishkan*]. And Moses was not able to enter into the tent of the congregation, because the cloud abode [*shakan*] thereon, and the glory of the Lord filled [*male*] the tabernacle.

The "glory of the Lord" is not the Shekinah, nor is it God himself; "for it was a matter of fixed Jewish belief that God is invisible . . . the brilliance is an effluence from Deity."[19] We are in the realm of metonymy and of the spatial imagination: if the word *Shekinah* is a concept standing for God's immanence, as somehow imagined apart from his transcendence, the *glory* of the Shekinah is God's Presence conceived as light. What seems especially important in a reading of Edwards is that the Old Testament concept of divine glory or *kavod*, and the post-biblical concept of the Shekinah as divine effulgence, or as "universally diffused Divine Presence,"[20] are inseparable.

This inseparability has, however, been obscured in Greek translation. The connotations of *Shekinah* and of the Hebrew *kavod* are both rendered by the Greek *doxa*: "Since the Shekinah is light, those passages of the Apocrypha and New Testament which mention radiance, and in which the Greek text reads *doxa*, refer to the Shekinah, there being no other Greek equivalent for the word" (*The Jewish Encyclopedia*).[21] The secular or non-biblical meaning of *doxa* is "what one thinks," or "opinion." But according to the *Theological Dictionary of the New Testament*, there is "not a single example in either the NT or the post-apostolic fathers" of *doxa* used in the sense of "opinion." Instead, *doxa* has taken on the meaning of "radiance," "glory," which meaning "is not found in secular Greek."

In the NT . . . the word is used for the most part in a sense for which there is no Greek analogy whatever and of which there is only an isolated example in Philo. That is to say it denotes "divine and heavenly radiance," the "loftiness and majesty of God," and even the "being of God" and His world. How does the word come to have this new significance? To answer this question it is necessary that we study the Hebrew *kavod*.

Tracing the use of *kavod* in the Old Testament, and of *doxa* in the Septuagint and the New Testament, the entry (by von Rad and Kittel) alludes to the Shekinah idea of Rabbinic Judaism. "That the *shekinah* and the *kabod* are closely related may be seen from equivalents used in [Targum Jonathan]. When the *shekinah* comes to Sion, the *kabod* may be seen by all Israel." The Targum on Exodus 34:29ff. is cited also: "There shone the radiance of his [Moses] features which had come to him from the light of the glory of the *shekinah* of Yahweh." So Hastings's *Dictionary of the Bible*: "The *conception* of the Shekinah appears in Greek dress under the word *doxa*. In several instances *doxa* is used of Deity or a manifestation-form of Deity, and thus shows itself to be the equivalent of Shekinah . . . . In the NT there are several instances in which *doxa* is used as more or less the equivalent of Shekinah."

One example of such equivalence is Hebrews 1:3, where Christ is called "the brightness of his [God's] glory" (AV). The RSV reads: "He reflects the glory of God." Taken word by word, however, the Greek text would read: "who being brightness [reflection] of the glory" (*apaugasma tes doxes*). (The text of Hebrews 1:3 echoes and recalls the Apocrypha, wherein Wisdom [*sophia*] is called "the brightness [*apaugasma*] of the everlasting light [*photos aidiou*]" [Wisd. 7:26].) Another example of what Abelson calls "the Schechinah-Presence"[22] may be this: "when he [Christ] received honour and glory [*doxan*] from God the Father and the voice was borne to him by the Majestic Glory [*megaloprepous doxes*]" (2 Pet. 1:17; RSV). In James 2:1, according to the AV and the RSV, Christ is "the Lord of glory"; whereas the Greek text reads simply: "Jesus Christ the glory" [*Iesou Christou tes doxes*].[23] C. H. Dodd's remarks are apposite:

The term *doxa* in Greek means either "opinion" . . . or else "reputation," and in particular a good reputation, and so "honour," "distinction." It is still somewhat obscure how the word acquired a new meaning which made it capable of translating the Hebrew *kavod*, Aramaic *jekara*. It seems that it does not bear this meaning anywhere except where Jewish influence is probable. *Kavod* means the manifestation of God's being, nature and presence, in a manner accessible to human experience; and the manifestation was conceived in the form of radiance, splendour, or dazzling light . . . . In Judaism of the Christian era, the *shekinah* ("dwelling," or presence of God) was conceived as light.

In the Fourth Gospel, the ordinary Greek use of *doxa* is common . . . but in the four places which speak of "seeing" the glory of God or Christ . . . and in the one place which speaks of "manifesting" the glory . . . we must recognize the biblical meaning of the term. In xii.41 we have a reference to the vision of Isaiah described in ch.vi of his book. Isaiah says bluntly, "I saw the Lord." John, in accordance with the general tendency of contemporary Judaism, says *eiden ten doxan autou* [lit. "he saw the glory of him"]. Clearly, therefore, *doxa* here means the manifestation of God's presence and power, *kavod* or *jekara*. So when in xvii.24 Christ prays for his disciples, *ina theorosin ten doxan ten emen en dedokas moi hoti egapesas me pro kataboles kosmou* ["that they may behold my glory, which thou hast given to me because thou didst love me before the foundation of the world"], he is using language of Hebrew ancestry to denote the *visio Dei*.[24]

*   *   *

Edwards's Dissertation *Concerning the End for which God Created the World*, written in 1755, was published in 1765. The following is excerpted from Chapter II:

> Let us begin with the phrase the GLORY OF GOD – And here I might observe, that it is sometimes used to signify the second person in the Trinity; but it is not necessary at this time, to prove it from particular passages of Scripture. Omitting this, I proceed to observe some things concerning the Hebrew word *kavod* which is most commonly used in the Old Testament, where we have the word *glory* in the English Bible . . . . The noun *kavod* signifies *gravity*, heaviness, *greatness*, and abundance . . . . (116: 512)[25]
>
> The Hebrew word *kavod* which is normally translated *glory*, is

used in such a manner as might be expected from this signification of the words from whence it comes. Sometimes it is used to signify what is *internal, inherent,* or in the *possession* of the person: and sometimes for *emanation, exhibition,* or *communication* of this internal glory: and sometimes for the *knowledge* or *sense* of these, in those to whom the exhibition or communication is made; or an *expression* of this knowledge, sense, or effect. And here I would note, that agreeable to the use of this word in the Old Testament is the Greek word *doxa* in the New. For as the word *kavod* is generally translated by the just mentioned Greek word *doxa* in the Septuagint; so it is apparent, that this word is designed to be used to signify the same thing in the New Testament with the other in the Old. This might be abundantly proved .... (116; 513)

The word glory is used in Scripture often to express the *exhibition, emanation,* or *communication* of the internal glory: Hence it often signifies an effulgence, or shining brightness by an emanation of beams of light .... But in particular, the word is very often thus used when applied to God and Christ. (117; 516)

Key words in Edwards's text are "effulgence," "emanation," "expression": God's glory, Edwards tells us, is "often represented by an effulgence, or emanation, or communication of light, from a luminary or fountain of light. What can so naturally and aptly represent the emanation of the internal glory of God; or the flowing forth and abundant communication of that infinite sense of good that is God? Light is very often in Scripture put for comfort, joy, happiness, and for good in general*" (117–118; 521). The asterisk in Edwards's text sends his reader to the following note:

Isa.vi.3. – "Holy, holy, holy is the Lord of hosts, the whole earth is full [Hebrew *melo*; LXX *pleres*] of his *glory*." In the original, *His glory is the fulness of the whole earth*: which signifies much more than the words of the translation .... By *God's glory* here, there seems to be respect to those effulgent beams that filled the temple: these beams signifying God's glory shining forth and communicated. (118; 521n)

Edwards's phrase, "those effulgent beams that filled the temple," recalls the cloud of glory of Exodus 40:35, identified in *Work of Redemption* with the Shekinah. (A useful gloss on Isaiah 6:3 is found in the Targums, translated throughout, for the present study, by Robert Hayward: "Holy in the highest heaven is the house of his Shekinah. Holy upon the earth is the deed [or work] of his power. Holy throughout the ages is the Lord of Hosts. All the earth is full of the splendour of his glory.") Having linked the divine plenitude with glory, Edwards goes on to link metonymically the name of God with the divine glory, explaining that they often "signify the same thing in Scripture" (118; 523). Whereupon, citing passages from Exodus, he alludes directly to the pillar of cloud that "dwelt above the mercy-seat in the tabernacle":

> And the same illustrious brightness and *effulgence* in the pillar of cloud that appeared in the wilderness, and dwelt above the mercy-seat in the tabernacle and temple, (or rather the spiritual, divine brightness and effulgence *represented* by it,) so often called the *glory of the Lord,* is often called *the name of the Lord.* Because God's glory was to dwell in the tabernacle . . . . In like manner, the *name* of God is said to dwell in the sanctuary . . . . And in Psal. lxxiv.7.the temple is called *the dwelling-place* [Heb. *mishkan*; LXX *skenoma*] *of God's name.* (118; 524)

To summarize: according to Edwards, the end or purpose of God's Creation is the glory or name of God communicated; at the same time, the glory of God communicated is the end or purpose of Creation, defined by Edwards as "the emanation and true external expression of God's internal glory and fulness." Creation is the "*manifestation* of [God's] internal glory to created understandings. The *communication* of the infinite fulness of God to the creature." On rereading *End of Creation,* one discovers that in Edwards's layered and metonymic scheme, there is an "ultimate end" or "great end" to God's works that is radically related to the divine fiat of Genesis. No matter what that ultimate purpose is called, we are told, all its names are metonymy for the glory of God:

> For though it [God's ultimate end] be signified by various names, yet they appear not to be names of *different* things, but various names involving each other in their meaning; either different names of the *same thing,* or names of several parts of *one whole;* or of the same viewed in *various lights,* or in its *different respects* and relations. (119; 526)

Thus we see that the great end of God's works, which is so variously expressed in Scripture, is indeed but one; and this one end is most properly and comprehensively called the glory of God; by which name it is properly called in Scripture; and is fitly compared to an effulgence or emanation of light from a luminary. (119; 530)

In terms of the discussion below, one fact is central: Edwards considers creation to be the divine fulness or internal glory of God existing *ad extra*. Expressed otherwise by Edwards, creation is an *"emanation of God's glory;* or the excellent brightness and fulness of the divinity *diffused, overflowing,* and as it were *enlarged*; or in one word, *existing ad extra"* (119; 527). With the crucial phrase *ad extra,* Edwards alludes to the doctrine of *creatio ex nihilo.*

*   *   *

In order to arrive at a precise understanding of Edwards's model of creation, it will be useful to examine a typical misunderstanding. Here, for example, is Perry Miller's attempt to explicate *Concerning the End for which God Created the World*:

> God did not create the world, said Edwards, merely to exhibit His glory; He did not create it out of nothing simply to show that He could: He who is Himself the source of all being, the substance of all life, created the world out of Himself by a diffusion of Himself into time and space. He made the world, not by sitting outside and above it, by modeling it as a child models sand, but by an extension of Himself, by taking upon Himself the forms of stones and trees and of man. He created without any ulterior object in view, neither for His glory nor for His power, but for the pure joy of self-expression, as an artist creates beauty for the sake of beauty . . . . If He bothers to create, it is out of the fullness of His own nature . . . . Edwards did not use my simile of the artist.., but we may still employ the simile because Edwards invested his God with the sublime egotism of the great artist.[26]

This is a case of misreading through misremembering. For it is not just the simile of the artist that Edwards does not use. Nowhere in his closely-argued *End of Creation* is there even a hint of God's "taking upon Himself the forms of stones and trees" (Miller's phrasing recalls Wordsworth's Lucy poems). Nor does Edwards once use the word "extension," which to the modern reader recalls Spinoza, and no doubt "pantheism" (whether or not Spinoza's model of emanation is pantheistic). More, Miller's depiction of a Deity "who created the world out of Himself by a diffusion of Himself into time and space" evokes in this context, not Calvin's sense of "diffusion," but the Stoic God, who indeed emanates and generates the world out of his own substance, and who "does so as a material immanent force, a sort of perfectly good and wise gas."[27]

* * *

If we look closely at Jonathan Edwards, we find that while God's glory and fulness is expressed in and through creation, God is nevertheless undiminished, unchanged, immutable. In fact Edwards is entirely explicit in *End of Creation* that God's emanation is "*ad extra*, or without himself" (100; 433). To Edwards, creation "implies a being receiving its existence, and all that belongs to it, out of nothing" (97; 420). Once again, the doctrine of *creatio ex nihilo* is evoked: the world, including creatures in all their complexity, was created out of nothing prior to or other than God – there was no eternal matter at hand from which anything derives. In the words of the Westminster Confession: "It pleased God . . . to create, or make of nothing, the world, and all things therein." The first explicit statement we find of *creatio ex nihilo* (the concept is implicit in Genesis 1, and was so understood by the Rabbis) was recorded about 125 B.C.:

> I beseech thee, my son, look upon the heaven and the earth, and all that is therein, and consider that God made them of things that were not; and so was mankind made likewise. (2 Maccabees 7:28)[28]

Compare Hebrews 11:3:

> By faith we understand that the world was created by the word of God, so that what is seen was made out of things which do not appear. (RSV)

There is a radical difference between a model of creation whereby all things are produced from "things that were not" (from no thing) and a model whereby all things are produced from God's Substance, or from *any* pre-existing matter. Nonetheless, when the language of emanation (overflowingness, radiance, streams, fountains, diffusion, and so on) is used to explicate *creatio ex nihilo*, there is the possibility, even the danger, of confusion. In consequence Edwards, and indeed Calvin, have been accused of verging on pantheism. To paraphrase a warning of Copleston's, *all theories of emanation must be interpreted according to the doctrine of creation to which they adhere.*[29] In the context of the present study, one should also be aware that all Edwards's *metaphors* of emanation must be interpreted with regard to the doctrine of divine generation [*gennesis*] of the Son from the Father, often described by the early Church Fathers in terms of "light and its radiance, fountain and stream, root and plant."[30] The word *emanation* itself is "used by divines to denote 'generation' of Son and 'procession' of Holy Ghost" (*OED*); its root is the Latin *manare*, to flow.

Creation out of nothing does not mean, as Gnosticism would have it, "that there was once a 'Nothing' out of which God created the world, a negative primal beginning, a Platonic me on, a formlessness, a chaos, a primal Darkness. The 'ex' of the *creatio ex nihilo* does not suggest any kind of 'matter' – however vague and shadowy – but it means the fact that God alone brought the world into being" (Emil Brunner is here cited).[31] In the doctrine of *creatio ex nihilo*, there "never was a 'nothing' alongside of God, as it were, but God alone," who creates the world through his Word or Wisdom or Torah, not by shaping or "emanating" some aboriginal substance. Compare Psalm 33:9: "For he spake, and it was done."

Compare also Ecclesiasticus (Ben Sirach) 43:26: "by his word [*logo*] all things consist." Likewise Wisdom of Solomon 9:1: "O God of my fathers, and Lord of mercy, who hast made [*poiesas*] all things with thy word [*en logo sou*]." So the Syriac Apocalypse of Baruch: "When of old there was no world with its inhabitants, thou didst devise and speak with a word, and forthwith the works of creation stood before thee" (14:7).[32] To take just one of countless patristic instances, Clement of Alexandria writes: "The logos issuing forth was the cause of Creation."[33] Implicit in *creatio ex nihilo* are two radical concepts: first, the world was created by means of the expressed and communicated Word of God; second, the world has a beginning (Gr. *En arche*; Heb. *Bereshith*).

Greek philosophy, on the other hand, wherein God and matter are coeternal, "knows no beginning of the world."[34] Plato, for example (according to St. Athanasius), "said that God had made all things out of pre-existent and uncreated matter, just as the carpenter makes things of wood that already exists."

> But [Athanasius argues] those who hold this view do not realize that to deny that God is Himself the Cause of matter is to impute limitation to Him, just as it is undoubtedly a limitation on the part of the carpenter that he can make nothing unless he has the wood.[35]

Nor in Platonic thought do *we* come from nothing into being. The most important distinction that must be made between the Platonic and the Judaeo-Christian concepts of being is the way in which being is divided. For Plato, as Andrew Louth has emphasized, the soul was

> pre-existent and immortal. *The most fundamental ontological distinction in such a world was between the spiritual and the material.* The soul belonged to the former realm in contrast to its body which was material: the soul belonged to the divine, spiritual realm and was only trapped in the material realm by its association with the body. But the doctrine of creation *ex nihilo* implies that *the most fundamental ontological divide is between God and the created order, to which latter both soul and body belong.*[36] (italics added)

To posit a "fundamental ontological divide . . . between God and the created order," and then to imagine, as Jonathan Edwards does, that God's "disposition" is to make himself known "by his *words* and *works*, i.e. in what he *says* and in what he *does*" (98; 422), suggests that God may somehow bridge that fundamental divide. It further suggests that Edwards, like Calvin and Augustine, views creation as a matter of grace, as "a . . . purely superfluous [cf. "overflowing"] expression of pure disinterested generosity."[37] For Edwards, as we have seen, God's purpose in creation is to express himself in order that we might understand Him. ("If it be fit that God's power and wisdom, &c. should be exercised and *expressed* in some effects, and not lie eternally dormant, then it seems proper that these exercises should appear, and not be totally hidden and unknown" [99; 431]). And that which God expresses, *ex nihilo*, without himself, is something Edwards terms the "internal glory or fulness." A passage from

Ecclesiasticus or Sirach (190 B.C.) is a valuable gloss on Edwards's *End of Creation*:

> I will now remember the works of the Lord, and declare the things that I have seen: In the words of the Lord are his works. The sun that giveth light looketh upon all things, and the work thereof is full [*pleres*] of the glory [*doxes*] of the Lord. The Lord hath not given power to the saints to declare all his marvellous works, which the Almighty Lord firmly settled, that whatsoever is might be established for his glory [*doxe*] . . . . He hath garnished the excellent works of his wisdom [*sophias*], and he is from everlasting to everlasting: unto him may nothing be added, neither can he be diminished. (42:15ff.)

That the world is filled with the grandeur of God – that God's grandeur is the fulness of the whole earth – is due to what Edwards calls God's "propensity" or "*disposition* to cause an emanation of his glory and fulness – which is prior to the existence of any other being" (100; 438). These words allude unmistakably to the doctrine of divine pre-existence. First of all, Edwards's assertion that God's glory and fulness is "prior to the existence of any other being" evokes Wisdom or *hochma* of the Hebrew Scriptures: "The Lord by wisdom [*hochma*] hath founded the earth; by understanding hath he established the heavens" (Prov.3:19).

> The LORD possessed me [i.e. *hochma*] in the beginning [Heb. *reshith*] of his way, before his works of old. I was set up from everlasting, from the beginning, or ever the earth was . . . . (Proverbs 8:22 ff.)

As given in the New Jewish Publication Society translation of the Hebrew Scriptures, the passage directly above reads:

> The LORD created me at the beginning of His course
> As the first of His works of old.
> In the distant past I was fashioned,
> At the beginning, at the origin of earth.
> There was still no deep when I was brought forth . . . .
> When He fixed the foundations of the earth,
> I was with Him as a confidant . . . .

Apparently in post-biblical Rabbinic writings, the concept of *hochma* tended to merge with the concept of Torah. The famous Midrash on Genesis 1 (Bereshith Rabbah) interprets God's Wisdom or *hochma* as the pre-existent Torah, living "with God as with a tutor, reared as it were by the Almighty."[38] If we move to Hellenistic Judaism, and trace what R. H. Fuller has called "the *hochma-sophia* tradition,"[39] we discover that in the Apocrypha it is Wisdom or *sophia* who was created "from the beginning before the world" (Ecclus. 24:9). In the Wisdom of Solomon we read that *sophia* "was with thee [God]: which knoweth thy works, and was present when thou madest the world" (9:9).[40]

More centrally, Edwards's *End of Creation* evokes the *logos* or Word who was "in the beginning [*en arche*] with God" (John 1:2); who, like *hochma* and *sophia*, existed "before the foundation of the world" (John 17:24); and "Who verily was foreordained [foreknown] before the foundation of the world, but was manifest in these last times for you" (1 Pet.1:20). Jesus himself speaks of "the glory [*doxe*] which I had with thee [God] before the world was" (John 17:5). Similarly, in Colossians 1:17, St. Paul declares: "And he [Christ] is before all things, and by him all things consist." Without such background, this remark of Edwards is indecipherable:

> Whatever that be which is *in itself* most valuable, and was so originally, prior to the creation of the world, and which is *attainable* by the creation . . . *that* must be worthy to be God's *last* end in the creation . . . . (97; 421)

Phrased otherwise, God's "last end" in the creation is radically involved with whatever was "most valuable . . . prior to the creation of the world." Floated out of its theological context, Edwards's text may well suggest the pre-existence of matter; for in *creatio ex nihilo*, as we know, there is *no thing* prior to the creation but God himself. That is why any informed reading of Edwards's *End of Creation* must take into account the doctrine of the pre-existent *logos*, whereby the Son is present with the Father before the foundation of the world. Formulated in the Nicene Creed: Christ is "Begotten of his Father before all worlds, God of God, Light of Light, Very God of very God, Begotten [*gennetos*], not made, Being of one substance with the Father, By whom all things were made." Or let us turn to Calvin on "The eternity of the Word":

nothing should be more intolerable to us than to fancy a beginning of that Word who both was always God and afterward was the artificer of the universe . . . . For because something begins to be manifested at a certain time, we ought not therefore to gather that it never existed before. Indeed, I conclude far otherwise: the Word had existed long before God said, "Let there be light" and the power of the Word emerged and stood forth. Yet if anyone should inquire how long before, he will find no beginning . . . . Therefore we again state that the Word, conceived beyond the beginning of time by God, has perpetually resided with him. (*Institutes* I.xiii.8)[41]

Edwards's view of divine pre-existence is revealed most clearly in his *Miscellaneous Observations* (pub. 1793), where he maintains that the "works of *creation* [are] ascribed to Christ." Furthermore, and this is not insignificant, Edwards identifies the pre-existent Word with Wisdom or *hochma* of the Old Testament:

If Christ in the beginning created the heavens and the earth, he must be from eternity; for then he is before the beginning, by which must be meant, the beginning of time; the beginning of that kind of duration which has *beginning* and *following*, before and after, belonging to it . . . . In Proverbs viii.22. it is said, "The Lord possessed me [i.e. *hochma*] before his works of old;" and therefore before those works which in Genesis i.1. are said to be made in the beginning. God's eternity is expressed thus, Psalm xc.2."Before the mountains were brought forth, or ever thou hadst created the earth and the world, even from everlasting." So it is said, Prov.viii.22.&c. "The Lord possessed me in the beginning of his way, before his works of old. I was set up from everlasting, from the beginning, or ever the earth was," &c.[42]

We are told by Edwards that "the phrase the Glory of God . . . is sometimes used to signify the second person in the Trinity" (116; 512). We are told also: "It is a thing infinitely good in itself, that God's glory should be known by a glorious society of created beings" (99; 431). At this point, if not earlier, one realizes that Edwards's *End of Creation* is a *midrash* or commentary on Creation in terms of the Incarnation (or on the *logos* of Creation in terms of the Incarnate *logos*, the *logos* of Redemption or Salvation); and also a *midrash* on the Incarnation in terms of *creatio ex nihilo*. Jaroslav

Pelikan sketches out the typological model that joins Creation with Redemption:

> As is evident from John 1:3 and its background in Proverbs 8:30, the doctrine of the preexistent logos was . . . a means of correlating the redemption accomplished in Jesus Christ with the doctrine of Creation. Creation . . . revelation . . . and redemption could all be ascribed to the logos."[43]

A further aspect of Edwards's *End of Creation* that needs to be considered is how it carefully unravels the language of the Fourth Gospel, especially the proem, which returns us to the beginning of Genesis, to Proverbs, and to the Jewish Apocrypha:

> In the beginning [*En arche*] was the Word [*logos*], and the Word was with God, and the Word was God. The same was in the beginning [*en arche*] with God. All things were made [*egeneto*] by him; and without him there was not anything made that was made. In him was life; and the life was the light [*phos*] of men. (John 1:1–4)

> And the Word [*logos*] was made flesh, and dwelt [*eskenosen* cf. *skene*] among us, and we beheld his glory [*doxan*], the glory as of the only begotten [*monogenous*] of the Father, full [*pleros*] of grace and truth . . . . And of his fulness [*pleromatos*] have we all received, and grace for grace. (1:14,16)

Here is a central but lesser-known passage from Sirach or Ecclesiasticus, one of a series of inter-testamentary writings that lead from the Hebrew Bible into Rabbinic Judaism and into the New Testament:

> Wisdom [*sophia*] shall praise herself . . . . I came out of the mouth of the most High, and covered the earth as a cloud. [Cf. Prov.2:6: "For the Lord giveth wisdom: out of his mouth cometh knowledge and understanding."] I dwelt [*kateskenosa*; cf. *skene*] in high places and my throne is in a cloudy pillar . . . .
> With all these I sought rest: and in whose inheritance shall I abide? So the Creator of all things gave me a commandment, and he that made me caused my tabernacle [*skenen*] to rest, and said, Let thy dwelling [*kataskenoson*] be in Jacob and thine inheritance

in Israel. He created me from the beginning before the world and I shall never fail.

In the holy tabernacle [*skene*] I served before him; and so was I established in Sion. (24: 1–10)

Let us now turn to Edwards's treatment of *pleroma*, a key word in the proem to the Fourth Gospel that we have so far ignored. The word *pleroma* means, "that which fills," "fulness," "plenitude": "And the Word . . . dwelt among us . . . full [*pleros*] of grace and truth. . . . of his fulness [*pleromatos*] have we all received." In Edwards's model of Creation, it is the divine "fulness," the "infinite fulness of all possible good" (99; 432), that is expressed and communicated by God.[44] What seems especially important is that "fulness" and "glory" are closely related: the "emanation of divine fulness" is "called in Scripture, *the glory of God*" (119; 529). Throughout his *End of Creation*, Edwards makes a confused (and often confusing) distinction between the *internal* glory or fulness (which is presumably invisible, just as the divine name is ineffable) and the *external* fulness – the perceptible glory of God, or in other terms, the glory of the Shekinah. To consider Edwards's invisible-visible model further is to sense that St. Paul is not far away: in Colossians, Christ is called the "image [*eikon*] of the invisible God" (1:15), just as in the Apocrypha, Wisdom is called the *eikon* of God's goodness (Wisdom 7:26). Edwards's first Miscellany on the Trinity describes the Son as the "express and perfect image of God."[45]

To follow Edwards further: the visible or external glory of God is the "expression of God's internal glory and fulness": "As there is an infinite fulness of all possible good in God . . . and as this fulness is capable of communication, or emanation *ad extra*; so it seems a thing amiable and valuable in *itself* that this infinite fountain of good should send forth abundant streams" (99; 433).

> So far as the stream may be looked upon as anything besides the fountain, so far it may be looked on as an increase of good. And if the fulness of good that is in the fountain, is itself excellent, then the emanation, which is as it were an increase, repetition, or multiplication of it is excellent. Thus it is fit, since there is an infinite fountain of light and knowledge, that this light should shine forth in beams of communicated knowledge and understanding [Cf. Prov. 2:6: "out of his mouth cometh knowledge and understanding."] . . . . And that, as there is an infinite fulness

of joy and happiness, so these should have an emanation, and become a fountain flowing out in abundant beams, as beams from the sun.

Thus it appears reasonable to suppose that it was God's last end, that there be a glorious and abundant emanation of his infinite fulness of good *ad extra*, or without himself; and that the disposition to communicate himself, or diffuse his own FULNESS,* was what moved him to create the world. (100; 433)

With the asterisk after the word "FULNESS," Edwards sends us to an explanatory note: the phrase "God's fulness," he writes, signifies "all the good which is in God natural and moral." As well, St. Paul "often useth the phrase in this sense." So we are referred directly to the divine *pleroma* (the word appears some dozen times in the Pauline Epistles), conceived by Edwards as something that overflows from God *ad extra* in the act of creation.[46]

Already we have seen the words *fulness* and *abundant* used by Edwards to describe creation. (1) The world is a "*manifestation* of [God's] internal glory to created understandings. The *communication of the infinite fulness of God to the creature*." (2) Creation is an "*emanation of God's glory*; or the excellent brightness and fulness of the divinity *diffused, overflowing*, and as it were *enlarged*; or in one word, *existing ad extra*." (3) "What can so naturally and aptly represent the emanation of the internal glory of God; or the flowing forth and abundant communication of that infinite sense of good that is God?" (4) " ... it seems a thing amiable and valuable in *itself* that this infinite fountain of good should send forth abundant streams." (5) The Hebrew word "*kavod* signifies *gravity*, heaviness, *greatness*, and abundance." (The words *abundance* and *abundant*, cognate with *abound*, stem from the Latin *abundare*, "to overflow." Cf. Paul's statement in Philippians 4:18: "But I have all, and abound: I am full [*pepleromai*].")

According to Delling's entry on *pleroma* and its word group in the *Theological Dictionary of the New Testament*, the idea of "God as the One who Fills the World" is found in the Old Testament and in post-biblical Judaism. The central text may be Jeremiah 23:24, with its divine assertation: "Do I not fill [*male*] heaven and earth?" (in the LXX, the Hebrew verb *male* becomes *plero*). Of this verse, Delling remarks pointedly: "the reference is not to the filling of the universe by the *pneuma* in the Stoic sense of an impersonal material power. God fills the world and he also sustains it." One should compare

1 Kings 8:27: "But will God indeed dwell on earth? Behold, heaven and the highest heaven cannot contain thee; how much less this house that I have built!" The Targum offers a useful and apposite gloss: "God is above all heavens and He upholds the world; they cannot embrace Him. It is His grace, His good pleasure, to let his Shekinah dwell among men." When the Targumists assert that the Shekinah is everywhere, they assert that even the smallest particle of creation reveals the Divine Presence. At no time, however, do they identify God with his creation. He is both here and there, immanent and transcendent. George Foot Moore explicates the Jewish idea of God:

> In reality God is everywhere present . . . . Because he is in one place he is no less elsewhere. In R. Levi's comparison: "The tabernacle was like a cave that adjoined the sea. The sea came rushing in and flooded the cave; the cave was filled, but the sea was not in the least diminished. So the tabernacle was filled with the radiance of the divine presence, but the world lost nothing of that presence." Another comparison for this all-pervading presence of God in the world is the soul of man. As the soul fills the body, so God fills his world, as it is written, "Do I not fill heaven and earth? saith the Lord." [47]

The biblical concept of "God as the One Who fills all things" was taken up by Philo, from whom Delling cites the following: "The whole cosmos . . . would not be a place worthy of God, since God is his own place (*topos*) and is Himself full . . . . He fills (*pleron*) and embraces all else, that which is deficient and waste and empty, but he is embraced by nothing." Thus, Delling explains, "In full self-sufficiency God is distinct from the world"; moreover, when Philo "speaks of God as the *peplerokos* he is describing God as the One who was at work in the creation of the world and who is still at work in its preservation." That is to say, by referring to God as the *peplerokos*, Philo "is not calling God the world soul. His super-terrestial concept of God prevents him from doing this." If for Philo, God is the One Who fills all things, God is at the same time immutable, undiminished, and outside the world, for there is nowhere in or outside creation where God is not: "for God fills all things and pervades all things, and has left nothing, no matter how solitary, void of himself. What kind of a place can man occupy in which God is not?"[48] (In this context, see Browning's "Saul": "And thy love fill infinitude wholly, nor leave up nor down/One spot for the creature to stand in!" [ll. 302–303].)

As we have seen, Philo conceives of God in spatial terms: "There I am, and everywhere, Who have filled [*pepleroka*] all things."[49] This model of thought may inform Paul's text in Colossians 1:19, cited here in three translations: "For it pleased the Father that in him [Christ] should all fulness dwell" (AV); "For in him all the fullness of God was pleased to dwell" (RSV); "For in him, the complete being of God, by God's own choice, came to dwell" (NEB). All three versions are an ideological gloss on the Greek text, where the words "Father" and "God" do not appear at all. It is simply, as Paul writes, that all the fulness [*pan to pleroma*] was well pleased to dwell in Christ.

Just as the divine *pleroma* is said to dwell in Christ, so Christ is said to fill all things: "He [Christ] that descended is the same also that ascended . . . that he might fill all things" [*plerose ta panta*] (Eph. 4:10). Compare Colossians 2:9–10:

> For in him [Christ] dwells all the fulness of the Godhead bodily [*pan to pleroma tes theotetos somatikos*]. And you are complete [lit. you have been filled, *peploromenoi*] in him.

*   *   *

To conceive spatially of the divine *pleroma* dwelling in Christ is to recall the point in Edwards's *End of Creation* where he explains that the Tabernacle and the Temple are "the dwelling-place" of the glory of God and of the divine name:

> And the same illustrious brightness and *effulgence* in the pillar of cloud that appeared in the wilderness, and dwelt above the mercy-seat in the tabernacle and temple, (or rather the spiritual, divine brightness and effulgence *represented* by it,) so often called the *glory of the Lord*, is often called *the name of the Lord*. Because God's glory was to dwell in the tabernacle . . . In like manner, the *name* of God is said to dwell in the sanctuary . . . . And in Psal. lxxiv.7 the temple is called *the dwelling-place* [*mishkan*; LXX *skenoma*] *of God's name*. (118; 524)

Several analogues come to mind, all of them concerned with divine places. (1) As the fulness or *pleroma* is said to dwell in Christ, so in the Hebrew Scriptures, the name and glory of God are said to dwell in the Tabernacle. (2) In the Targums, the glory of the Shekinah dwells in the Tabernacle – see Targum Neofiti on Exodus 25:8: "And they shall build for my name the house of the sanctuary, and I shall cause the glory of my Shekinah to dwell in their midst." (3) In Exodus 40:35, "the glory of the LORD [*kavod YWHW*] filled [*male; LXX pleres*] the tabernacle [*mishkan*]"; whereas in the Targums, it is the glory of the Shekinah that fills the tabernacle: "It was not possible for Moses to enter the *mishkan zimna* because the cloud of glory was dwelling on it. And the glory of the Shekinah of the Lord filled the *mishkan*."

In the New Testament, the word "tabernacle" or *skene* becomes metonymy for Christ: in the vision of St. John the Divine, a voice cries out, "Behold, the tabernacle [*skene*] of God is with men, and he will dwell [*skenosei*] with them" (Rev.21:3). One recalls also the well-known connection between the second Temple and the "temple" of the body of Christ (see John 2:19–20), itself metonymy for the Church. In Hebrews 9:11, Christ is "a greater and more perfect tabernacle [*skenous*], not made with hands" (cf. 2 Cor. 1:1–5). So far we are on familiar ground. But what is remarkable about the following excerpt from *A History of the Work of Redemption* is Edwards's firm conviction that the pre-incarnate *logos* "dwelt" in the second Temple "till he came to dwell in human nature":

> The building of the [second] temple was a great type of . . . Christ, especially his human nature; of the church; and of heaven . . . .
>
> *This was the house where Christ dwelt, till he came to dwell in human nature*. That his body was the antetype of the temple, appears from what he says, "Destroy this temple, and in three days I will raise it up," speaking of the temple of his body, John ii.19,20. (557; 225, italics added)

Several pages on, in the passage cited partially on the first page of the present study, Edwards contends that the second Temple, rebuilt in 516 B.C., "was nothing in comparison" with the first: that along with the tablets of the law, and the fire upon the altar, one of the things lacking in the Temple was "the Shechinah, or cloud of glory over the mercy seat" (563; 252–54). Several pages later he remarks: "We before observed . . . how the cloud of glory withdrew, before Christ, the brightness of the Father's glory appeared" (566; 269). Still later, we are reminded by Edwards that before the Babylonian captivity, "God used to dwell among them [the Jewish people] . . . visibly revealing himself to them by the Shechinah . . . " (570; 288).

One clue to Edwards's model of light-overtaking-light is Haggai 2:9, and God's promise to fill the second Temple with glory: "The glory of this latter house shall be greater than the former, saith the Lord of Hosts: and in this place will I give peace . . . . " Read christologically, the verse from Haggai is an accepted prophecy of the Incarnation. Edwards says of the second Temple: "Now that very temple was built that God would fill with glory by Christ's coming into it, as the prophets Haggai and Zechariah told the Jews in order to encourage them in building it" (565; 265). The allusion is to Haggai 1:8 ("build the house . . . that I may appear in my glory"), a verse interpreted by the Targumists as: "build the house . . . that I may cause my Shekinah to dwell in it."

Now the theological stumbling-block in Edwards's passage cited above is this: for Edwards the rebuilt, second Temple is not simply a type of the Incarnation, but already, five centuries before the birth of Christ, *the dwelling-place of the pre-incarnate Christ*, who "dwelt" there "till he came to dwell in human nature," or in the "temple of his body." In other words, that the Shekinah or "cloud of glory withdrew" from the first Temple is not only a type or prophecy of the Word made flesh. The withdrawal of the Shekinah also prefigures the indwelling of the pre-incarnate *logos* in the second Temple. Rephrased: in Edwards's view, the pre-incarnate *logos* has re-placed, has taken over the dwelling place (and with it the literary *topos*) of the Shekinah or Divine Presence, said by "the ancient accounts of the Jews" (Edwards's phrase) to be absent from the second Temple.[50]

*   *   *

Explicating God's reason for creating the world, Edwards asserts that there is "a communicative *disposition* in general, or a disposition in the fulness of the divinity to flow out and diffuse itself."

> This propensity in God to diffuse himself, may be considered as a propensity to himself diffused; or to his own glory existing in its emanation. A respect to himself, or an infinite propensity to and delight in his own glory, is that which causes him to incline

to its being abundantly diffused, and to delight in the emanation of it.... (100; 439)

The verb *to diffuse* stems from the Latin *diffundere*, meaning "to pour out or abroad." Likewise in English, *diffuse* may mean: "to pour or send forth as from a centre of dispersion"; "to spread widely, shed abroad, disperse, disseminate" (*OED*). In what I take to be a central passage from *End of Creation*, we learn that God,

> from his goodness, as it were enlarges himself.... This is by communicating and diffusing himself; and *so*, instead of *finding*, he *makes* objects of his benevolence – not by taking what he finds distinct from himself, and so partaking of their good, and being happy in them, but – by flowing forth, and *expressing himself in them*, and *making them to partake of him*, **and then rejoicing in himself expressed in them, and communicated to them.** (105; 461–62, bold italic added)

Edwards's text is filled with participles (communicating, diffusing, finding, taking, partaking, flowing, expressing, making, rejoicing), all partaking of the nature of adjective and verb and noun, and all imitating the inflowing of the visible glory into creation. Thus one's attention is directed to the role of language itself as the medium of creation. By God's "expressing himself" in "objects of his benevolence," and "making them to partake of him," God creates the world. But as we know, in Edwards's model at least, God expresses himself without himself through the agency of his creating and poetic Word. In brief, if the works of God indeed "partake" of divinity, they do so by partaking of God's Word or Wisdom or Torah or *logos*. So that as Edwards says, "all that is good and worthy in the object, and its very *being*" proceed from the emanation and diffusion and overflowing of God's fulness (105; 462). Creation is a superfluity and surplus of divine meaning.

To understand Creation as an overflowing, purely *ad extra*, of the divine fulness and glory is to regard things as partaking of that glory – the glory, that is, not of God, who is invisible, but of his Shekinah. Metonymy is the figure of contiguity, and there can, as we have seen, be no contiguity between the Creator and Creation. The things of the world, then, are not metonymies of God but metonymies of his Shekinah. Neither mediating between Creator and Creation, nor part of Creation, the Shekinah enables the Divine to reveal himself visibly within the space of Creation. All things, for Edwards, can be signs of God's Presence because they participate in what the late Edmond Jabès, in a visionary gloss on the Shekinah, named "His dazzling absence."[51]

Notes

1: Emerson: This Almost Insignificant Signifier

1. Jacques Derrida, *Dissemination*, trans. Barbara Johnson (Chicago: University of Chicago Press, 1981), pp. 143–44. The original passage appears in *La dissémination* (Paris: Editions du Seuil, 1972), p. 165. I have modified Johnson's translation slightly.
2. With certain exceptions, citations of Emerson's writings are inserted in parentheses directly into the text. For the convenience of my readers, and to avoid unnecessary clutter, page numbers refer to Ralph Waldo Emerson, *Essays & Lectures* (New York: Library of America, 1983). As is customary, *The Journals and Miscellaneous Notebooks of Ralph Waldo Emerson*, ed. William H. Gilman et al. (*JMN*), 16 volumes (Cambridge: Harvard University Press, 1960–1982) are cited with their appropriate volume and page number. In cases where a cited work by Emerson is not included in his *Essays & Lectures*, references appear in the notes.
3. *Theological Dictionary of the New Testament*, ed. Gerhard Kittel and Gerhard Friedrich (Michigan: William B. Eerdmans, 1964–74), Vol. III, p. 661.
4. Jaroslav Pelikan, *The Christian Tradition: A History of the Development of Doctrine*, Volume 3, *The Growth of Medieval Theology (600–1300)* (Chicago and London: University of Chicago Press, 1978), p. 152. St. Bernard's text reads: "Et modus quidem Dei exananitio est; fructus vero nostri de illo repletio"; in *Sancti Bernardi, Opera Genuina* (1845), Vol. 3, p. 477. Compare Emerson, writing in his Journal for 1827: "The Trinitarian urges a natural & sublime deduction from his creed when he says of the Saviour that as he became a partaker in our humanity so we also shall become partakers in his divinity" (*JMN* III: 74).
5. R. P. Martin, *Carmen Christi: Philippians ii. 5–11 in Recent Interpretation and in the Setting of Early Christian Worship* (Cambridge: Cambridge University Press, 1967), pp. 166–67.
6. Excerpted from Walter Lock's entry on *kenosis* in Hastings's *Dictionary of the Bible* (Edinburgh, 1899).
7. Emerson, "The Poet," in *The Early Lectures of Ralph Waldo Emerson*, Vol. III, 1838–1842, ed. Robert E. Spiller and Wallace E. Williams (Cambridge Mass.: Harvard University Press, 1972), p. 365.
8. "Poetry and Imagination" (1875) in *The Complete Works of Ralph Waldo Emerson*, ed. Edward Waldo Emerson, Centenary Edition (Boston: Houghton Mifflin, 1903–4), Vol. VIII, p. 17. The final form of "Poetry and Imagination" results from the editing of James Eliot Cabot. Objecting to what he saw as needless repetition in Emerson's proof copy, Cabot revised it heavily for publication.

9. Cited in Maurice Gonnaud, *An Uneasy Solitude: Individual and Society in the Work of Ralph Waldo Emerson*, trans. Lawrence Rosenwald (Princeton, N.J.: Princeton University Press, 1987), p. 135, n. 99.
10. "Poetry and Imagination," p. 10.
11. "Poetry and Imagination," p. 11.
12. "Poetry and Imagination," p. 20.
13. From Emerson's poem "Woodnotes II," lines 321–22, in *Poems of Ralph Waldo Emerson* (London, New York: Oxford University Press, 1914), p. 60.
14. "Poetry and Imagination," p. 15.
15. G. Oegger, *The True Messiah*, reprinted in Kenneth Walter Cameron, ed., *Emerson the Essayist: An Outline of His Philosophical Development through 1836* (Raleigh, North Carolina: Thistle Press, 1945), pp. 83–99. In a note to Oegger's text, Cameron writes: "This work is a translation of the introductory portions of Oegger's *La Vrai Messie*, Paris, 1829, apparently made by Miss Peabody herself. It was probably her uncorrected manuscript that Emerson used in July and August, 1835" (83). Philip F. Gura explicates Oegger: "Because God never acted from mere whim, Oegger thought, but rather with a premeditated divine purpose, the visible Creation could not be anything but 'the exterior circumference of the invisible and metaphysical world' and as such spoke to man of what was behind its natural facade. Once the world was regarded as the perimeter of divine Creation, an extension of Logos, it became apparent that 'material objects [were] necessarily *scoriae* of the substantial thoughts of the Creator ... '": *The Wisdom of Words: Language, Theology, and Literature in the New England Renaissance* (Middletown, Conn.: Wesleyan University Press, 1981), pp. 86–87.
16. Kenneth Burke, "I, Eye, Ay – Emerson's Early Essay 'Nature': Thoughts on the Machinery of Transcendence," in *Transcendentalisn and its Legacy*, ed. Myron Simon and Thornton H. Parsons (Ann Arbor: University of Michigan Press, 1966), p. 20.
17. Oegger, *The True Messiah*, p. 90.
18. If indeed Emerson *did* conceive "the realm of matter as nothing other than God's offal," as Burke suggests, offal is nothing more or less that its cognate, the German *Abfall*, something that falls or is thrown off: compare *precipitate*. Offal may be cast off as dross in melting metals; or it may comprise any sort of fragment that falls off in breaking or in using or in distributing anything. As cited in the *OED*, Foxe in *Acts & Martyrs* refers specifically to divine and awe-full offal: "There were left twelve baskets, twelve maunds full of brokelets and offalls at that meal." In Matthew's (and in Luke's) version of the miracle of the loaves and fishes, the left-over bread is described as "the fragments that remained" (Matt. 14:20). The "fragments" of the AV renders the Greek *klasmaton*, a word which, according to Liddell and Scott, means "that which is broken off, a fragment, piece, morsel." Further, Emerson's Journal for August 1837 includes what one might consider an appropriate response to Burke: "The secret of the scholar or intellectual man is that all nature

is only the foliage, the flowering, & the fruit of the Soul and that every part therefore exists as emblem & sign, of some fact in the soul. *Instantly rags & offal are elevated into hieroglyphics*; as the chemist sees nothing unclean so the poet does not" (*JMN* V: 366; italics added).

19. "Poetry and Imagination," p. 14.
20. "Poetry and Imagination, p. 11.
21. This passage moves into Emerson's lecture "Holiness," in *The Early Lectures of Ralph Waldo Emerson*, Vol. II, 1836–1838, ed. Stephen E. Whicher *et al.* (Cambridge Mass.: Harvard University Press, 1964) pp. 352–53.
22. *Journals of Ralph Waldo Emerson*, ed. Edward Waldo Emerson and Waldo Emerson Forbes (Boston: Houghton Mifflin, 1909–14), Vol. X, pp. 189–90.
23. *The Complete Works of Ralph Waldo Emerson*, ed. Edward Waldo Emerson, Vol. VII, pp. 175–76. In his study of Emerson, Maurice Gonnaud remarks: Emerson "never succeeds in driving from his mind that he is a misfit, almost an outlaw" (p. 193). Compare Herbert's "Redemption": "I straight return'd and, knowing his great birth, / Sought him accordingly in great resorts;/In cities, theatres, gardens, parks, and courts;/At last I heard a ragged noise and mirth/Of thieves and murderers – there I him espied . . . ."
24. "A fact is only a fulcrum of the spirit. It is the terminus of a past thought but only a means now to new sallies of the imagination & new progress of wisdom . . . .

    A man, I, am the remote circumference, the skirt, the thin suburb or frontier post of God but go inward & I find the ocean; I lose my individuality in its waves. God is Unity but always works in variety. I go inward until I find Unity universal, that Is before the World was; I come outward to this body a point of variety" (*JMN* V: 177).
25. See Stanley Cavell who, defending Emerson's "uncanonical" style of argumentation, remarks on "its sometimes maddening quality of seeming never to come to the point": *Conditions Handsome and Unhandsome: The Constitution of Emersonian Perfectionism* (Chicago and London: University of Chicago Press, 1990), p. 138. For Emerson: "The value of the universe contrives to throw itself into every point" (289). As early as 1850, Theodore Parker said of his friend Emerson: "He lacks the power of orderly arrangements to a remarkable degree. Not only is there no obvious logical order, but there is no subtle psychological method by which the several parts of an essay are joined together . . . . This often confuses the reader; this want appears the greatest defect of his mind," in *The Recognition of Ralph Waldo Emerson*, ed. Milton R. Konvitz (Ann Arbor: University of Michigan Press, 1972), p. 37.

    On the subject of the apparent disconnectedness of Emerson's prose, see Barbara Packer: "Emerson once praised Landor for having 'the merit of not explaining.' Like most of Emerson's comments about rhetoric, this tribute celebrates the virtues of absence, the exhilirations of discontinuity. Later in life he remarked to a young admirer that the best writing is that which does not quite satisfy the reader. 'A little guessing does him no harm, so I would assist him with no connections'": B. L. Packer, *Emerson's Fall: A New Interpretation of the Major Essays* (New York: Continuum, 1982), p. 1. (Packer is citing Charles J. Woodbury's *Talks with Ralph Waldo Emerson* [1890].) According to Emerson's essay on Montaigne: "Truth, or the connection between cause and effect, alone interests us. We are persuaded that a thread runs through all things: all worlds are strung on it, as beads: and men, and events, and life, come to us only because of that thread: they pass and repass, only that we may know the direction and continuity of that line" (701).

26. *The Complete Sermons of Ralph Waldo Emerson, Volume 2*, ed. Teresa Toulouse and Andrew Delbanco (Columbia and London: University of Missouri Press, 1990), p. 192.
27. Henry James, "Emerson," in *The American Essays*, ed. Leon Edel (New York: Vintage, 1956), p. 76. First published in Macmillan's Magazine, December 1887, this essay was reprinted by James in his *Partial Portraits* (1888). On the subject of renunciation, see Emerson's "Divinity School Address": "The man who renounces himself, comes to himself" (77). See also Emerson's comments on his contemporary, the Reverent Edward Taylor: "His sovereign security results from a certain renunciation & abandonment" (*JMN* IX: 259).

2: *In Nomine Diaboli*: An Extreme Interpretation of *Billy Budd*

1. Geoffrey H. Hartman, "The Fate of Reading," in *The Fate of Reading and other Essays* (Chicago and London: Midway Reprint/University of Chicago Press, 1985), pp. 265-66.
2. Merman Melville, *Billy Budd Sailor (An Inside Narrative)*, Reading Text and Genetic Text, Edited from the Manuscript with Introduction and Notes by Harrison Hayford and Merton M. Sealts, Jr. (Chicago and London: University of Chicago Press, 1962). Hereafter citations *according to Leaf number* of this edition appear parenthetically in the text.
3. Hartman, "The Fate of Reading," pp. 265-66.
4. Derek Attridge, "Unpacking the Portmanteau, or Who's Afraid of *Finnegans Wake*," in *On Puns: The Foundation of Letters*, ed. Jonathan Culler (Oxford: Basil Blackwell, 1988), p. 140.
5. Christopher Ricks, *Milton's Grand Style* (Oxford: Oxford University Press, 1963), p. 110. See Hans Aarsleff on Adamic language: "languages even now, in spite of their multiplicity and seeming chaos, contain elements of the original perfect language created by Adam when he names the animals in his prelapsarian state. In the Adamic doctrine the relation between signifier and signified is not arbitrary; the linguistic sign is not double but unitary. Still retaining the divine nature of their common origin, languages were in fundamental accord with nature, indeed they were themselves part of creation and nature. They were divine and natural, not human and conventional."

From Locke to Saussure: Essays on the Study of Language and Intellectual History (Minneapolis: University of Minneapolis Press, 1982), p. 25.

6. F. O. Matthiessen, *American Renaissance: Art and Expression in the Age of Emerson and Whitman* (1941; rpt. Oxford and London: Oxford University Press, 1968), p. 503.

7. Nathaniel Hawthorne, "The Birth-mark," in *Tales and Sketches* (Library of America, 1982), pp. 765–66.

8. Page numbers following citations from Emerson's essays refer to Ralph Waldo Emerson, *Essays & Lectures* (New York: Library of America, 1983). As is customary, *The Journals and Miscellaneous Notebooks of Ralph Waldo Emerson*, ed. William H. Gilman et al. (*JMN*), 16 volumes (Cambridge: Harvard University Press, 1960–82) are cited in the text with their appropriate volume and page number.

9. Stanley Cavell's recently published *Conditions Handsome and Unhandsome: The Constitution of Emersonian Perfectionism* (Chicago: University of Chicago Press, 1990) takes its title and epigraph from Emerson's passage. Alluding to it, Cavell writes: "You may either dismiss, or savor, the relation between the clutching fingers and the hand in handsome as a developed taste for linguistic oddity, or you may further relate it to Emerson's recurring interest in the hand (as in speaking of what is at hand, by which, whatever else he means, he means the writing taking shape under his hand and now in ours) . . . " (p. 38).

10. Frederick Ahl, "Ars Est Caelare Artem (Art in Puns and Anagrams Engraved)," in *On Puns: The Foundation of Letters*, ed. Jonathan Culler (Oxford: Basil Blackwell, 1988), p. 22.

11. In his Introduction to the Penguin edition of *Billy Budd*, Harold Beaver suggests that the name John Claggart may be "conflating 'clerk' plus 'haggard'" (p. 42). Howard P. Vincent hardly does better: "'Claggart' has ugly associations in its echoes: *braggart, haggard, ragged, staggered, laggard, slacker, lack, clog, clang, clangor, anger, angered, girt, guard, grr, ger* (Indo-European, 'to cry,' and a root in words like *crow* and *crane*) and *grate*. There is the rural English word *claggen* meaning 'to daub with mud,' the Danish *klagge*, 'mud.'" In Vincent's Introduction to *Twentieth Century Interpretations of* Billy Budd, *A Collection of Critical Essays* (Englewood Cliffs N.J.: Prentice-Hall, 1971), p. 8.

12. Ernest Klein, *A Comprehensive Etymological Dictionary of the English Language*, "Dealing with the origin of words and their sense development thus illustrating the history of civilization and culture" (1966; rpt. Amsterdam, Oxford, New York: Elsevier, 1971).

13. In her *Melville's Use of the Bible* (Durham N.C.: Duke University Press, 1949), Nathalia Wright, discussing *Moby-Dick*, points to "Melville's reliance on Kitto's *Cyclopaedia of Biblical Literature*" (p. 13). In their notes to Leaves 129 and 130 of *Billy Budd*, Hayford and Sealts maintain that Melville's phrase "that lexicon . . . based on Holy Writ" does not allude to a particular work, but "rather to the special vocabulary of biblical theology" (p. 162).

14. Geoffrey H. Hartman, *Saving the Text: Literature/Derrida/Philosophy*

(Baltimore and London: The Johns Hopkins University Press, 1981), p. 111.
15. Jonathan Culler, "The Call of the Phoneme," in *On Puns: The Foundation of Letters*, ed. Jonathan Culler (Oxford: Basil Blackwell, 1988), p. 10.
16. Jacques Derrida, *Glas*, English Translation by John P Leavey, Jr., and Richard Rand (Lincoln and London: University of Nebraska Press, 1986), p. 5b.
17. Herman Melville, *Moby-Dick or The Whale* (Library of America, 1983), p. 1315 (Chapter 113).
18. *Moby-Dick*, p. 967 (Chapter 36).
19. Derek Attridge, "Unpacking the Portmanteau, or Who's Afraid of *Finnegans Wake*," p. 141.
20. Maureen Quilligan, *The Language of Alegory: Defining the Genre* (Ithaca and London: Cornell University Press, 1979), pp. 33–34.
21. Milton, *Paradise Lost*, VI, 564–67.
22. The pun on "overture" made by Milton's Satan implies: 1) an offer to negotiate; 2) an opening or aperture (L *apertura*), *Paradise Lost*, VI, 562.
23. *Moby-Dick*, p. 968 (Chapter 36).
24. Cf. Luke 6:19: "And the whole multitude sought to touch him: for there went virtue [*dynamis*] out of him, and healed them all."
25. Matthiessen, *American Renaissance*, p. 506.
26. Compare the diabolic metamorphosis in Melville's *The Confidence-Man*: "Out of old materials sprang a new creature. Cadmus glided into the snake" (Library of America, 1984), p. 1035 (Chapter 32).
27. Introducing the Penguin edition of *Billy Budd*, Harold Beaver is more or less unimpressed with the text, contending that Melville "worked and reworked at the story . . . till the narrative, overloaded with meanings and double meanings, allegory and allusions, almost ground to a standstill. Technically, while intent on drama, his bias remained static, unable to resist interplay (on the page) at the expense of a forward propulsion (in time), imagery at the expense of a plot. Admittedly *Billy Budd, Sailor* is unfinished, but as incident after incident became transformed, Melville's imaginative – purely aesthetic – grip no longer seemed to exercise the firm hold of thirty years earlier . . . "(39). One notices with some satisfaction Beaver's electrical metaphors: the story is "overloaded" (or surcharged); Melville's bias is "static"; because he cannot "resist" interplay, there is little "forward propulsion"; as incidents become "transformed," Melville loses his *grip*.
28. A *Treatice on Magnetism* from 1870 reads: "This suggests the idea that the whole magnetism peculiar to that end of the magnet is collected into that one point: and that point is called a 'pole'" (*OED*).
29. Nathaniel Hawthorne, *The Blithedale Romance*, in *Novels* (Library of America, 1983), p. 806 (Chapter 33).
30. Herman Melville, *The Confidence-Man: His Masquerade* (Library of America, 1984), p. 1092 (Chapter 43).

31. Elizabeth S. Foster, ed., *The Confidence-Man: His Masquerade*, New York: Hendricks House, 1954, p. 362.

3: Giving Umbrage: The Song of Songs which is Whitman's

1. "Preface" to *Leaves of Grass* (1855), in Walt Whitman, *Complete Poetry and Collected Prose* (Library of America), p. 25.
2. Ralph Waldo Emerson, "An Address" to the Senior Class in Divinity College, Cambridge, July 15, 1838, in *Essays & Lectures* (New York: Library of America, 1983), pp. 84–85: "I once heard a preacher who sorely tempted me to say, I would go to church no more . . . . A snow storm was falling around us. The snow storm was real; the preacher merely spectral . . . . "
3. See E. Ann Matter, *The Voice of My Beloved: The Song of Songs in Western Medieval Christianity* (Philadelphia: University of Pennsylvania Press, 1990), p. 7: "That veritas is found hidden *sub umbra et figura* is an essential concept of medieval hermeneutics in general . . . . " See also Matter's discussion on p. 94: "allegory reveals the divine truth hidden *sub umbra et figura*."
4. Brian Stock, *Listening for the Text, On the Uses of the Past* (Baltimore and London: The Johns Hopkins University Press, 1990), p. 39.
5. The seventeenth-century writer John Rawlinson, cited in Stanley Stewart, *The Enclosed Garden: The Tradition and the Image in Seventeenth-Century Poetry* (Madison, Milwaukee, London: University of Wisconsin Press, 1966), note 31, p. 193.
6. John Bunyan, *The Pilgrim's Progress*, edited with introduction by N. H. Keeble (Oxford, New York: Oxford University Press, 1984), p. xxiii (The World's Classics).
7. Cited in Jon Whitman, "From the *Cosmographia* to the *Divine Comedy*: An Allegorical Dilemma," in *Allegory, Myth, and Symbol*, ed. Morton W. Bloomfield, Harvard English Studies 9 (Cambridge Mass. and London: Harvard University Press, 1981), p. 63.
8. See Robert Gordis, *The Song of Songs, A Study, Modern Translation and Commentary* (New York: The Jewish Theological Seminary of America, 5714–1954), p. 2: "its canonicity was reaffirmed at the Council of Jamnia in 90 C.E., never to be seriously challenged again."
9. E. Ann Matter, *The Voice of My Beloved*, p. 4.
10. Christian David Ginsburg, *The Song of Songs, Translated from the Original Hebrew, with a Commentary, Historical and Critical* (London, 1857), pp. 84ff.
11. Ginsburg, *The Song of Songs*, p. 94.
12. Daniel Boyarin, "The Song of Songs: Lock or Key?" in *The Book and the Text*, ed. Regina Schwartz (Oxford, Cambridge Mass.: Basil Blackwell, 1990), p. 214.
13. Ginsburg, *The Song of Songs*, pp. 36–37.
14. *The Anchor Bible, Song of Songs*, A New Translation with Introduction

and Commentary by Marvin H. Pope (Garden City N.Y.: Doubleday, 1977), p. 17.
15. Pope, *The Anchor Bible*, p. 17.
16. Robert Alter, *The Art of Biblical Poetry* (New York: Basic Books, 1985), p. 185.
17. Gordis, *The Song of Songs*, p. 1.
18. Gordis, *The Song of Songs*, p. 8.
19. Thomas Percy, Bishop of Dromore, *Preface to the Song of Solomon, newly translated from the original Hebrew, with a Commentary and Annotations* (London, 1764), cited in Ginsburg, pp. 84–85.
20. J. G. Herder, *The Spirit of Hebrew Poetry*, trans. James Marsh (Burlington, Vermont, 1833; rpt. Naperville, Ill.: Aleph Press, 1971), Vol. II, p. 120. Although neither the Brooklyn Library nor the Astor Library had a copy of Marsh's translation of Herder, Floyd Stovall believes that it was "no doubt accessible" to Whitman. See *The Foreground of Leaves of Grass* (Charlottesville: University Press of Virginia, 1974), pp. 185ff. (James Marsh, President of the University of Vermont from 1826–1833, edited Coleridge's *Aids to Reflection* [1829], a work that had a formative influence on Emerson.) Whitman also had access to Robert Lowth's *Sacred Poetry of the Hebrews*, translated into English in 1787 by G. Gregory, and reprinted in 1816 and 1847 (a copy of the 2nd edition of 1816 was in the Brooklyn Library).
21. From J. G. Herder's *Salomon's Lieder der Liebe* (1778). Cited in Ginsburg, p. 90.
22. According to Floyd Stovall, in *The Foreground to Leaves of Grass*, p. 187.
23. George R. Noyes, *A New Translation of the Proverbs, Ecclesiastes and The Canticles with Introductions, and Notes, Chiefly Explanatory* (Boston: James Munroe, 1846), pp. 119 ff.
24. George Noyes, p. 132.
25. George Noyes, p. 119.
26. Moses Stuart's *Critical History and Defence of the Old Testament Canon* (1845) is cited in Ginsburg, p. 95.
27. George Noyes, p. 125.
28. John Cotton, *A Brief Exposition of the Whole Book of Canticles Or, Song of Solomon* (London, 1648), p. 7. (Copy at Houghton Library, Harvard University). For valuable background on "The Canticles Tradition" as it moves into American thought, see Mason I. Lowrance, Jr., *The Language of Canaan: Metaphor and Symbol in New England from the Puritans to the Transcendentalists* (Cambridge Mass.: Harvard University Press, 1980), pp. 41–54.
29. Paul Ricoeur, "Biblical Hermeneutics," *Semeia* 4 (1975), 29–148; p. 48.
30. Beryl Smalley, *The Study of the Bible in the Middle Ages*, 2nd edn revised (Oxford: Basil Blackwell, 1952), p. 1.
31. See Matter, *The Voice of My Beloved*, p. 4: "even Nicholas of Lyra, champion of the historical sense of the Bible, argued that the Song of Songs has no literal sense." Stanley Stewart remarks of the Song of Songs: "so great was this allegorical view, that certain

writers ... were led to deny the literal meaning of the text entirely," *The Enclosed Garden*, p. 17. On Nicolas of Lyra, see also Ginsburg, p. 68.

32. William E. Phipps, "The Plight of the Song of Songs," in Harold Bloom, ed., *The Song of Songs* (New York, New Haven: Chelsea House, 1988), p. 11; reprinted from *JAAR* 42, No. 1 (March 1974). On Origen's approach to the "literal" meaning of the text, see Harry Austryn Wolfson, *The Philosophy of the Church Fathers*, Vol. 1, Third Edition Revised (Cambridge Mass.: Harvard University Press, 1970), p. 58.
33. Angus Fletcher, *Allegory, The Theory of a Symbolic Mode* (Ithaca: Cornell University Press, 1984), p. 18.
34. Matter, *The Voice of My Beloved*, p. 32. See Northrop Frye on the Song of Songs, most recently in *Words with Power: Being a Second Study of "The Bible and Literature"* (New York, London: Harcourt Brace, 1990), pp. 195–97 and passim.
35. Daniel Boyarin, p. 224.
36. Paul de Man, "The Rhetoric of Temporality," in *Blindness and Insight: Essays in the Rhetoric of Contemporary Criticism*, 2nd edition, revised (Minneapolis: University of Minnesota Press, 1983), p. 207.
37. Andrew Louth, *The Origins of the Christian Mystical Tradition: From Plato to Denys* (Oxford: Clarendon, 1981), p. 76. On shells and kernels of meaning, see Vincent Arthur De Luca's important study of Blake and the sublime: "'Allegory' means 'other-speaking,' but in such a state of sublimity as we get at the end of *Jerusalem*, 'Sublime Allegory' becomes an 'other-speaking' that cancels its own otherness and becomes simply speaking; the only 'other' here is the text itself. The text, the signified of its own signifiers, should not be conceived as a shell covering the meaty kernel of meaning, to use a favorite trope of traditional accounts of the allegorical relation. Even the most profound of his critics can lapse into talk of cracking shells and extracting kernels, but Blake never speaks in such terms. Although Blake's worlds are full of conventional allegorization, Sublime Allegory is not a conventional system of obscured referentiality": *Words of Eternity: Blake and the Poetics of the Sublime* (Princeton: Princeton University Press, 1991), p. 35.
38. Daniel Boyarin, pp. 224–225.
39. Paul de Man, "The Rhetoric of Temporality," p. 203.
40. Walt Whitman, *Notes and Fragments*, ed. R. M. Bucke (1899; rpt. Folcroft Pa.: Folcroft Press, 1972), Part I, p. 27, note 65.
41. *Notes and Fragments*, ed. Bucke, Part IV, p. 170, note 72. In "The Bible as Poetry," Whitman writes this about Hebrew Poetry: "The metaphors daring beyond account, the lawless soul, extravagant by our standards, the glow of love and friendship, the fervent kiss – nothing in argument or logic, but unsurpass'd in proverbs, in religious ecstasy .... faith limitless, its immense sensuousness immensely spiritual ... "; in *November Boughs* (Library of America edition of Whitman, pp. 1140 ff.).
42. See "A Few Drops Known" in *Leaves of Grass*: "A little of Greek and

Roman, a few Hebrew canticles, a few death odors as from graves from Egypt."
43. In fact, recalling Solomon's attributes, we *should* have been alerted to the presence of the Song of Songs by Emerson's letter to Whitman of July 21, 1855, praising *Leaves of Grass* as "the most extraordinary piece of wit & wisdom that America has yet contributed." Emerson's letter is most readily available in the Norton Critical Edition of *Leaves of Grass*, ed. Sculley Bradley and Harold W. Blodgett, pp. 731–32.
44. The 1855 text of "Song of Myself" is cited throughout; for the reader's convenience, section numbers refer to the numbering of later editions.
45. George Burrowes, *A Commentary on The Song of Solomon*, (Philadelphia, 1853; rpt. London, Pennsylvania: The Banner of Truth Trust, 1958), p. 91. A footnote in Ginsburg, p. 100, indicates that the Rev. George Burrowes was Professor in Lafayette College, Easton, Pennsylvania.
46. George Noyes, p. 149.
47. *Notes and Fragments*, ed. Bucke, Part II, p. 55, note 1.
48. Whitman "Preface" in *Complete Poetry and Collected Prose*, p. 11.
49. *Notes and Fragments*, ed. Bucke, Part I, p. 49, note 173.
50. Jon Whitman, "From the *Cosmographia* to the *Divine Comedy*, p. 64.
51. Brian Stock, *Listening for the Text*, p. 41.
52. Cited from Clifton Joseph Furness's Introduction to the facsimile reprint of the first (1855) edition of *Leaves of Grass* (New York: Columbia University Press, 1939), p. viii.
53. *Leaves of Grass*, 1856 edition, "Bunch Poem"; later called, "Spontaneous Me." Compare "Song of the Open Road" (in 1856, Poem of the Road"): "Why are there men and women that while they are nigh me the sunlight expands my blood? / Why when they leave me do my pennants of joy sink flat and lank?" (section 7).
54. Cited in Whitman, *Complete Poetry and Collected Prose*, notes to *Calamus* poems, p. 1356.
55. In the Song of Songs, the Hebrew word for calamus is *queneh*; the same word is used in Exodus 30:23, where calamus is described as one of the "principal spices."
56. For Vendler, the passage from section 24 is Whitman's "unequaled representation of the body, treated in a liturgy of worship. (Each phrase of rendering in this passage is followed by a phrase of ritual veneration, the verbal equivalent of a salaam – 'It shall be you.') Behind this extended imagining of the self, there must lie a long reflection on the body and on its visual and kinesthetic correspondence to the natural world. How to render the pelvis and the shoulder blades? they are 'ledges and rests.' How to render the penis? it is like a plowshare, going ahead into a furrow. How to imagine semen? well, it is milky in appearance, and one could, after all, liken the action of masturbation to the action of stripping a cow's udder of its milk . . . . How to imagine urine? like maple sap trickling from a branch. The scrotum? a nest of two eggs. The penis (in another aspect), so shy and yet so quickly aroused? a 'timorous

pond-snipe.' In his thirties, writing this passage, Whitman, aware of a new relation with his own body – its desires, its shape, its effluents – could find nothing more worthy of worship and of expression." "Body Language: *Leaves of Grass* and the Articulation of Sexual Awareness," *Harper's Magazine*, October, 1986, p. 66.

57. *Notes and Fragments*, ed. Bucke, Part I, p. 40, note 135.
58. Ernst Robert Curtius, *European Literature and the Latin Middle Ages*, trans. Willard R. Trask (Princeton: Princeton University Press [Bollingen] 1953), p. 311.
59. Curtius, p. 314. Curtius's unspoken topos of the phallus as writing implement merges in Whitman's text with the absent topos of the tongue as pen. See, for example, Psalm 45:1: "My tongue is the pen of a ready writer" (AV), given in the Vulgate as, "Lingua mea calamus scribae velociter scribentis."
60. For a modern version of the topos, see Wallace Stevens's early poem, "Ploughing on Sunday."
61. *Notes & Fragments*, ed. Bucke, Part IV, p. 178, note 124.
62. Robert Burns, *Poems and Songs*, ed. James Kinsley (London, New York: Oxford University Press, 1971), poem 69, pp. 101–102. For Whitman on Burns, see, *Notes and Fragments*, Part I, p. 91, note 32:
63. John James Audubon, *The Birds of America* (New York: Macmillan, 1965), plate 253.
64. J. F. Lansdowne with John A. Livingston, *Birds of the Northern Forest* (Toronto, Montreal: McClelland and Stewart, n.d.), plate 14.
65. Jean Starobinski, *Words upon Words: The Anagrams of Ferdinand de Saussure [Les mots sous les mots]*, trans. Olivia Emmet (New Haven and London: Yale University Press, 1979), p. 17.
66. See *Notes & Fragments*, ed. Bucke, Part IV, p. 172, note 84: "ribs – waist – breast-side – back – spine – hips – man-nuts – thig hs – man-balls – man-root – thigh strength." Cf. "I Sing the Body Electric," final version, section 9, 140ff. In a review of the 1856 *Leaves of Grass*, the Boston *Christian Examiner* called it "an ithyphallic audacity that insults what is most sacred and decent among men": cited in Roger Asselineau, *The Evolution of Walt Whitman: The Creation of a Personality* (Cambridge Mass.: Harvard University Press, 1960), Vol. 1, p. 90.
67. See Frederick Ahl, "Ars Est Caelare Artem (Art in Puns and Anagrams Engraved)," in *On Puns: The Foundation of Letters*, ed. Jonathan Culler (Oxford: Basil Blackwell, 1988), p. 31. "We do not regard anagrams as proper figures of speech, and we are less trained to recognize or generate them than to create puns or sophisticated patterns of metrics and rhyme. What we do not do, we tend to assume our predecessors did not do, or were silly to have done. If forced to acknowledge anagrams, we resort to the knee-jerk response that they are not meaningful, or are accidental" (p. 29).

4: Recycling Language: Emily Dickinson's Religious Wordplay

1. Jack L. Capps, *Emily Dickinson's Reading, 1836–1886* (Cambridge, Mass.: Harvard University Press, 1966), p. 116. The most recent review of Dickinson's relation to Emerson is Paul Ferlazzo's "Emily Dickinson," in *The Transcendentalists: A Review of Research and Criticism*, ed. Joel Myerson (New York: MLA, 1984), pp. 320–327.
2. With certain exceptions, citations of Emerson's writings are inserted in parentheses directly into the text. For the convenience of my readers, and to avoid unnecessary clutter, page numbers in parentheses refer to Ralph Waldo Emerson, *Essays & Lectures* (New York: Library of America, 1983).
3. Richard Wilbur, "Sumptuous Destitution," in *Emily Dickinson: A Collection of Critical Essays*, ed. Richard B. Sewall (Englewood Cliffs, N.J.: Prentice-Hall, 1963), p. 161.
4. Glauco Cambon's suggestion that we must find some reference from Dickinson's world "to the other worlds of language, experience, and thought with which it shares at least part of its substance and space" anticipates the nature of this study. By moving back and forth between Dickinson's world and other worlds of language, I work to establish points of reference. In Cambon's words, "No poem is a closed monad"; "Emily Dickinson and the Crisis of Self-Reliance," in *Transcendentalism and its Legacy*, ed. Myron Simon and Thornton H. Parson (Ann Arbor: Univ. Michigan Press, 1966), p. 123.
5. Northrop Frye, *The Great Code: The Bible and Literature* (Toronto: Academic Press, 1982), pp. 6–7.
6. Margaret Schlauch, *Modern English and American Poetry: Techniques and Ideologies* (London: Watts, 1956), p. 30.
7. Kenneth Burke, *The Rhetoric of Religion: Studies in Logology* (Berkeley: University of California Press, 1970), p. 7.
8. I am concerned here with the models of thought behind Emerson's recycling of religious language, not with his "infidelity." Santayana said that "at bottom," Emerson "had no doctrine at all." If "doctrine" means a theoretical system, then neither Emerson nor Dickinson had a doctrine. Both were unsystematic. To read analyses of Emerson's and Dickinson's beliefs is to hear literary criticism echoing itself. Roy Harvey Pearce, for example, says of Dickinson, "In effect she refuses to settle down to a definite theology.... What are God and Immortality to me? She asks again and again.... Trying to answer her own questions, she finds a new answer each time"; *The Continuity of American Poetry*, rev. edn (Princeton: Princeton University Press, 1977), p. 177. Compare Santayana on Emerson: "Every day he said, 'Let there be light,' and every day the light was new. His sun, like that of Heraclitus, was different every morning"; "Emerson," in *Emerson: A Collection of Critical Essays*, ed. Milton R. Konvitz and Stephen E. Whicher (Englewood Cliffs, N. J.: Prentice-Hall, 1962), pp. 31–32. Or see Richard Chase on Dickinson: "In her imaginative life she lived with a loose and contradictory complex of ideas historically akin to Calvinism, Romanticism,

Transcendentalism, Stoicism, Gnosticism, and even revolutionary Futurism"; *Emily Dickinson* (New York: William Sloane, 1951), p. 187. Compare Joseph Warren Beach on Emerson: "His mind was one in which contraries lived happily together in a sort of benign solution"; *The Concept of Nature in Nineteenth-Century English Poetry* (1936; rpt. New York: Pageant, 1956), p. 339.

9. Alexis de Toqueville, *Democracy in America*, ed. Phillips Bradley (1945; rpt. New York: Vintage, n.d.), II, 32–33.

10. Thomas Carlyle, *Sartor Resartus* (1908; rpt. London: Dent, 1956), pp. 194–95. Compare Emerson's *Nature* : "If the stars should appear one night in a thousand years, how would man believe and adore; and preserve for many generations the remembrance of the city of God which had been shown! But every night come out these envoys of beauty, and light the universe with their astonishing smile."

11. *The Letters of Emily Dickinson*, ed. Thomas H. Johnson and Theodora Ward (Cambridge Mass.: Harvard University Press, 1958); hereafter cited by letter number. The couplet, part of letter 280, is numbered 685 in *The Poems of Emily Dickinson Including Variant Readings Critically Compared with All Known Manuscripts*, ed. Thomas H. Johnson (Cambridge Mass.: Harvard University Press, 1955); also cited hereafter by poem number.

12. *The Complete Works of Ralph Waldo Emerson*, ed. Edward Waldo Emerson (Boston: Houghton Mifflin, 1903–4), Centenary Edition, Vol. IX, p. 53.

13. R. W. B. Lewis, *The American Adam : Innocence ,Tragedy and Tradition in the Nineteenth Century* (Chicago: University of Chicago Press, 1955), p. 22.

14. Thoreau, *Walden*, ed. J. Lyndon Shanley (Princeton: Princeton University Press, 1971), p. 88. Among the books presumably marked by Dickinson, now in the Houghton Library at Harvard, is an 1863 edition of *Walden*. She knew what Thoreau was about: in a letter to her Norcross cousins she writes, "The fire-bells are oftener now, almost, than the church-bells. Thoreau would wonder which did the most harm" (letter 691).

15. Lewis, p. 23: "Transcendentalism drew on the vocabularies of European romanticism and Oriental mysticism; but the only available local vocabulary was the one that the hopeful were so anxious to escape from, and a very effective way to discredit its inherited meaning was to serve it up in an unfamiliar context."

16. Thoreau, *Walden*, p. 69. On Thoreau's Wordplay, see Michael West's brilliant "Scatology and Eschatology: The Heroic Dimensions of Thoreau's Wordplay," *PMLA*, 89 (1974), 1043–1064. See also David Skwire, "A Check List of Wordplays in *Walden*," *American Literature*, 31 (1959), 282–289; and also Larzer Ziff, *Literary Democracy: The Declaration of Cultural Independence in America* (New York: Viking, 1981), pp. 204–205. Joseph J. Moldenhauer, in "Emily Dickinson's Ambiguity: Notes on Technique" (which does not touch on the kinds of wordplay I explore), maintains that "Thoreau's ambiguities, however complex, can be resolved by reference to the firm philosophical and ethical assumptions which underlie his entire

argument. Emily Dickinson . . . argues only occasionally and never seeks to proselytize"; *Emerson Society Quarterly*, No. 44 (3rd quarter 1966), p. 37. I disagree with his appraisal of Dickinson, whose wordplay can indeed be resolved by reference to her ethical and religious assumptions.

17. Whitman, "Song of Myself," in *Leaves of Grass: A Textual Variorum of the Printed Poems*, ed. Gay Wilson Allen, Sculley Bradley et al. (New York: New York University Press, 1980), Vol. I, 48, line 790; capitalization is added in the 1860 and later editions.

18. James Joyce, *Stephen Hero*, ed. Theodore Spencer, rev. edn (London: Granada, 1979), p. 188. "He believed that it was for the man of letters to record these epiphanies with extreme care, seeing that they themselves are the most delicate and evanescent of moments."

19. John Hollander, *The Figure of Echo, A Mode of Allusion in Milton and After* (Berkeley: University of California Press, 1981), p. 113.

20. Martin Bickman, "Kora in Heaven: Love and Death in the Poetry of Emily Dickinson," *Emily Dickinson Bulletin* 32 (1977), 100. And see Geoffrey Hartman: "If the Christian poets of the Renaissance wondered how they could use pagan forms and themes, the neo-Puritan writers wonder how they can use the Christian superstitions"; "The Romance of Nature and the Negative Way," in *Romanticism and Consciousness*, ed. Harold Bloom (New York: Norton, 1970), p. 296.

21. I have used the 1883 text of Poem 1068 which Dickinson sent to Thomas Niles, editor of the publishing house of Roberts Brother, as part of letter 813. "Further in Summer" was incorporated in the letter preceding the poet's signature and represents, to my mind, her final authorial intent. Why Johnson chose for the *Complete Poems* the 1866 version (which Dickinson enclosed in letter 314 to Higginson) is not clear. In his *Emily Dickinson's Poetry: Stairway of Surprise* (New York: Holt, Rinehart and Winston, 1960), pp. 150–151, Charles R. Anderson uses the late version of the poem also.

22. From the time she was fourteen, Dickinson used the 1844 edition of Webster's *American Dictionary of the English Language*. See Willis J. Buckingham, "Emily Dickinson's Dictionary," *Harvard Literary Bulletin*, 25, (1977), 489–92. Throughout this chapter I use the 1828 edition in the new facsimile reprint. The 1844 edition is essentially the same but contains several thousand additional words added in 1841 and in 1844.

23. Charles R. Anderson glossed the liturgical language years ago; moreover he noted the crickets' "pre-Christian nature rite whose meaning is lost in the dim past," pp. 151–52. My point here is that these words (as well as other words and phrases that Anderson mentions) have both a secular and a sacred connotation; that both meanings appear in the poet's dictionary; and that words like "Ordinance" and "Grace" retain their Christian meaning even when associated with pre-Christian rites. When two meanings are packed into one word, as I have said, we have a pun, a cunning ploy to reclaim the rhetoric of religion for secular use. The obvious pun on "Mass" forces the reader first to acknowledge the doubleness that runs throughout

24. the poem, then to question it. Ultimately, the reader and Dickinson may question the whole idea of set-apartness, of supernaturalism as opposed to natural supernaturalism, of exclusivity and hierarchies.
24. Frye writes, "the chief difference between sophisticated and naive irony is that the naive ironist calls attention to the fact that he is being ironic, whereas sophisticated irony merely states and lets the reader add the ironic tone himself"; *The Anatomy of Criticism: Four Essays* (1957; rpt. Princeton: Princeton University Press, 1973), p. 41. One of the challenges of reading Dickinson, Margaret Homans says, is that "it is often very difficult to know when she is being ironic and when we are to take her at her word, and often she seems to have contrived this difficulty"; *Women Writers and Poetic Identity: Dorothy Wordsworth, Emily Brontë, and Emily Dickinson* (Princeton: Princeton University Press, 1980), p. 177.
25. Cited in Elizabeth Sewell, *The Field of Nonsense* (London: Chatto and Windus, 1952), p. 178.
26. Gelpi, *The Tenth Muse: The Psyche of the American Poet* (Cambridge, Mass. and London: Harvard University Press, 1975), p. 178.
27. No published explication of poem 239 points out its pervasive Miltonic echoes, nor does anyone suggest that Dickinson is making an etymological pun on "spurned." If *Paradise Lost*, specifically Book IX, is Dickinson's subtext, as I suggest, what is it doing beneath her poem?
28. See Byron's extended Gilt/Guilt pun in *Don Juan*, II, 127; and also Lady Macbeth: "I'll gild the faces of the grooms withal,/For it must seem their guilt" (*Macbeth* II.ii.55–56).
29. Walter Ong, "Wit and Mystery: A Revaluation of Medieval Latin Hymnody," *Speculum*, 22 (1947), 315, 312; cited by Maureen Quilligan, *The Language of Allegory: Defining the Genre* (Ithaca and London: Cornell University Press, 1979), pp. 161–62, p. 297.
30. See, for example, Herbert's "The Sonne": "How neatly doe we give one onely name/To parents issue and the sunnes bright star !/A sonne is light and fruit; a fruitfull flame/Chasing the father's dimnesse . . . " (lines 58–61).
31. In the packet copy of Poem 324, "God" is in quotation marks. I use the text enclosed in a letter to Higginson of July 1862. The packet copy dates from no later than 1860. At one point "Surplice" was spelt "Surplus"; the words share a column in Dickinson's lexicon. Again, no one has discussed this pun or, indeed, focussed on the kinds of religious wordplay examined here. George Frisbie Whicher, for example, writes, "The doctrinal sermons that she heard in girlhood did little more than give her a theological vocabulary, so that when she used such technical terms as *predestination, justification, election,* and *grace* in her poems, she used them understandingly, albeit sometimes with a mischievous twist"; *This Was a Poet: A Critical Biography of Emily Dickinson* (1938; rpt. Archon Books, 1980), p. 162. Surely we are dealing with more than the mischievous twists of a naughty girl. Charles Anderson's chapter on Dickinson's wit is especially fine, pp. 3–29.

32. *The Canterbury Tales* in *The Works of Geoffrey Chaucer*, ed. F. N. Robinson, second edition (Boston: Houghton Mifflin Company, 1957).
33. The Surplice/Surplice model of wordplay, as well as my interpretation of it, may help to unravel Dickinson's Poem 724, "It's easy to invent a Life," with its chilling, unspoken Gambol/Gamble pun. "The dice of God are always loaded," says Emerson, revising Sophocles (289).
34. Hollander, *The Figure of Echo*, p. 141. I cannot find a discussion of Dickinson's technique of substitution anywhere, yet it runs throughout the poetry. Here are some obvious examples: "The Sweeping up the Heart/And putting Love away" (Poem 1078) – one normally sweeps up the Hearth; "And then he drank a Dew/From a convenient Grass" (328) – one normally drinks from a Glass.
35. Rich, "Vesuvius at Home: The Power of Emily Dickinson," in *Critical Essays on Emily Dickinson*, ed. Paul Ferlazzo (Boston: G.K. Hall, 1984), p. 181.
36. See Philip Wheelwright, *Metaphor and Reality* (Bloomington: Indiana University Press, 1968), p. 59: "The phenomenon of plurisignation has been recognized under various names by critics generally, but sometimes it has been defined inaccurately. Robert Bridges has gone to the length of declaring that all the particulars denoted by a word are brought into play in a poem." In this study I avoid the word "ambiguity," particularly in the case of puns. Elizabeth Sewell, in *The Field of Nonsense*, p. 36, declares: "A pun is not simple but it is not ambiguous. It is of the very nature of the pun that its meanings are separate, and are therefore still within the mind's control."
37. "Song of Myself," 844.
38. For Dickinson's consolatory allusions to Isaiah 53 see letters 564, 875, 932. See also prose fragment 20, which alludes to Dickinson's father: "Acquainted with Grief through Father's dying it grieves me (us) that neighbours so thoughtful of us must make its acquaintance." Compare "He is despised and rejected of men; a man of sorrows, and acquainted with grief" (Isa. 53:3).
39. Sewall, *The Life of Emily Dickinson* (New York: Farrar, Straus Giroux, 1974), I, 24: "The revival spirit ... was very much alive in Emily Dickinson's time and caused her anguish. No fewer than eight revivals swept Amherst ... during her formative years, roughly between 1840 and 1862. She could never see herself as a sinner in the hands of an angry God. She could never testify, as so many of her pious friends did, to that direct visitation of the spirit which was essential to membership in the church." See also Dickinson's letter 35 to Jane Humphrey (1850): "Christ is calling everyone here, all my companions have answered, even my darling Vinnie believes she loves, and trusts him, and I am standing alone in rebellion, and growing very careless." Readers interested in Dickinson's relationship to Christian ritual and its historical background in New England may consult Rowena Revis Jones, "'A Royal Seal': Emily Dickinson's Rite of Baptism," in

Religion and Literature 18 (1986), 29–51, with its useful endnotes. The author's conclusions are essentially mine: "Viewed from an overall perspective, Dickinson emerges a poet of doubt, critical of the traditional doctrines of Congregational orthodoxy"; "Her final stance is that of the 'inspired perceiver' who in the last analysis has substituted her personal identity for an external covenant and imposed her own patterns upon the received traditions of New England"; p. 46.

40. Frank, "Some Uses of Paronomasia in Old English Scriptural Verse," *Speculum*, 47 (1972), 212. I am indebted to my colleague Roberta Frank for sending me this provocative study.

41. *The Complete Works of Ralph Waldo Emerson*, ed. Edward Waldo Emerson (Boston: Houghton Mifflin, 1903–4), IX, 126.

42. From the late essay "Poetry and Imagination," *The Complete Works of Ralph Waldo Emerson*, ed. Edward Waldo Emerson, Vol. VIII, 35. Observing that Dickinson's poetry was "almost wholly instinctive," F. O. Matthiessen wrote, "it should never be forgotten that Emerson was the great figure in her foreground, and that her conception of poetic language, of how 'the word becomes one with the thing' in the moment of inspired vision, was basically his"; "The Private Poet: Emily Dickinson," *Kenyon Review*, 7 (1945), 593–594; rpt. *The Recognition of Emily Dickinson*, ed. Caesar R. Blake and Carlton F. Wells (Ann Arbor: Univ. of Michigan Press, 1968), p. 232.

43. Compare Dickinson's first letter to Higginson, letter 260: "Are you too deeply occupied to say if my Verse is alive? . . . Should you think it breathed – and had you the leisure to tell me, I should feel quick gratitude."

44. Christopher Ricks observes that "with the Fall of Man, language falls too"; in *Milton's Grand Style* (Oxford: Oxford University Press, 1963), p. 109.

45. Maureen Quilligan, following Michel Foucault, notes "the fundamental importance of words that not only designated but were the origins of essences . . . . In the *Cratylus* Plato had argued that reasoning by etymology was inferior to dialectic, but the Middle Ages appear to have forgotten the lesson; it was not unusual for men to contemplate the etymology of a beast's name and that name's synonyms along with the beast's habitat, methods of movement, and reproduction . . . as equally valid bits of information for understanding its essential being" (*The Language of Allegory* pp. 158–59).

5: Robert Frost: The Design of Violence

1. *Natural Theology*, in *The Works of William Paley* (Philadelphia: Crissy and Markley, 1857), p. 387.
2. *Natural Theology*, pp. 388–89.
3. *Paradise Lost*, ed. Scott Elledge (New York and London: Norton,

1975). Book and line numbers in parentheses following Milton's text refer to this edition.
4. Ralph Waldo Emerson, "Compensation," in *The Collected Works of Ralph Waldo Emerson*, ed. Alfred R. Ferguson et al., Vol. I (Cambridge Mass.: Harvard University Press, 1979), p. 63.
5. Michael Edwards, *Towards a Christian Poetics* (London: Macmillan, 1984), p. 154. Beckett's quip, cited by Edwards, comes from *Murphy*.
6. Christopher Ricks, "Robert Lowell: 'The War of Words,'" in *The Force of Poetry* (Oxford and New York: Oxford University Press, 1987), p. 265.
7. Page numbers in parentheses following Girard's text refer to *Things Hidden since the Foundation of the World*, trans. Stephen Bann and Michael Metteer (Stanford: Stanford University Press, 1987). The English translation includes Girard's revisions to the original French text, *Des Choses cachées depuis la fondation du monde* (Paris: Grasset, 1978).
8. René Girard, *Violence and the Sacred*, trans. Patrick Gregory (Baltimore and London: The Johns Hopkins Univerity Press, 1977), p. 37. The original French text, *La Violence et le sacré*, was first published in 1972.
9. *Violence and the Sacred*, p. 2.
10. See *Things Hidden* . . . , passim; and also *Violence and the Sacred*, p. 148: "*Mimetic desire* is simply a term more comprehensive than *violence* for religious pollution."
11. "In White" was sent by Frost in a letter to Susan Hayes Ward on January 15, 1912; see *Selected Letters of Robert Frost*, ed. Lawrance Thompson (New York: Holt, Rinehart and Winston, 1964), pp. 44–45. The original text of the poem is reprinted in *The Early Years 1874–1915*, Volume I of Lawrance Thompson's three volume biography of Frost (1966), p. 582; and also in Richard Poirier's *Robert Frost: The Work of Knowing* (Oxford and New York: Oxford University Press, 1977), pp. 248–49. "Design," the final version of "In White," was published in *American Poetry, 1922, A Miscellany*, and appeared fourteen years later in Frost's *A Further Range*, 1936. Why Frost ignored "Design" from 1922 to 1936 (years in which he published two volumes of poetry), is apparently a mystery: see Poirier, p. 255.
12. *The Poetry of Robert Frost*, ed. Edward Connery Lathem (New York: Holt, Rinehart and Winston, 1969), p. 302.
13. Trilling's controversial speech, given at Frost's eightieth birthday dinner, was published as "A Speech on Robert Frost: A Cultural Episode," *Partisan Review* 26 (1959), 445–52.
14. Although Frost and critics of Frost (including the present one) have assumed that the white heal-all is an albino that ought to be blue, perhaps we are all mistaken. In England, at any rate, there is another member of the genus, the *Prunella laciniate*, "a rare plant with cream flowers which occurs on chalk grassland," according to J. G. Barton's *Wild Flowers* (London: Spring Books, 1963).

15. See John Hollander's important discussion of "the x of y" construction in English, which "can be either a genitive or a partitive construction. In the first instance it may or may not be plain (e.g. 'the middle of the night' but 'the hand of God'); in the second it is metonymic or synecdochic, doing the work of a compound in Greek or German. Historically, the decision of the Jacobean Bible translators to use 'the x of – ' for the Hebrew construct state may have had great rhetorical consequences for English . . . . And thus with a resonant phrase like 'stagger-wine' of the Psalmist, alluding to its intoxicating strength; in the King James Bible it becomes 'the wine of astonishment,' and the necessary metonymy then works to personify Astonishment (a witch who lives on the shady side of the mountains? Is her wine dark? How is she related to Desire, to Repose? to Violence . . . ?) This kind of construction inhabits a domain where trope lives as secret an existence under the legitimate cover of the literal as it does in the land of Etymology": in Hollander's Introduction to Harold Bloom, *Poetics of Influence*, ed. John Hollander (New Haven: Henry R. Schwab, 1988), xxxviii. See also Hollander's thoughtful essay "Psalms": "It would be many years before I knew both enough Hebrew and enough about English to understand that the KJV's peculiar way of translating the Hebrew construction led to all sorts of latent allegorizing. The paths of righteousness, what were they? Were they the paths that led to a place – alas, somewhat distant – called Righteousness? Were they the paths someone called Righteousness used to take striding along on business or taking his ease . . . ?": In *Congregation: Contemporary Writers Read the Hebrew Bible*, ed. David Rosenberg (San Diego, New York: Harcourt, Brace, 1987), p. 296.
16. Herman Melville, *Moby-Dick or The Whale* (Library of America, 1983) pp. 993–1001. See also the compacted line of Wilfred Owen"s "Anthem for Doomed Youth": "The pallor of girls' brows shall be their pall." For Emily Dickinson, the mortician is "the man/Of the Appalling Trade" (Poem 389): death is an appalling trade in a number of senses.
17. Edwards, *Towards a Christian Poetics*, p. 219.
18. René Girard, *The Scapegoat*, trans. Yvonne Freccero (London: Athlone, 1986), p. 166.
19. Girard: "Violence is the enslavement of a pervasive lie; it imposes upon men a falsified vision not only of God but also of everything else. And that is indeed why it is a closed kingdom. Escaping from violence is escaping from this kingdom into another kingdom, whose existence the majority of people do not even suspect. This is the Kingdom of love . . . (197).
20. Walter Ong, "Wit and Mystery: A Revaluation of Medieval Latin Hymnody," *Speculum*, 22 (1947), 315. For a discussion of puns that get along, see the foregoing chapter on Emily Dickinson's Religious Wordplay.
21. See Philippe Sollers: "The [religious] institution is there to channel this crisis of doubles, the access to the Other for everyone. But if the

institution no longer holds, it is the murderous unleashing without pause of Egos, the great waltz of the equal sign taken to its climax. The sacrificial round becomes "infernal," our century known this and is dying of it, essentially, everywhere": "Is God Dead? "The Purloined Letter of the Gospel," trans. Robert Postawko, in *To Honor René Girard*, Stanford French and English Studies, XXXIV (Saratoga, Calif.: Anma Libri, 1986), p. 196.

Revising the present study, I came across John Leonard's *Naming in Paradise: Milton and the Language of Adam and Eve* (Oxford: Clarendon, 1990). Pointing to R. A. Shoaf's *Milton: Poet of Duality* (Yale, 1985) with its "talk of a 'free play of signification' and 'the arbitrariness of the sign,'" Leonard contends that Shoaf's "own prompt recourse to such ready-made terminology allows him too little freedom. It is a hollow celebration of 'free play' which always falls into obedient and predictable line. There is such a thing as 'free play'; but play may be organized as well as free, and freedom need not exclude responsibility" (p. 9).

6: Understanding Understatement: Biblical Typology and "The Displaced Person"

1. Northrop Frye, *The Great Code: The Bible and Literature* (Toronto: Academic Press, 1982), p. 80.
2. *The Great Code*, p. 79.
3. Erich Auerbach, "'Figura,'" trans. Ralph Manheim, *Scenes from the Drama of European Literature* (Minneapolis: University of Minnesota Press, 1984), p. 30.
4. Joseph A. Galdon, *Typology and Seventeenth-Century Literature* (The Hague, Paris: Mouton, 1975), p. 23.
5. Auerbach, "Figura," p. 29.
6. Flannery O'Connor, *The Habit of Being*, ed. Sally Fitzgerald (New York: Vintage, 1979), p. 118.
7. Mariella Gable, "The Ecumenic Core in Flannery O'Connor's Fiction," *American Benedictine Review* 15:2 (June 1964), 129.
8. Joel Wells, "Off the Cuff," in *Conversations with Flannery O'Connor*, ed. Rosemary M. Magee (Jackson: University Press of Mississippi, 1987), p. 87.
9. *The Great Code*, p. 78.
10. Jean Daniélou, *From Shadows to Reality: Studies in Biblical Typology of the Fathers* (London: Burns & Oates, 1960), p. 61. (Translation of *Sacramentum Futuri: Études sur les Origines de la Typologie biblique*).
11. Auerbach, "St. Francis of Assisi in Dante's 'Commedia,'" trans. Catherine Garvin, *Scenes from the Drama of European Literature*, p. 97. Cf. Auerbach's *Mimesis: The Representation of Reality in Western Literature*, trans. Willard Trask (1953; rpt. Princeton: Princeton University Press, 1974), p. 73.
12. Auerbach, *Mimesis*, 195–196.

13. Beryl Smalley, *The Study of the Bible in the Middle Ages*, second revised edn (Oxford: Basil Blackwell, 1952), pp. 6–7.
14. *The Great Code*, p. 226.
15. *The Great Code*, p. 80.
16. *The Great Code*, p. 92.
17. Page numbers in parentheses following quotations from "The Displaced Person" refer to Flannery O'Connor, *The Complete Stories* (1971; New York: Farrar, Straus and Giroux, 1987).
18. *The Habit of Being*, p. 92.
19. In a passage from Teilhard de Chardin's *Le Milieu Divin*, marked by O'Connor, he writes: "In fact, from the beginning of the Messianic preparation, up till the Parousia, passing through the historical manifestation of Jesus and the phases of growth of His Church, a single event has been developing in the world: the Incarnation, realised, in each individual, through the Eucharist"; noted in Arthur F. Kinney, *Flannery O'Connor's Library: Resources of Being* (Athens: University of Georgia Press, 1985), p. 33.
20. *The Habit of Being*, p. 227.
21. Unless otherwise noted, the Bible is cited from the Authorized Version.
22. "Figura," pp. 50–51. See Frank Kermode on the joining of the Old and New Testaments: "This joining, which occurred late in the second century, was of a kind that permitted Christian interpreters to assume that the more obvious sense of the Old Testament, including its historical meaning, were of small or no importance, were dangerous illusions, even. The Old Testament made sense only insofar as it prefigured Christianity. The rest of it – a great deal – was deafness, blindness, forgetfulness"; *The Genesis of Secrecy: On the Interpretation of Narrative* (Cambridge, Mass. and London: Harvard University Press, 1979), p. 18.
23. "Figura," p. 40.
24. Robert Fitzgerald, "The Countryside and the True Country," *Sewanee Review* 70 (1962), 388.
25. It is precisely the confusion of methodology with claim – according to Jonathan Arac at least – that underlies Harold Bloom's disagreement and break with Frye: "Since Frye had begun our whole current attention to 'reading' by defining the key to Blake as his reading of the Bible . . . this disagreement was fundamental," Arac writes. "Bloom could not accept Blake's [or Frye's] Christian understanding of the so-called 'New Testament' as completing and purifying the 'Old Testament' . . . . From this refusal followed the general impossibility of 'fulfillment' in literary tradition, the recognition that fulfillment involved insidious judgments, that Frye's criticism depended on decisively evaluating the relation of the Hebrew Bible to the Christian Bible. Thus Frye proved a canonizer, another Matthew Arnold," *Critical Genealogies: Historical Situations for Postmodern Literary Studies* (New York: Columbia Univerity Press, 1987), p. 20.
26. *Mimesis*, p. 158.

27. *The Great Code*, p. 160.
28. *From Shadows to Reality*, p. 88.
29. *From Shadows to Reality*, p. 101.
30. What O'Connor called "the short version" of "The Displaced Person" appeared in *The Sewanee Review* 62 (1954) 634–54. It was accepted for publication in March, 1954. On November 15, 1954, O'Connor wrote to her editor Robert Giroux, explaining that the manuscript of *A Good Man is Hard to Find* included "only the long version [the three-part version] of 'The Displaced Person' but if you don't like it, we can substitute the short one" [published in *SR*]. On December 6, 1954 O'Connor sent Giroux "a new first page" for "The Displaced Person" (*The Habit of Being*, pp. 72–73). See Roy R. Male, "The Two Versions of 'The Displaced Person,'" *Studies in Short Fiction* 7 (1970), 450–457.
31. For O'Connor, scripture was *Heilsgeschichte*, the true history of salvation. Those interested in O'Connor's religious convictions should consult Sr. Mariella Gable's "Ecumenic Core in Flannery O'Connor's Fiction." In a tribute to O'Connor published after her death, Sr. Mariella reports: "Though she was only a month away from death, she exerted herself to tell me that my article . . . came nearer the truth about her writing than any other criticism. With characteristic humility she said, 'I shall learn from it myself and save my breath by referring other people to it'" (*Esprit* [University of Scranton, Scranton PA] Vol. 8, No 1 [Winter 1964], 26).
32. And for slave ships. The present chapter does not address this aspect of the story directly. O'Connor alludes to the slave trade – the forced Exodus of the Blacks from Africa – in the pointed exchange between Mr. Shortley and Sulk: "'Well, if you behave yourself it isn't any reason you can't stay here,' Mr. Shortley said kindly. 'Because you didn't run away from nowhere. Your granddaddy was bought. He didn't have a thing to do with coming. It's the people that run away from where they come from that I ain't got no use for'" (232).
33. Noted in *Flannery O'Connor's Library*, p. 47.
34. *The Great Code*, p. 145.
35. Sr. M. Bernetta Quinn identified Mrs Shortley as a false prophet years ago, "Flannery O'Connor, a Realist of Distances," in *The Added Dimension: The Art and Mind of Flannery O'Connor*, 2nd edition rev., ed. Melvin J. Friedman and Lewis A Lawson (New York: Fordham University Press, 1977), p. 169. Sr. Kathleen Feeley calls the vision "a comic parody of the warnings of the Old Testament prophets," *Flannery O'Connor: Voice of the Peacock* (New Brunswick N.J.: Rutgers University Press, 1972), p. 174; Sr. M. Joselyn calls it "pseudo-apocalyptic," in "Thematic Centers in 'The Displaced Person,'" *Studies in Short Fiction* 1 (1964), 89. Frederick Asals remarks that Mrs. Shortley's "Sunday afternoon revelation comes out of a suspicious matrix of recollections of newsreels of concentration camps, dark distrust of things foreign and Catholic, studies of the Bible that assure her of her importance of the divine plan," in *Flannery O'Connor: The Imagination of Extremity* (Athens: University

of Georgia Press, 1982), p. 208. Unless the reader identifies the "gigantic figure" on the "stage" as a perversion of the divine tetragrammaton of the Old Testament, he/she misses the point: following her "vision," Mrs Shortley sees the "distinguished person" on the "dirty calendar" holding up his marvellous arcanum. In fact that person is both avatar and counterpart of the "gigantic figure" she sees in the so-called "vision"; both figures are tricksters.

36. "The Countryside and the True Country," 389.
37. *From Shadows to Reality*, p. 259.
38. *From Shadows to Reality*, p. 248.
39. *From Shadows to Reality*, p. 247.
40. *Sewanee Review* 62 (1954), 634.
41. *The Habit of Being*, p. 130.
42. What critics of Hawthorne and Melville and Faulkner and O'Connor, just to mention American authors, call "Christ figures," even "transfigurations of Christ," is, to my mind at least, a misuse of critical terms and a parody of typology: an *imitatio Christi* is not a "figure." In a reading of *The Faerie Queen*, for example, as Rosemond Tuve observes, "Typology is not needed to understand the most important ways in which Red Crosse 'becomes' or 'takes on' Christ.... Types properly precede the figure that fulfills them, Moses before Christ. Only a divine Author can so write history that the types foreshadow the revelation of pure truth in another historical occurrence...": *Allegorical Imagery: Some Medieval Books and Their Posterity* (Princeton: Princeton University Press, 1966), p. 47. I refer the interested reader to Edwin M. Moseley, *Pseudonyms of Christ in the Modern Novel: Motifs and Methods*, Pittsburgh: University of Pittsburg Press, 1962. Moseley's study moves almost entire into Theodore Ziolkowski's *Fictional Transfigurations of Jesus* (Princeton: Princeton University Press, 1972). Ziolkowski's rationalism leads him to the following: "Figural thinking developed only after his [Christ's] death, and notably in the later Gospels... *for propagandist purposes*" (51; italics added).
43. So well disguised that, so far as I know, no published reading of "The Displaced Person" discloses it.
44. See Rosemary Woolf's discussions of the Isaac/Christ typology in *The English Mystery Plays* (London: Routledge & Kegan Paul, 1972), pp. 145–52; and in "The Effect of Typology on the English Mediaeval Plays of Abraham and Isaac," *Speculum* 32 (1957), 805–825.
45. *From Shadows to Reality*, p. 120.
46. K. J. Woollcombe, "The Biblical Origins and Patristic Development of Typology," in G. W. H. Lampe and K. J. Woollcombe, *Essays on Typology* (London: SCM, 1957), p. 73; Galdon, *Typology and Seventeenth-Century Literature*, p. 41.
47. *From Shadows to Reality*, pp. 128–30.
48. *The Habit of Being*, pp. 365–66.
49. *The Great Code*, pp. 80–81.

7: His Dazzling Absence: The Shekinah in Jonathan Edwards

1. For each citation from Edwards's *Work of Redemption* I give two page numbers. The first number refers to Jonathan Edwards, *A History of the Work of Redemption* (short title, *Work of Redemption*) in *The Works of Jonathan Edwards*, edited by Edward Hickman (London: William Ball, 1837), Vol. 1. The second number refers to *A History of the Work of Redemption*, transcribed and edited by John F. Wilson, in *The Works of Jonathan Edwards*, Vol. 9 (New Haven and London: Yale University Press, 1989). I use the 1837 Hickman edition throughout, and cite the Yale edition for the convenience of my readers.

2. Jerusalem Talmud *Ta'anith* 65a; Babylonian Talmud *Yoma* 21 a; 52b; 9b. To cite the entry on *Shekinah* in Hastings's *Encyclopedia of Religion and Ethics* (Vol. 11): "The Rabbis affirm that the Shekinah first presided in the Tabernacle prepared in the wilderness by Moses, into which it descended on the day of its consecration, into the figure of a cloud." The imagined absence of the Shekinah is based upon the Rabbis' interpretation of Haggai 1:8. See also the Introduction to Lamentations Rabbah XXIV: "No sooner was the Temple burnt than the Holy One (blessed be He) said: Now will I withdraw my Schechinah from it and I will go up to my former habitation." Cited in J. Abelson, *Jewish Mysticism* (London: G. Bell and Sons, 1913), p. 69.

3. Writing on Edwards's *Work of Redemption*, several scholars have discussed his use of biblical typology; see, for example, John F. Wilson, "Jonathan Edwards as Historian," *Church History* 46 (March 1977) 5–18. None of the studies I have seen, however, takes any notice of Edwards's Shekinah-Christ typology.

4. Herman Melville, *Mardi*, ed. Harrison Hayford *et al.* (Evanston and Chicago: Northwestern/Newberry, 1970), p. 636. The word "Shekinah" appears in *Clarel* (IV. ix. 47) and also in Melville's "In the Desert." (Under *Shekinah* in the *OED* there is no citation from Melville's writings.) See also Henry Rowlands, *Mona Antiqua Restaurata* (1723): "it seems to me that god in those antient Times, before he determin'd his *Schekinah* and Divine Presence into the Mosaick Tabernacles and the *Jewish* Temple, had his sacred places in several parts of these Countries ... "; cited in Vincent Arthur De Luca, *Words of Eternity: Blake and the Poetics of the Sublime* (Princeton: Princeton University Press, 1991), pp. 183–184.

5. The *OED* cites the first line of Wesley's hymn – "Arise my Soul Arise" – but not its title. Verse 6 of "Hymn on the Titles of Christ" reads: "Our eyes on earth survey/The Dazzling *Shechinah*!/Bright, in endless glory bright, / Now on earth He stoops to dwell,/God of God, and Light of Light,/Image of the Invisible." Verse 7 begins: "He shines on earth adored,/The *Presence of the Lord*." According to my colleague Dr. Margaret Procter, who kindly provided me with the complete text of Wesley's hymn, verse 6 is almost always omitted from modern hymn books. *The Poetical Works of John and Charles Wesley*, Vol. 1, collected and arranged by G. Osborn (London,

1868), pp. 146–48.
6. *Biblia Sacra Polyglotta*, ed. Brian Walton, London MDC.LVII; "Paraph. Chald. cum Versione Latina."
7. John Bowker, *The Targums and Rabbinic Literature: An Introduction to Jewish Interpretations of Scripture* (Cambridge: Cambridge University Press 1969), p. 3. Readers wishing to consult the Targums might note that the publishers T & T Clark (Edinburgh) have announced the publication of *The Aramaic Bible: The Targums*.
8. Bowker, *The Targums and Rabbinic Literature*, p. x.
9. J. Abelson, *The Immanence of God in Rabbinical Literature* (London: Macmillan, 1912), p. 78.
10. A note of gratitude: the present study was both inspired and informed by a course in post-biblical Judaism given by Dr. Robert Hayward of the Department of Theology, University of Durham. Without his command of Hebrew, Aramaic, and Greek, and without his guidance in matters of Scripture, Targum, Talmud, the Apocrypha, and Christian doctrine, this chapter would lack whatever scholarly merit it may be found to possess. "Two that sit together and are occupied in words of the Torah have the Shekinah among them" (Pirque Aboth iii:3). For the translations of the Aramaic Targums, and for the translations and transliterations from the Hebrew Bible, I am entirely indebted to Dr. Hayward. Quotations from the Bible and from the Apocrypha are cited according to the Authorized or King James Version (used by Edwards), unless the sense of the passage demands the Revised Standard Version (RSV).
11. Abelson, *The Immanence of God in Rabbinical Literature*, p. 79. According to Robert Hayward, A. M. Goldberg "argues that the term [Shekinah] originated in the attempt to explain God's dwelling both in heaven and in the Temple, and that its most primitive usage is confined to the representation of the local presence of God (*Localbezug*). Later the Shekinah came to be used as the subject of revelation and manifestation, without reference to place": Robert Hayward, *Divine Name and Presence: The Memra* (New Jersey: Allanheld, Osmun, 1981), p. 112, note 17 (Publications of the Oxford Centre for Postgraduate Hebrew Studies).
12. *Encyclopedia Judaica*, entry on *Shekinah*.
13. A passage from Blau's most valuable entry on *Shekinah* in the *Jewish Encyclopedia* (1905) is here paraphrased.
14. Hayward, *Divine Name and Presence*, p. 5.
15. See the entry on *Shekinah* in Hastings's *Dictionary of the Bible* (1902): "Under the conception that 'God is Light,' the Shekinah is God's mere 'manifestation form.'"
16. It cannot be unimportant that St. Paul refers to the body as "our earthly house of this tabernacle" [*skenous*] (2 Cor. 5:1), adding, "we that are in this tabernacle [*skenei*] do groan" (5:4).
17. This and the quotation following are taken from the nine-volume *Theological Dictionary of the New Testament*, ed. Gerhard Kittel and Gerhard Friedrich (Michigan: William B. Eerdmans, 1964–74). See the extended entries under *doxa* (and its cognates) and under *skene*.

18. Abelson, *The Immanence of God in Rabbinical Literature*, p. 81.
19. Hastings's *Dictionary of the Bible*, under *Shekinah*.
20. The phrase is taken from Abelson's entry on Jewish mysticism in Hastings's *Encyclopedia of Religion and Ethics* (1917). The entry can be found under "Mysticism."

    See also Arthur Michael Ramsey's *The Glory of God and the Transfiguration of Christ* (London: Longmans, Green, 1949): "The Shekinah is not the glory . . . . Nor is the Shekinah a personal or hypostatic intermediary with attributes and functions. Rather is it a way of speaking about God such as conveys the truth of His omnipresence, accessibility and special activity within the created world without infringing the doctrine of His transcendence" (19).
21. From Blau's entry on *Shekinah* in the *Jewish Encyclopedia* (1905). He adds: "Thus according to Luke ii.9 the "glory of the Lord" [*doxa Kyrios*] shone round about them." To the passage from Luke, Blau compares, 2 Peter 1:17; Ephesians 1:6; 2 Corinthians 4:6.
22. Abelson, *Jewish Mysticism*, p. 45.
23. According to A. M. Ramsey's *The Glory of God and the Transfiguration of Christ*, several passages in the New Testament "seem to contain an identification of Christ with the glory or Shekinah." One such passage, Ramsey says, is James 2:1, of which J. B. Mayor "urged that the proper translation is 'our Lord Jesus Christ, the glory': Christ is Himself the Shekinah in the midst of the congregation, and they must not confound their faith in His presence among them with snobbish thoughts and actions. This interpretation makes good sense," according to Ramsey, "and it fits the Greek better than the others" (pp. 148–49).
24. C. H. Dodd *The Interpretation of the Fourth Gospel* (1953; rpt. Cambridge: Cambridge University Press, 1988), pp. 206–207. Interpolations in square brackets are mine.
25. For each citation from *End of Creation* I give two page numbers. The first number refers to Jonathan Edwards, *Concerning the End for which God Created the World* (Short title, *End of Creation*) in *The Works of Jonathan Edwards*, edited by Edward Hickman (London: William Ball, 1837), Vol. 1. The second number refers to *Concerning the End for which God Created the World*, in *Ethical Writings*, ed. Paul Ramsey, *The Works of Jonathan Edwards*, Vol. 8 (New Haven and London: Yale University Press, 1989). I use the 1837 Hickman edition throughout, and cite the Yale edition for the convenience of my readers.
26. Perry Miller, "From Edwards to Emerson," in *Errand into the Wilderness* (Harper Torchbooks, 1956), p. 194. To cite (approvingly) Stephen J. Stein: "Miller's discomfort with Reformed orthodoxy and his personal inclination toward the naturalism of the Enlightenment blinded him to certain traditional theological patterns. He wrenched Edwards out of context, ignoring the primary commitments the latter had made to Reformed dogmatics, scriptural interpretation, and the collective experience of the faithful. Instead, he attempted to create an image of the New England minister that could inspire 'a generation facing an anxious future' at the middle of the twentieth

century. Miller succeeded in that objective, perhaps even beyond his own expectations, but at considerable cost to the accuracy of his portrait. The Edwards emerging from his pages is a modern intellectual hero . . . . " In Stein's view, "Miller, Ola Winslow, and other interpreters were altogether uncomfortable with Edwards's theology – in large part . . . because they misunderstood it." In Stein's Foreword to Conrad Cherry, *The Theology of Jonathan Edwards: A Reappraisal* (Bloomington and Indianapolis: Indiana University Press, 1990), pp. xi, xxiii.

Convinced that "Edwards was first and last a Calvinist theologian," Conrad Cherry alludes to those who "still feel uncomfortable with Edwards's Calvinism. To alleviate the pain of embarrassment, features of Edwards's thought are frequently searched out which 'transcend' his Calvinism or which prefigure the post-Puritan era of American thought" (p. 6, p. 2). In his Introduction to Edwards's *Ethical Writings*, Paul Ramsey reminds us: "it is a grave error . . . to separate Edwards's philosophy from his theology" (p. 11).

27. The marvellous phrase appears in A. H. Armstrong and R. A. Markus, *Christian Faith and Greek Philosophy* (London: Darton, Longman & Todd, 1960), p. 4. Cf. Perry Miller's *Jonathan Edwards* (1949; rpt. Delta, American Men of Letters Series, n.d.): "In one sense Edwards was . . . so much a materialist that he could join hands with Spinoza" (p. 188).

28. See Edwards's allusions to Maccabees in *Work of Redemption*, Sermon Twelve. To cite John F. Wilson's footnote to the relevant passage: "Much of the material in this section refers to events described in the apocryphal books of I and II Maccabees. Although JE would have viewed these books as noncanonical, he took them to be historically reliable" (274n, Yale edn).

29. Frederick Copleston, *History of Philosophy*, Vol. 2, p. 117. In an explanatory footnote to *End of Creation*, Paul Ramsey writes: "The word *emanation* . . . is in the context of communication . . . . A crucial question is whether 'communication' governs the meaning of emanation, 'flowing forth,' and the images of fountain and light that JE uses; or whether emanation governs the meaning of communication and those images. If the first, one's reading of *End of Creation* will be more biblical, communication expressing an action, disposition, or will in God. If the second, one's reading will be more Neoplatonic, emanation meaning some sort of procession of or from God" (433, Yale edn). Surely only a *misreading* of Edwards can be in any way Neoplatonic: the doctrine of *creatio ex nihilo* should leave no room in his theology for Neoplatonism. Again, for Edwards, creation "implies a being receiving its existence, and all that belongs to it, out of nothing" (97; 420).

30. Robert L. Ottley, *The Doctrine of the Incarnation*, 4th edition revised (London: Methuen 1908), p. 582. See Edwards's *End of Creation*: "But the diffusive disposition that excited God to give creatures existence was rather a communicative disposition in general, or a disposition in the fullness of divinity to flow out and diffuse itself. Thus the

disposition there is in the root and stock of a tree to diffuse and send forth its sap and life, is doubtless the reason of the communication of its sap and life to its buds, leaves and fruits, after these exist" (p. 435, Yale edn). Of God's "delight in the emanation" of his own glory, Edwards says: "Thus that nature in a tree, by which it puts forth buds, shoots out branches, and brings forth leaves and fruit . . . . And so the disposition in the sun to shine, or abundantly to diffuse its fullness . . . " (p. 439, Yale edn). In his notes to *Ethical Writings*, Ramsey cautions the reader "not to overlook references to the Trinity in both *End of Creation* and *True Virtue*" (432n, Yale edn).

31. Emil Brunner, *The Christian Doctrine of Creation and Redemption* (*Dogmatics*, Vol. 2), trans. Olive Wyon (London: Lutterworth Press, 1952), p. 10.
32. The Syriac Apocapypse of Baruch is cited in Hayward, *Divine Name and Presence*, p. 128.
33. Pelikan, *The Christian Tradition: A History of the Development of Doctrine*, Vol. 1, *The Emergence of the Catholic Tradition (100–600)* (Chicago and London: University of Chicago Press, 1971), p. 189.
34. Brunner, *The Christian Doctrine of Creation and Redemption*, p. 15.
35. St. Athanasius, *On the Incarnation*, trans. and ed. by "A Religious of C.S.M.V." (London & Oxford: Mowbray, n.d.), p. 27.
36. Andrew Louth, *The Origins of the Christian Mystical Tradition: From Plato to Denys* (Oxford: Clarendon, 1981), p. 76, p. 77.
37. The phrase appears in Armstrong and Markus, *Christian Faith and Greek Philosophy*, p. 25.
38. Compare Edwards's *Work of Redemption*, Sermon Nine: "The church under the Old Testament was a child under tutors and governors and God dealt with it as a child" (p. 230, Yale edn). On Genesis 1, see the Midrash Rabbah (Bereshith Rabbah): "Thus God consulted the Torah and created the world, while the Torah declares, IN THE BEGINNING GOD CREATED, BEGINNING referring to the Torah, as in the verse, The Lord made me as the beginning of His way (Prov. viii, 22)." *The Midrash Rabbah*, ed. H. Freedman and M. Simon, 10 Vols. (Soncino Press, 1939), Vol. 1.
39. Reginald H. Fuller, *The Foundations of New Testament Christology* (London: Lutterworth Press, 1965), p. 96. Fuller's discussion of the *hochma-sophia* tradition should be consulted by anyone concerned with the background of the *Logos* doctrine. According to Fuller, the concept of *sophia* "offered the possibility of an interpretation of Christ as the pre-existent agent of creation" (p. 75). "Both Philo and the Book of Wisdom witness to a gradual substitution within Hellenistic Judaism of the term *logos* for *sophia*" (p. 76). As Fuller points out, the proem to the Fourth Gospel "borrows from the *sophia* myth but goes beyond it" (p. 208). Which is to say: "Down to v. 13 there is nothing which could not have been derived from the *sophia-logos* myth" (p. 226). That the Redeemer should be God incarnate, however, is "without precedent" (p. 210).
40. According to A. M. Ramsey: "there seems to be good evidence that

the early Church thought of Jesus as Himself the manifestation of the glory of God. A parallel in rabbinic literature may be seen in the comment of Simeon ben Jochai on Ps. ii, where he speaks of 'The Lord of the serving angels, the son of the Highest, yea, the Shekinah.' And in Justin Martyr, *Dialogue against Trypho*, 61, we read: 'God begat from Himself a certain immaterial Dynamis, which is called the glory of the Lord, and sometimes the Son, and sometimes the Wisdom'" (p. 150).

41. John Calvin, *Institutes of the Christian Religion*, ed. John T. McNeill, trans. Ford Lewis Battles (London: SCM, 1961), The Library of Christian Classics, Vol. XX.
42. *Miscellaneous Observations*, in *The Works of Jonathan Edwards*, ed. Edwards Hickman (London: William Ball, 1837), Vol. II, p. 500.
43. Pelikan, *The Christian Tradition*, Vol. 1, p. 188.
44. "When God was about to create the world, he had respect to that emanation of his glory, which is actually the consequence of the creation . . . " (Edwards, *End of Creation*, p. 532, Yale edn).
45. Cited in Paul Ramsey's Introduction to Edwards's *Ethical Writings*, pp. 41–42.
46. According to Paul Ramsey, the biblical concept of *pleroma* "concretely exhibited the oneness JE sought between God's will to communicate himself and his will to himself communicated, between his effectual fullness and his fullness in effect, between Christ and the church . . . " (*End of Creation*, p. 432n, Yale edn).
47. George Foot Moore, *Judaism in the First Centuries of the Christian Era*, Vol. I, The Age of the Tannaim (Cambridge: Harvard University Press, 1950), p. 370. Moore's footnote to this passage directs us to Augustine's figure of the boundless sea and the sponge in *Confessions* vii.5,1.
48. Moore, *Judaism*, Vol. 1, p. 372.
49. F. R. Montgomery-Hitchcock, "The Pleroma of Christ," *Church Quarterly Review*, Vol. 125, No. 249 (October–December 1937), p. 13.
50. Rabbi Eleazar ben Pedat maintained that even after the destruction of the first Temple, the Shekinah "still abode on the ruined site." Cited in Moore, *Judaism*, p. 369.
51. Edmond Jabès, *The Book of Questions*: II & III, *The Return to the Book*, trans. Rosmarie Waldrop (Middletown Conn.: Wesleyan University Press, 1976), p. 228.

Index

Aarsleff, Hans, 166n
Abelson, J., 139, 141, 143,
accommodation, *see* Incarnation
Ahl, Fredrich, 45, 173n
Alcott, Amos Bronson, 33
allegory: 51, 67–69, 72–73; distinguished from typology, 121; Puttenham's definition of, 67; temporal gap in, 73, 82; *see also* nut
Alter, Robert, 69
anagrams, 82, 173n
Anderson, Charles R., 176n
animal magnetism, *see* mesmerism
antitype, *see* typology
apple of knowledge, 42, 92–94
Arac, Jonathan, 183n
argument from design, 107
Asals, Frederick, 184n
Asselineau, Roger, 173n
Athanasius, St., 150
Attridge, Derek, 42, 49
Auerbach, Erich, 119–23, 124
Augustine, St., 123, 125, 134, 191n

Barth, Karl, 126
Beach, Joseph Warren, 175n
Beaver, Harold, 167n, 168n
Bernard, St., 24
Bickman, Martin, 90
Blake, William, 116
Bloom, Harold, 183n
Bowker, John, 138
Boyarin, Daniel, 72–73
Browning, Robert, 98, 157–58
Brunner, Emil, 149
Bunyan, John, 67
Burke, Kenneth, 32–33, 85–86, 164n
Burns, Robert, 81
Burrowes, George, 75, 172n

Cabot, James Eliot, 163n
calamus: as phallus, 80; as rushes or flags, 79; as writing instrument, 79
Calvin, John, 89, 148, 150, 152–53
Calvinism, 189n; vocabulary of, 83, 86
Cambon, Glauco, 174n
Canticles, *see* Song of Songs
Carlyle, Thomas, 86–87
Carroll, Lewis, 92; Humpty-Dumpty, 108; Mock Turtle, 97; Tweedledum and Tweedledee, 116
Cavell, Stanley, 165n, 167n
Chaucer, Geoffrey, 95–96
Cherry, Conrad, 189n
Chrysostom, St. John, 125
Confession, Westminster, 148
Copleston, Frederick, 149
correspondence: atemporal, 73; between body and natural world, 80; between mind and matter, 30; between surface-structure of body and surface-structure of text, 72, 76; Platonic-Pauline theory of correspondence, 72; as "tallying," 76
Cotton, John, 71
creatio ex nihilo, 73, 147–50, 152, 189n
Creed, Nicene, 152
Culler, Jonathan, 46
Curtius, Ernst Robert, 80–81, 173n

Daniélou, Jean, 121, 124–25, 129, 133–34
De Luca, V. A., 171n, 186n
De Man, Paul, 72–73
Derrida, Jacques, 22, 46–47, 52
diabolos: 46–65; pun or quibble on the name of, 47–65; and envy, 116
Dickinson, Emily, 83–106

Index

displacement: in the Bible 122; the Fall as type of, 126; *see also* kenosis
docetism, 71–72
Dodd, C. H., 143–44
doxa, *see* glory

Edwards, Jonathan, 27, 136–62; *Concerning the End for which God Created the World*, 144–62; *A History of the Work of Redemption*, 136–37, 140, 142, 145; *Miscellaneous Observations*, 153
Edwards, Michael, 109, 116
emanation, 27, 29, 31–32, 145, 149, 151, 155–56, 160, 190n
Emerson, Ralph Waldo, 22–39, 44; on language, 26, 34, 84–85, 44; "The American Scholar," 35; "Bacchus," 104; "Beauty," 34; "Circles," 26, 27–28, 30, 87; "Compensation," 29, 31, 52–53, 54, 86, 108; "Divinity School Address," 27, 39, 66, 84, 88, 91; "Experience," 28, 31, 37, 44, 475; "Fate," 26, 30; "History," 25, 27, 37; letter to Whitman, 172n; "Manners," 37; "The Method of Nature," 27; *Nature* 25, 28–31, 44, 48, 84–85, 90, 175n; "Nature," 25, 31; "The Over-Soul," 25; "Plato; or the Philosopher," 31; "The Poet," 26, 44, 83–84, 104; "Poetry and Imagination," 26, 27, 28, 30, 31, 36, 104; "Prudence," 31, 34, 44; 27, 29; "Self Reliance," 30, 95, 104; Sermon LXXVI, 38; "Spiritual Laws," 27, 38; "Woodnotes II," 30, 88; "Works and Days," 37
equivocation, *see* wordplay

figura, *see* typology
Fitzgerald, Robert, 123, 128
Fletcher, Angus, 72
Flood, Noah's, as type of Christ, 124–25, 132
Foster, Elizabeth S., 63

Frank, Roberta, 103, 179n
Frost, Robert, 107–18; "Design," 111–15, 180n; "In White," 111, 180n; "Once by the Pacific," 114
Frye, Northrop, 84, 119, 123, 124, 126, 135, 171n, 177n, 183n
Fuller, Reginald H., 152, 190n

Galdon, Joseph, 119
Gelpi, Albert, 92
Ginsburg, Christian David, 169n
Girard, René, 110–18; *see also* rivalry, mimetic; *see also* violence
Giroux, Robert, 184n
glory, 24, 139, 142–47, 150, 153, 155, 158–60; *see also* Shekinah
Gonnaud, Maurice, 164n, 165n
Gordis, Rabbi Robert, 69
Gura, Philip F., 164n

Handel, George Friedrich, 45
Hartman, Geoffrey, 40–47, 50, 176n
Hawthorne, Nathaniel, "The Birth-mark," 43; *The Blithedale Romance*, 62; letter from Melville, 47
Hayford, Harrison, 48
Hayward, Robert, 139–40, 146, 187n
Herbert, George, 94, 165n, 177n
Herder, J. G., 68, 70
Higginson, Thomas Wentworth, 87, 91
Hollander, John, 89, 97, 181n
Homans, Margaret, 177n
humilitis-sublimitas, *see* kenosis; *see also* reputation
Humpty-Dumpty, 108
hypogram, 82

imitatio Christi, 102, 132; *see also* servant, suffering
Incarnation: as antitype of the Fall, 126; as divine displacement, 122; defined by O'Connor, 123; in Emerson, 22–39; as

fulfillment of Messianic vision, 123–24. *See also* kenosis
Isaac, as type of Christ, 103, 122, 133–34, 185n

Jabès, Edmond
James, Henry, 39
Jones, Rowena Revis, 179n
Joyce, James, 89, 176n

kavod, see glory
kenosis: 23–25, 33, 123; *see also* Incarnation
Kermode, Frank, 183n
Kinney, Arthur F., 183n
Kirby, William, 107
Kitto, *Cyclopaedia of Biblical Literature*, 46, 167n
Klein, Rabbi Ernest, 46, 52, 65

language, fallen: 41, 106, 108, 109, 179; *see also* Ricks, Christopher; *see* also Humpty-Dumpty
Leonard, John, 182n
Lewis, R. W. B., 88, 175n
lexicon: "based on Holy Writ," 46; Dickinson's, 91, 105–106, 176n
Livingston, John A., 81
Lock, Walter, 24
Louth, Andrew, 150
Lowth, Robert, 170n

magnetism, 52–53, 57–62
Martin, R. P., 24
Matter, E. Ann, 68, 72,
Matthiessen, F. O., 42, 179n
Melville, Herman, 40–65; *Billy Budd*, 40–65; "Billy in the Darbies," 51; *The Confidence-Man*, 62, 168n; letter to Hawthorne, 47; *Mardi*, 40, 137; *Moby-Dick*, 47–48, 54, 115
Memra, 139–40
Mesmer, F. A., 61–62
mesmerism, 61–63
Miller, Perry, 147–48, 188n, 189n
Milton, John, *Paradise Lost*, 45, 52, 66, 93, 108–10, 122
Montgomery-Hitchcock, F. R., 191n

Moore, George Foot, 157

Newness, the, 36–37
Nicholas of Lyra, 71, 170n
Noyes, George R., 70–71,
nut: and kernel of truth, 73; man-nuts, 82; as shell or husk of literal meaning, 67. *See also* allegory

O'Connor, Flannery, 119–35
Oegger, Guillaume, 32–33
offal, God's, 32, 164n
Ong, Walter, 94, 99, 117
Origen, 72, 77, 79, 121
Ottley, Robert L., 189n
Owen, Wilfred, 181n

Packer, Barbara, 165n
Paley, William, 107–8
pall, 112, 115, 181n
pantheism, 149
Parker, Theodore, 165n
parody, demonic: 103, 122, 125, 126–27
paronomasia, *see* wordplay
Peabody, Elizabeth, 32
Pearce, Roy Harvey, 174n
Pelikan, Jaroslav, 24, 154
Percy, Bishop Thomas, 69
Philo of Alexandria, 121, 157–58, 190n
Plato, 149–50
Platonism, 70, 72–73, 189n
pleroma, 24, 155–58
plurisignation, *see* wordplay
Poirier, Richard, 180n
polarity, 35, 52, 61
Pope, Alexander, 41, 97
Pope, Marvin H., 68, 74
pun, *see* wordplay

quibble, *see* wordplay
Quilligan, Maureen, 51, 177n, 179n
Quinn, M. Bernetta, 184n

Rahab, as type of Gentiles, 129
ram, as type of Crucifixion, 134

Index

Ramsey, Arthur Michael, 188n, 190n
Ramsey, Paul, 189n, 191n
reputation, 22–23, 33; *see also* kenosis
Rich, Adrienne, 98
Ricks, Christopher, 42, 109, 117, 179n
Ricoeur, Paul, 71
rivalry, mimetic, 110–18; *see also* violence; *see also* Girard, René

sacrifice: in "The Displaced Person," 134; of meaning, 116; of the scapegoat, 110
Santayana, George, 174n
Satan: 40, 43, 45–64, 52; as conjuror, 93; as arch designer, 108; etymology of name, 46; and imitation, 116; as name for the mimetic process, 111, 116; as mimetic model, 116; and puns that quarrel, 111; as serpent, 42, 108–109; Satan's fall from heaven, 126
Saussure, Ferdinand de, 82
Schlauch, Margaret, 85
scoriae, 31–33, 164n
Sealts, Merton M., 48
servant, suffering, as type of Christ, 33, 132–33
Sewall, Richard, 103, 178n
Sewanee Review, The, 130
Sewell, Elizabeth, 177n
Shakespeare, William, *Hamlet*, 40; *Macbeth*, 113–15; *Othello*, 40; *Richard III*, 42
Shekinah, 136–62; as type of Christ, 137, 140, 186n, 188n; relation to *doxa*, 143; relation to *skene* and *mishkan*, 140–42
Shoaf, R. A., 182n
skandalon, 49–51, 60
Smalley, Beryl, 121
snake-charming, *see* mesmerism
snipe, 81–82
Sollers, Philippe, 181n
Song of Songs, 67–82, 91
Spence, William, 107

Spenser, Edmund, 51
Spinoza, Baruch, 147
Starobinski, Jean, 82
Stein, Stephen J., 188n
Stevens, Wallace, 108
Stewart, Stanley, 169n
Stock, Brian, 67, 78
Stovall, Floyd, 70, 170n
Stuart, Moses, 71

Targum Jonathan, 139, 143
Targum Onqelos, 139
targums, 138–62
Temple, as type of Christ, 160
texts, as weavings, 78
Theology, Natural, 107
Thoreau, Henry David, 88–89
Tocqueville, Alexis de, 86
Trilling, Lionel, 112
Tweedledum and Tweedledee, 116
typology: 102–103, 105, 123–24; definition of, 119–20; distinguished from allegory, 121; in Edwards, 154; in Emerson, 33, 36; in O'Connor, 119–35; and "Christ figures," 132, 185n.

umbrage: as body of text, 71; giving and taking, 66, 82; as shade, 66; truth hidden *sub umbra*, 67; *umbra* in Song of Songs, 76

Vendler, Helen, 79, 172n
Vincent, Howard P., 167n
violence: legitimate and illegitimate, 110–16; as the subject of violence, 117. *See also* rivalry, mimetic; *see also* Girard, René; *see also* Tweedledum and Tweedledee

Walton, Brian, 138
Wesley, Charles, 138, 186n
Wheelwright, Philip, 178n
Whicher, George Frisbie, 177n
Whitman, Jon, 169n, 172n
Whitman, Walt, 66–79; *Calamus* poems, 79; "Song of Myself,"

74–89; *Notes and Fragments*, 74, 173n
Wilbur, Richard, 83, 92
Wilson, John F., 186n, 189n
Woolf, Rosemary, 185n
wordplay: bilingual, 45; in Browning, 98; in Dickinson, 83–106; 108–18; in Emerson, 29, 44–45; in Herbert, 94–95; in Latin hymnody, 94; in Melville, 40–43, 49–51, 115; in *Macbeth*, 177n; in Milton, 53–54, 66–67, 82, 93, 108–9, 168n; in Pope, 97; in Spenser, 51; puns that get along and puns that quarrel, 109–10; puns and ambiguity, 49, 178n; paronamasia in Anglo-Saxon verse, 103; substitution as wordplay, 97–99, 102–3, 178n. *See also* language, fallen.
Wordsworth, William, 148
Wright, Nathalia, 167n